Renaissance and Reformations

Blackwell Introductions to Literature

This series sets out to provide concise and stimulating introductions to literary subjects. It offers books on major authors (from John Milton to James Joyce), as well as key periods and movements (from Old English literature to the contemporary). Coverage is also afforded to such specific topics as 'Arthurian Romance'. All are written by outstanding scholars as texts to inspire newcomers and others: non-specialists wishing to revisit a topic, or general readers. The prospective overall aim is to ground and prepare students and readers of whatever kind in their pursuit of wider reading.

Published

Renaissance and Reformations

An Introduction to
Early Modern English Literature

Michael Hattaway

Blackwell
Publishing

BLACKWELL PUBLISHING
350 Main Street, Malden, MA 02148-5020, USA
9600 Garsington Road, Oxford OX4 2DQ, UK
550 Swanston Street, Carlton, Victoria 3053, Australia

First published 2005 by Blackwell Publishing Ltd

1 2005

Library of Congress Cataloging-in-Publication Data

Hattaway, Michael.
Renaissance and reformations : an introduction to early modern English
literature / Michael Hattaway.
p. cm.—(Blackwell introductions to literature)
Includes bibliographical references and index.
ISBN-13: 978-1-4051-0044-1 (hardcover : alk. paper)
ISBN-10: 1-4051-0044-3 (hardcover : alk. paper)
ISBN-13: 978-1-4051-0045-8 (pbk. : alk. paper)
ISBN-10: 1-4051-0045-1 (pbk. : alk. paper)
1. English literature—Early modern, 1500–1700—History and criticism.
2. Renaissance—England. 3. Reformation—England. I. Title. II. Series.

PR421.H27 2005
820.9'003—dc22
2005006591

A catalogue record for this title is available from the British Library.

Set in 10/13pt Meridien
by Graphicraft Limited, Hong Kong

For further information on
Blackwell Publishing, visit our website:
www.blackwellpublishing.com

Contents

Illustrations

Acknowledgements

Andrew McNeillie had enough confidence in me to commission this book: his support and encouragement were exemplary, and I commend the collegial help I received from the editorial and production teams at Blackwell. My friend and colleague Malcolm Jones inspired me with his great knowledge of the visual records of the age. Students and colleagues, past and present, at the universities of Wellington, Cambridge, Kent, British Columbia, Massachusetts, and Sheffield have accompanied me along the paths that led to this work. It was a particular privilege as a graduate student to have been supervised by Muriel Bradbrook and later to have taught alongside Reg Foakes, Howard Mills, Reg Ingram, Peter Laven, Malcolm Jack, Patrick Collinson and Norman Blake. Finally, I would like to thank my wife Judi, who tolerated my taking a laptop on a holiday in the Luberon where this book was planned. The actual writing of it has given her a lot more to put up with since.

Introduction:
New Worlds of Words

John Florio, an Italian living in London, called his Italian–English dictionary of 1611 *Queen Anna's New World of Words*. His metaphor links Atlantic voyages of discovery with mental explorations, so reminding us that concern for speech and language was central to almost every endeavour in the period. Florio's contemporaries were attentive to the complexities of using words to make sense of the world – perhaps more than most of us today who can be all too ready to overlook the functions of language.

I assume in this book that our enjoyment of literature comes from delight in a writer's verbal skills, from the satisfaction that comes from recognizing literary forms, and from reflection upon the complex ways by which texts might be related one to another and upon how they touch our own experience. The study begins by examining how methods for speaking and writing were taught and used. It then turns to a description of how books were produced, consumed and, in the case of plays, reproduced in performance. Its third chapter investigates the ways in which writers 'discovered' – the word then meant 'uncovered' or 'revealed' – not only new mental territories but ancient and modern linguistic forms and literary genres. From there we track the ways in which authors participated in the creation of national identity by concerning themselves with history (chapter 4), joined with debates about the present (chapter 5), wrote about people and places (chapter 6), and, finally, how they explored languages fit for religious experience (chapter 7).

Browsing through this book will reveal that it contains many quotations, some moderately long. These signal two of its purposes. The first: to help modern readers, using specific examples, appreciate the ways in which writers of about five hundred years ago fashioned their verbal artefacts, tried to made words work – and enjoyed making them play. It asks 'how' questions, not 'what' questions. The second: to create contexts for our readings of their texts. To do this, we must think not only about 'history' and 'society' but also about the metaphors commonly used to describe relationships between words and the world. Many of these are misleading because they derive from the visual arts: 'reflection', 'portrait', 'image' and so on. Contemporaries in their own critical practice did, of course, use many of these difficult metaphors, along with some taken from another sister art, music. This notwithstanding, when we try to connect literature with history or society, it is, I submit, far more enlightening to focus on verbal practice within our chosen texts, on the interpretative metaphors and other rhetorical figures from the age, the metaphors women and men lived by, than simply to describe matters of substance or speak blandly of 'themes'.

If I have been successful, I will have helped readers to think not about, say, history *and* 'literature', but about history *in* literature – and vice versa. Language is at the centre of my concern because I believe that the period witnessed a great coming together, a conflux of what Donne called 'new philosophy' and a delight in the categorization and description of literary forms. This process defamiliarized language, made people aware of its most exciting power, as a tool for exploring or 'discovering' both outer and inner experience.

To use another distinctive Renaissance metaphor, this book is an anatomy, a dissection that seeks to uncover the practices of writing and the concerns of writers as these impinged upon educational, material, cultural and religious processes. It ranges over a period of about 150 years: the age that runs roughly from Sir Thomas More to John Milton. It is only incidentally a history of the literature of the period, and is not arranged around studies of authors or genres. Nor is it the sort of book that will theorize or build models out of those abstract processes that are listed, perhaps rather shamelessly, in the first sentence of this paragraph. Help of this kind is at hand, however, within the covers of many books listed in the Bibliography.

Writing at the time was more of a systematic craft than it is now, and students spent much time developing highly formalized skills of eloquence (see chapter 1). This means that writers and speakers shared techniques and habits of expression (the great 'genius' Shakespeare being no exception). Readers and listeners took as much pleasure from expectation and recognition as they did from surprise, and were trained to register and enjoy a gamut of verbal styles, schematic techniques of characterization and set patterns of narrative. This may seem strange to today's readers, brought up in a post-Romantic age to privilege singularity and originality, to devalue the typical, to assume that 'ideas' can be 'expressed' in a text, to look for meaning in the intention of the author, to test his or her works for 'sincerity', and to assume that, in order to be successful, authors need to create fictive characters that are 'true to life' or with whom readers or playgoers might 'identify'. I hope that a consideration of those earlier habits, now unfamiliar, will generate insight and, more importantly, pleasure.

It would also have been troublesome to have had chapters devoted to the reigns of England's kings and queens: habits of thought were not changed and memories of form and commonplace could not be purged with the death of a monarch. This is not, however, to deny the differences in cultural tone between the reigns of Protestant Edward VI (1547–53) and Catholic Mary Tudor (1553–8). Individual chapters in this book, however, do rest on appropriate chronological foundations.

My laying out of the skeleton, sinews and arteries of this great body of texts means that I can offer neither a description of 'background' – another misleading metaphor from the visual arts and illusionist theatre – nor a history of 'ideas'. It is naïve and misleading to write about what lies *behind* texts rather than the plays of mind evidenced *within* them. A love poem by John Donne turns out to be 'about' the making of maps, a verbal map of Guyana by Sir Walter Ralegh 'about' sexual conquest. Both Catholic Robert Southwell and Protestant George Herbert use homely metaphors to explore religious yearnings: perhaps God, like love, can be known only through metaphor.

Nor does this study concentrate solely on 'literature', a canon that until recently was held to comprise mainly fictions, narrative and dramatic, and verse – with 'golden' lyric in that category privileged over other 'drabber' kinds. We need to follow the habits of Renaissance students who not only wrote imitations of fictive texts written by the authors ('authorities') they studied, but also turned their hands to non-fictional treatises, polemics, as well as praises of great men and formalized letters. In a study of this length there is no space to draw alternative maps that chart new worlds of Renaissance 'literature', but I hope that, as in maps of old, I have been able to indicate where marvels and sites of interest might be sought out.

This was a time of huge cultural changes and some technological advance, notably the spread of printing. Many tensions apparent in the period derive from efforts to explain emergent social or cultural patterns using traditional or residual forms or paradigms. It was also a time when those distinctions between the secular and the 'religious' or 'supernatural' that we take for granted would not have been recognized. In order to begin to understand some of these tensions we might not only look at textual practices but also remember that the production, reproduction or consumption of *'literature'* can constitute an historical 'event', and, conversely, that *history* is textualized. It is mediated through the perceptions and cultural assumptions of those who report or document it, peopled with 'characters', and structured according to formulaic narratives. Furthermore, although the word had not been invented, leading minds understood 'ideology', the use of value systems, traditional, revealed, or 'natural', for social and political control. We can find examples in 'literary' texts that a previous generation might have considered to be 'impure' or contaminated by history. The Duke of Guise, Machiavellian and Catholic, in Marlowe's *The Massacre at Paris* (1593), a documentary play about the slaughter of French Protestants that started on St Bartholomew's Day, 1572, puts it succinctly in a soliloquy:

> My policy hath framed religion:
> Religion? *O Diabole!* (1.2.65–6)

This is not fundamentalism but politics – as most varieties of fundamentalism are.

It would have been naïve to scrutinize the fast-changing forms and pressures of this age from one point of view – which is why this book has a somewhat lengthy title. It starts with *Renaissance*. Some contemporaries did debate the concept (see chapter 3), but the word itself was not used in English until the nineteenth century. It is always a difficult word, requiring writers to make clear whether they are using it to designate a period or a movement. The label can seldom be conclusive: the visual style of figure 2 (see p. 80), which is taken from Sir John Harington's translation of Ariosto's *Orlando Furioso* (1591), is obviously 'renaissance', but what it represents derives ultimately from medieval romance. It is important to realize that in England any notion of a fresh start was a political instrument: it was useful to the generation of Henry VIII to 'medievalize' the past in order to enhance political power and cultural domination. For anyone writing about the period, however, it is necessary to demonstrate continuities as well as changes: to the poets of the age of Shakespeare Chaucer was as important as Ovid.

Some concepts of Renaissance suggest not just new literary forms – sonnets and Senecan tragedies – but rapid secularization. The period did see a revival of arts of eloquence that were central to *litterae humaniores* ('the more humane disciplines of learning'). These had been neglected by a concentration on logic by the scholastic thinkers of 'medieval' Europe. The adjective *'humaniores'* encourages the association of a concept of 'Renaissance humanism' with the works and outlook of learned coteries and particular scholars such as Marsilio Ficino of Florence (see chapter 7) and Desiderius Erasmus of Rotterdam (see chapter 1), both of whom helped create new structures of thought and feeling in England. However, the humanism of the sixteenth century was not akin to modern humanism, which easily embraces atheism, but was a Christian humanism, a fusion of classical and Christian thought. Its main achievement may have been the revival of an elegant Latin style that, along with the development of printing, helped create a republic of letters across Europe.

Although students and intellectuals did read Virgil and Ovid, Tacitus and Plato, if we analyse the output of English printing presses we may come to believe that more cultural energy was expended in religious debate and polemic than in the resuscitation of classical writings. This is why I have attempted to give emphasis not only to Renaissance channels of learning but also to the currents driven by the religious *Reformations* of the period (see chapter 7). Again, it is misleading to think of a clean break with the past in the reign of Henry VIII: his new religious superstructures were soon struck down in the reign of Mary Tudor, a Catholic and wife of Philip of Spain, and scores of Protestant martyrs were burnt at the stake. However, had he lived, the fiercely Protestant Edward VI who preceded her might well have imposed a lasting and unyielding Protestantism upon his country. Elizabeth I sympathized with Protestantism but was unwilling to offer substantial support to those rebelling against Spanish domination in The Netherlands. In 1563, however, five years after her accession, John Foxe published his *Acts and Monuments*, popularly known as *Foxe's Book of Martyrs*, which kept alive for the next hundred years the memories of those who had died for their faith under Mary. Another surge of reformation in the early seventeenth century is signalled by what Patrick Collinson has called an alliance of magistracy and ministry,[1] to which Shakespeare's *Measure for Measure* (1603) bears testimony.

A third vantage point from which the age is commonly surveyed buttresses the description of *early modern*, a designation taken from social historians (see chapter 5). Again, there are difficulties and dangers: like 'Renaissance', this label elides continuity with the past. It does remind us that the period saw the posing of some of the great political and cultural questions that have shaped the forging of modernity. To quote again from *The Massacre at Paris*: the weak King Charles IX of France is rebuking Catherine of Medici, the Queen Mother, and the Duke of Guise, who are planning their act of state-sponsored terrorism:

> Besides, my heart relents that noble men,
> Only corrupted in religion,
> Ladies of honour, knights, and gentlemen,
> Should for their conscience taste such ruthless ends.   (1.4.9–11)

It was a long time, however, before this implicit endorsement of the ideal of modern Europe, liberty of conscience, became an acknowledged right in England. Notions of early modernism usefully encourage us to look in texts for scepticism and doubt rather than reconciliation, harmony and 'closure', but they also invite the importation back into our period of cultural paradigms that we associate with eighteenth-century Enlightenment and even the revolutionary epoch of the early nineteenth century.

In this volume all spelling and punctuation have been silently modernized, except in passages quoted from Spenser's *The Faerie Queene* (in that text Spenser deliberately used archaic spellings and syntactic forms in order to suggest affinities with antique traditions). Likewise, in quotations, key words or phrases picked up in the discussion that surrounds them have been silently italicized. Footnoting has been kept to a minimum.

I have cheerfully referred to and quoted from texts that are not to be found in the most widely available anthologies. The intention was to explode 'the canon'. Electronic archives have made many of these rarer pieces quickly available, and readers' computer searches can continue the explorations I have made in this way.

CHAPTER 1

Speaking and Writing

'Literature' and 'Fiction' in Early Modern Culture

> HAMLET My tables – meet it is I set it down
> That 'One may smile and smile and be a villain'.
> (*Hamlet*, 1600–1, 1.5.108–9)

Hamlet, fine student that he is, carries a notebook in his pocket, his 'tables' or table-book in which to inscribe not only feelings and observations but also pleasing words and phrases. At this moment in the play he is thrilled at having exposed the hypocrisy of Claudius, at having inferred a political maxim, and at having deployed a simple repetitive verbal scheme ('smile and smile'). He stores away his small rhetorical artefact for future use. Many writers of the present do likewise, but from Hamlet's action we can work towards insights into how, during the Renaissance, the practice of writing was regarded in ways very different from the way in which most of us think of it now.

A primary difference between Renaissance and modern concepts of writing involves meanings for 'literature' and for 'fiction'. As surviving library catalogues reveal, contemporaries of Donne and Shakespeare did not recognize the groupings that determine the display of books in modern bookshops and which split the curriculum in schools and universities between 'creative' writing and everything else. In the Renaissance, the modern category of 'literature' was yet to develop. The word designated not a body of fictions characterized by 'literariness', but a faculty or skill, a person's acquaintance with learning. In 1598 the expatriate Italian compiler of dictionaries John Florio glossed the word *letteratura* as 'learning, knowledge in letters, lore, cunning';[1] this is not the equivalent of today's notion of a 'literary sensibility'. Only from the eighteenth century was the word applied to select and generally imaginative texts, or to polite learning.[2]

Pupils certainly studied fictions: classical tragedies and comedies as well as poems such as Virgil's *Eclogues*, along with Renaissance imitations of them. Schoolmasters often used allegorical eclogues written by Johannes Baptista Spagnuoli (1447–1516) of Mantua (known often as 'Mantuan'). In his turn, Spenser imitated these in *The Shepheardes Calender* (1579).[3] Sir Philip Sidney heaped praise on another imitation, Norton and Sackville's *Gorboduc* (1562), a closet tragedy written for the Inner Temple. He found it 'full of stately speeches and well-sounding phrases, climbing to the height of Seneca's style'.[4] (Does the 'style/stile' pun create an irony?) However, students read these fictions alongside non-fictional texts, classical history and political analysis (for example, Livy and Tacitus), as well as moral and philosophical compositions (for example, Plutarch and Cicero). Aristotle had laid down similarities between historians and poets[5] – the familiar modern partition between imaginative and factual writing had not come into being.

As with the word 'literature', the word 'fiction' had an unfamiliar meaning. It designated anything made (out of words), although it was developing its modern meanings that relate to untruth or make-believe as well as to imaginative prose narratives. Conversely, writers of history were accustomed to invent 'characters' for the historical figures whose doings they chronicled. In the manner of Sir Thomas More in his *History of King Richard III* (c.1513) or John Foxe in what came to be known as 'Foxe's Book of Martyrs' (his *Acts and Monuments* of 1563), they wrote fictional orations and dialogue for them, speeches the historian felt they might or ought to have made.

In the Renaissance, therefore, a 'literature of fact' sat alongside a literature of fiction. Historians in the Middle Ages had tended to devote themselves to *interpretation*, inculcating moral or religious truths from what they took to be God's designs for mankind. Renaissance historians began to use techniques of *demonstration*, comparing and correcting ancient chronicles in their search for another kind of truth. So much so that truth of detail could be used as a selling point. Certain imaginative texts cheerfully carried claims for facticity and veracity, a convention parodied by Shakespeare:

AUTOLYCUS   Here's [a] ballad, of a fish that appeared upon the coast on Wednesday the fourscore of April, forty thousand fathom above water, and sung this ballad against the hard hearts of maids. It was thought she was a woman, and was turned into a cold fish for she would not exchange flesh with one that loved her. The ballad is very pitiful, and as true.

(*The Winter's Tale*, 1609, 4.4.265–70)

The passage also suggests a market for news, a market enabled, as we shall see, by the spread of printing.

The association of 'literature' with forms that ranged beyond, say, verse that dealt with inner experience and narratives of a fictional nature, came into being partly because at schools and universities students concentrated on disciplines of *language* right through to the conclusion of their studies. Writings, in this context, including history and philosophy, were not categorized by their content. Moreover, unlike authors today who almost always write their early works in their own language, Renaissance writers began their apprenticeship by translating from and writing in Latin. This was facilitating: the resultant responsiveness to language is manifest in an exuberant expansion of vocabulary. Words from Latin – as well as from European vernacular languages – were imported into English: in 1589 George Puttenham welcomed '"irrevocable", "irradiation", "depopulation" and such like . . . which . . . were long time despised for ink-horn [affected, abstruse] terms.'[6] Nine years later, John Florio celebrated the new lexical plenitude by calling his Italian–English dictionary *A World of Words*.

Writing in English

However, huge cultural changes – rising rates of literacy, new national identities that followed the English reformations of the sixteenth century – did create a market for texts in English. Four printed editions of Chaucer and two of Langland, along with the appearance in 1557 of *Songs and Sonnets*, an anthology edited by Richard Tottel (often known as 'Tottel's Miscellany'), which was reprinted eight times before 1587 and which included translations from Petrarch by Wyatt and Surrey, signal the emergence of an early canon of English literature. These and texts like Spenser's *Faerie Queene* (1590–1609), in which the traditions of chivalric romance and classical epic combined to create an allegory which looks to the consolidation of Protestantism, are also evidence of the way in which texts were instrumental in nation-building. Nevertheless, these books always occupied a position alongside classical models and practices.

Writing in English long remained a phenomenon worthy of comment. Latin and Greek were the main topics of study in schools and universities, and Latin had for centuries been the language of the Roman church. From the Norman Conquest until the reign of Edward III, 'law French', a form of Anglo-Norman, had been used in courts and legal documents, and for centuries many of its terms remained in use. In a dialogue by Florio of 1578 the question is put: 'What think you of this English?' The answer: 'It is a language that will do you good in England but, pass Dover, it is worth nothing ... It doth not like me at all because it is a language confused, bepieced with [so] many tongues ... that if every language had his own words again, there would be but a few remain for Englishmen, and yet every day they add.'[7] Basic poetic techniques were not taken for granted: Ben Jonson, turning against his native tradition, wrote a bravura attack on the use of rhyme in verse, 'A Fit of Rhyme against Rhyme' – Latin poetry does not rhyme. By contrast, George Chapman, in a verse epistle to his readers prefixed to his translation of Homer's *Iliad* (1598), praised English for a rhythmic facility generated by its comparatively large number of monosyllabic words.

The Study of Speech and Writing: The *Trivium*, Eloquence and Copiousness

Educational programmes of language and writing for these students of texts in Latin and Greek followed a classical model designated as the 'three paths' (the *trivium*), those of grammar, logic and rhetoric. These were the first three of the seven liberal arts. The 'liberal' arts were not only the necessary skills for learning but those designated to be worthy of 'free' (in Latin *liber*) men, as apposed to 'rude mechanicals' – the phrase Shakespeare applies to Bottom and his crew in *A Midsummer Night's Dream* (1595).

As a preliminary, at petty schools, children were taught the rudiments of reading in English along with the catechism, a set of elementary questions and answers for instruction in the Christian religion. Some progressed to learn writing which was taught independently. After that, girls tended to be educated separately, but although there was a growth in the number of 'academies' for girls in the period, they were not generally exposed to the full rigours of the *trivium* and were diverted towards decorative arts and domestic skills. At grammar school, boys studied the grammar of Latin and some Greek, and their rhetorical studies (see below) generated compositions in verse and prose. Formal disputations were common for which both logic and rhetorical proficiency were necessary. Nor was 'literature' in the modern sense included in what followed the *trivium*, the *quadrivium* or 'four paths' of arithmetic, geometry, astronomy, and music.

Familiarity with reasoning and the art of logic left its mark on all kinds of writing. Cicero had stated that the 'bond of reason and speech' was the basis of society,[8] and educated readers were attuned to logical configurations not only in prose but also in verse. John Dryden was to write in 1668: 'I am of opinion that they cannot be good poets who are not accustomed to argue well.'[9] The arts of logic and rhetoric in this context cannot be separated, and Renaissance poems often 'argue' – they are not just concerned with feelings. William Empson called this 'argufying', not nagging but 'the kind of arguing we do in ordinary life to get our own way'.[10]

Hamlet, therefore, would have studied logic as well as rhetoric: later in the play he asks whether it is better to accept adversity or rebel against it:

> To be, or not to be; that is the question:
> Whether 'tis nobler in the mind to suffer
> The slings and arrows of outrageous fortune,
> Or to take arms against a sea of troubles,
> And, by opposing, end them.   (3.1.58–62)

'Question' here is a technical term, meaning the main point in a disputed matter. Audiences may have noted how the prince strays from the logical path of his argumentation, sliding into a dream of an easeful death. Later they encounter displays of false logic – 'chop-logic' it was often called – that were common in theatrical clownage. Here is the Gravedigger drawing a sophistical conclusion, based on a false syllogism,[11] about the death of Ophelia:

if I drown myself wittingly, it argues an act; and an act hath three branches: it is to act, to do, and to perform. Argal [from Latin *ergo*, meaning 'therefore'], she drowned herself wittingly.   (5.1.10–13)

The text of *Hamlet*, therefore, would have appeared not only as a work of genius, a repository for memorable phrases, and a vehicle for a star player, but also as an exhibition of the disciplines of thought and an exercise in moral deliberation. It contributed to the debate about whether it could be right to take up arms against an anointed king if that king turned out to be a villain.

Reasoning could also be an attribute of lyric verse. Many wooing poems of the period deploy logical arguments to persuade a woman to succumb to masculine desire. Marvell's poem 'To his Coy Mistress' is generally printed as three verse paragraphs which correspond to the three parts of an 'enthymeme' or a syllogistic argument by a rhetorician. The argument goes like this:

1   If we inhabited a timeless world, I could spend an eternity in wooing you.
2   We live in a world ruled by time.
3   Therefore, time spent in wooing is wastefully consumed and we should now make love.

Marvell's tone and wit, however, invite the woman to see through the sophistry and, by irony, even imagines her reply – possibly acceptance, possibly a graceful but firm refusal of the offer.

Because of this exhibition of witty 'argufying', poems by, say, Donne and Marvell that appear sexist to modern readers are open to ironic readings. Many of the poems are 'apostrophes', pointed addresses to someone imagined to be present. They are 'dramatic' in that they both create a speaker or persona and imply a listener. They thereby invoke other kinds of experience: seemingly cavalier poems might be mannerly, even puritanical. Often the endings of such poems conclude a line of reasoning: consider what Donne himself said about poetry in Sermon 55 on the Penitential Psalms:

in all metrical compositions, of which kind the book of Psalms is, the force of the whole piece is, for the most part, left to the shutting up; the whole frame of the poem is a beating out of a piece of gold, but the last clause is as the impression of the stamp, and that is it that makes it current.[12]

A poem similar to that of Marvell, Thomas Carew's 'A Rapture', also implicitly invites its subject to inspect critically the virtuoso extended metaphor that sustains its insistent ardour:

> I will enjoy thee now, my Celia, come,
> And fly with me to Love's Elysium.
> The giant Honour that keeps cowards out
> Is but a masquer, and the servile rout
> Of baser subjects only bend in vain
> To the vast idol; while the nobler train
> Of valiant lovers sail between
> The huge Colossus' legs and pass unseen
> Unto the blissful shore.

Coming to the considered conclusion that honour is not an absolute value but an extravagant and hollow figure made to control attendance at a court entertainment is a major moral event, and might dissuade a mistress from agreeing to amorous consummation.

To return to Hamlet's 'tables'. It was held to be of great educational benefit to keep a notebook, and across Renaissance Europe many books about writing and eloquence are comprised of or include lists of 'topics'. 'Topic' derives from the Greek word for 'place', the (virtual) place in which a writer would seek observations or examples for treating a theme; a 'commonplace' was not simply a truism but a topic to be used in a variety of contexts. One of the best known of these compilations was the *De Copia Verborum* (1512), assembled by the great Dutch humanist Desiderius Erasmus (c.1467–1536). Writers employed this 'copy' along with material from the *Adagia* (1500), an Erasmian collection of proverbs or 'sentences' drawn from classical and scriptural texts, to help them generate hoards of words and phrases. As part of their work in rhetoric (studied in relation to both the classical languages and English), they amassed and memorized these nuggets of text (i.e. 'topics') that they stored away in commonplace books:[13] Hamlet's 'villain' sentence provides an example. With an eye to logical patterning, they could then themselves deploy these in exercise letters, poems, speeches, praises, or polemics. It was good to demonstrate 'copiousness', to write texts that abounded in matter as well as being eloquent in expression: both were marks of writerly distinction. If a poet has to 'wrench his words to help his rhyme', wrote George Puttenham, 'it is a sign that such a maker is not copious in his own language'.[14] 'Amplification', the means of generating that sense of copiousness, could, of course, generate the kind of fatuous verbosity displayed by Shakespeare's Polonius, and Erasmus, like most other writers on rhetoric, warned against excess of it.

Aemilia Lanyer's 'Description of Cookham' (1609–10) appeared in the first substantial book of poems published by an Englishwoman, *Salve Deus, Rex Judaeorum* (1611). The poem is a praise of her patron Margaret Clifford, Countess of Northumberland, who had stayed at the royal manor of Cookham in Berkshire. The effect of the following comes from our enjoyment of a theme gracefully amplified and of a list of particulars to which are attributed human motives and feelings:

> The house received all ornaments to grace it,
> And would endure no foulness to deface it.
> The walks put on their summer liveries,
> And all things else did hold like similes [*here* 'resemblances']:
> The trees, with leaves, with fruits, with flowers clad,
> Embraced each other, seeming to be glad,
> Turning themselves to beauteous canopies
> To shade the bright sun from your brighter eyes;
> The crystal streams with silver spangles graced,
> While by the glorious sun they were embraced;
> The little birds in chirping notes did sing,
> To entertain both you and that sweet spring,
> And Philomela [the nightingale] with her sundry lays
> Both you and that delightful place did praise.[15]

Like so many other similar passages from the period, this description is not of what might be *seen in* but what might be *attributed to* such a place: Lanyer offers the conventional features of the *locus amoenus* or pleasance that are reproduced from classical writings in a myriad of medieval and Renaissance texts. These include 'a tree (or several trees), a meadow, and a spring or brook. Birdsong and flowers may be added'.[16] However, Lanyer does not simply accumulate fine-sounding or picturesque details but embeds them in figures of speech and then deploys these in elegant array. The predominant figure here is what John Ruskin was to designate as the 'pathetic fallacy', the attribution of feeling to the non-human. Lanyer offers the kind of pleasure that, according to the author of one of the first Renaissance handbooks on the visual arts, Leon Battista Alberti, 'first . . . comes from the copiousness and variety of things'.[17] In the period, however, the description of the place would also have been recognized as part of the 'argument' for the virtue of the Countess.

A quick scan of a handbook like M. P. Tilley's *Dictionary of the Proverbs in England in the Sixteenth and Seventeenth Centuries*[18] reveals how pervasive the incorporation of particular categories of commonplace, proverbs and stock phrases was in the literature of Renaissance England and how these forms derived not only from folk wisdom but from classical antiquity as well as the Bible. Use of these and other succinct or pithy sayings generated another desirable quality: *sententiousness*. Weighty matter and artful forms are combined in comedy and political discourse alike:

> CELIA   Let us sit and mock the good housewife Fortune from her wheel, that her gifts may henceforth be bestowed equally.
> ROSALIND   I would we could do so: for her benefits are mightily misplaced, and the bountiful blind woman doth most mistake in her gifts to women.
>
> (Shakespeare, *As You Like It*, 1599–1600, 1.2.26–30)

> Forts may decay and forces decrease . . . either by variety of fortune or inconstancy of men's desires, but a man's own blood [i.e. children] cleaveth close unto him, not so much in the blisses of prosperity, which are equally imparted to others, as in the crosses of calamity, which touch none so near as those that are nearest by nature. (John Hayward, *The First Part of the Life and Reign of King Henry IV*, 1599, p. 1)

In England, some writers compiled rhetorical handbooks that centred on anthologies of 'figures' (many picked these from Sir Philip Sidney's prose romance, *Arcadia* [1590]). These exemplified patterns of speech as well as listing commonplaces. '*Anthos*' means 'flower' in Greek: Shakespeare's Holofernes became ecstatic when he thought of Ovid's capacity for 'smelling out the odoriferous flowers of fancy, the jerks of invention' (*Love's Labour's Lost*, 1594–5, 4.2.124–6).

Here is a sample of serendipity from what Thomas Blount, the compiler of such a book published in 1654, called a list of 'Little forms':

> He felt fiery arrows fly from her eyes, so sharp that they transfixed his heart with compassion.
> Love, anger, jealousy, suspicion, drew him with four horses.
> As innocently spoken, as treacherously interpreted.

They murmured as do the waves of a mutinous sea.

Exercise the vivacity of your wit.

In a vast ocean of affairs, he hath lived as fishes who keep silence within the loud noise of waves, and preserve their plump substance fresh in the brackish waters.

He sheltered himself with subtleties, as a hedgehog with his quills.

To behold (as in the glass of a bright mirror) on the one side —, on the other —.

As soon as break of day drew the curtain of heaven.

Virginity is as redolent balm, which ascends to heaven in a perpetual sacrifice.

Religion is the hive where the honey of good doctrine is made.

He put them in the furnace of tribulation to purify them.[19]

Here is another, by the poet Lady Anne Southwell (1573–1636), later married to Captain Henry Sibthorpe. Her manuscript book contains original poems, translations, letters (which often resemble essays), transcripts of poems that she obviously liked, accounts, theological reflections, a short bestiary, and also a collection of thirty 'Apothegms' or maxims:

1   He that knows not where to find the sea, let him take a river for his guide.

2   It is a happy necessity that makes a man better than he would be.

3   He that builds up virtue in words and destroys it in action is an audacious hypocrite, one that builds up fame with one hand and hell with another.

4   He that must depend upon God for his salvation and dare not trust him for a morsel of bread is a laborious [assiduous] atheist . . .

20 As rusticity befits not a gentleman, so ink-pot terms best become a pedagogue.[20]

The range of subjects covered in the extracts from Blount again confirms for us that 'literature' designated acquaintance with practically all recorded knowledge.

Although a modern reader might disparage books like these, scanning these commonplaces reminds us that distinctions between content and form, between thought and expression, matter and word, are generally difficult to sustain. Indeed, Francis Bacon thought that the collection of commonplaces generated more wisdom than the writing out of 'methods' or summaries:

I hold the diligence and pain in collecting commonplaces to be of great use and certainty in studying, as that which aids the memory, sub-ministers copy to invention [submits the text to the selection of topics to be treated], and contracts [sharpens] the sight of judgment to a strength.[21]

Language and Experience

As for verse, Renaissance students would not have thought of poetry as being primarily concerned with *expression* – the revelation of inward and private experience. For many eminent genres such as epic, pastoral or satire, of course, that notion is inappropriate, but even for lyric or love poetry it may be misleading. In 1805, Wordsworth was to describe 'all good poetry' as 'the spontaneous overflow of powerful feelings', a celebrated romantic formula, but one that does not really suit Renaissance verse. Wordsworth in fact went on to say: 'Though this be true, poems to which any value can be attached were never produced on any variety of subjects but by a man who, being possessed of more than usual organic sensibility, *had also thought long and deeply*.'[22] Yet, taken out of its context, it is the first part of Wordsworth's descrip-tion, which emphasizes subjective feeling, that has lodged in the consciousness of the English-speaking world as a touchstone for all poetry.

Such a definition, which purports to identify the *origins* of writings, overlooks *language*. It dulls awareness of the ways in which words can be made to work, an awareness that is so necessary to a poet. It would have seemed very strange at a time when poets were consid-ered not only as individuals possessed of particular sensitivities but as careful craftsmen. Renaissance scholars liked to point out that the Greek word *poetes* had meant 'maker'. Ben Jonson defined 'Poesy', the art of poetry, as the poet's 'skill or craft of making'.[23] In order to make a table, a joiner would draw upon the arts of wood-turning and carpentry that he had learned as an apprentice to a master of his trade. By analogy, a poet (in the Renaissance the word could designate a writer of prose as well as of verse) would have recourse to recognized skills in order to fashion a text out of the medium's material – which is language.

We can readily confirm these observations concerning Renaissance poetics by attempting to write a response to or continuation of a poem from the period, particularly one that uses complicated stanzas like many poems by Donne. Romantic descriptions of poetry as 'expression' give no hint of the *work*, the revising, polishing, getting it right, that goes into the fabrication of any work of art. Sir Philip Sidney famously wrote in his *Apology for Poetry* (1595): 'Only the poet . . . lifted up with the vigour of his own invention, doth grow in effect, into another nature, in *making* things either better than Nature bringeth forth, or quite anew, forms such as never were in Nature.'[24] Sidney delicately avoids the suggestion that the poet resembles the Great Artificer, God himself, but certainly regards the profession of poets as something like a craft guild.

Imitation

As we have seen, training for writers included time spent at school and university constructing 'imitations' of texts written by masters of the trade, not only mimicking the forms and content of classical poetry, but composing orations as well as speeches for and praises of historical figures. This form of education admirably combined academic study with the practice of a writers' workshop – in some ways, students resembled apprentices. It was the Italian poet and scholar Francesco Petrarca ('Petrarch', 1304–74, whose life overlapped that of Geoffrey Chaucer) who had advocated both the concept and the practice of keeping commonplace books and thus accelerated the Renaissance cult of eloquence. 'Originality' (the very concept is anachronistic) was not a necessary marker for authenticity or quality. Indeed, Ben Jonson wrote that a requisite 'in our poet or maker is imitation, to be able to convert the substance or riches of another poet to his own use'.[25] For many, it was more important to write about common and familiar material in a way that was pleasing and appropriate than to seek out new or unfamiliar subjects.

We might react by reflecting that the continual writing of exercises in imitation must have prevented authors appearing 'sincere', finding individual voices. However, readers valued 'originality' less than assurance and skill, the former deriving from a writer's ability to use appropriate authorities for both substance and style. Authorities could be either writers or texts, and the 'authority' a reader might find in a text would not come from a sense of the writer's personality.

Certainly there are reams of undistinguished and mechanical Elizabethan sonnets of the kind that Shakespeare parodied in 'My mistress' eyes are nothing like the sun', and John Donne tended to avoid the references to classical deities that lace so many Renaissance texts. Surely, however, familiarity with a range of styles is for an author an enabling rather than a restricting faculty. Most writers start off, unconsciously perhaps, by producing imitations or pastiches; they imitate 'art' rather than represent 'life'. In a context like this, therefore, we may conclude that writing precedes speaking in that a poet may use language to construct a voice or persona, rather than finding a way for feelings or thoughts to create language.

Later, romantic writers came to distrust any kind of imitation that might harden into 'rules' and stifle creativity. However, their distrust of traditional word skills was not widespread in the Renaissance. Many writers, particularly those writing for a coterie audience, rejoiced in displays of 'wit': in this context, the word designates 'knowingness' as well as vivacity of thought or fancy. T. S. Eliot spoke of a union of thought with feeling, and then, in an essay on Marvell: '[Wit] is more than a technical accomplishment, or the vocabulary and syntax of an epoch; it is, what we have designated tentatively as wit, a tough *reasonableness* beneath the slight lyric grace.'[26] Texts in which allusions or forms of words and thought were instantly recognizable made for closeness between writer and reader.

Any text, however, that was studded with abstruse words – Anne Southwell's 'ink-pot terms' – or which offered only clumsy or showy logical or rhetorical practices, might attract the charge of 'courtesan-like painted affectation'.[27] In *Hamlet*, Osric's style of speech defies a widespread classical and Renaissance assumption that a crucial function of art was to conceal art.[28] This is spelt out in Baldassare Castiglione's widely read courtesy book, *The Book of the Courtier* (1528) where the author speaks of the need for writing to be possessed of 'grace', for a work to display *sprezzatura*. What is most important is

to eschew as much as a man may, and as a sharp and dangerous rock, too much curiousness [inquisitiveness, strangeness], and (to speak a new word) to use in everything a certain 'disgracing' [disfiguring or imperfection] to cover art withal, and seem whatsoever he doth and saith to do it without pain and (as it were) not minding it.[29]

Over-profuse displays of copiousness or over-ingenious imagery, on the one hand, or studied perfection, on the other, offend against the criterion of this kind of liveliness or grace. In his 'Ode: Of Wit' Abraham Cowley invoked a similar criterion for success:

> In a true piece of wit all things must be,
>   Yet all things there agree,
> As in the ark, joined without force or strife,
> All creatures dwelt, all creatures that had life.

The comparison between complexity in a text and Noah's loaded ark is itself ingenious and implicitly challenges us to decide whether the simile in fact displays 'force or strife'.

Ben Jonson's wonderful tribute to Shakespeare, printed at the beginning of the first collected edition of Shakespeare's *Comedies, Histories, and Tragedies* (the first folio of 1623), praises Shakespeare as a 'natural' poet, but then turns to describe the *work* required to attain to that status:

> Yet must I not give nature all: thy art,
> My gentle Shakespeare, must enjoy a part.
> For though the poet's matter nature be,
> His art doth give the fashion; and that he
> Who casts to write a living line, must sweat,
> (Such as thine are) and strike the second heat
> Upon the Muses' anvil; turn the same
> (And himself with it) that he thinks to frame,
> Or, for the laurel, he may gain a scorn;
> For a good poet's made, as well as born.

Does the awkwardness or the placing of the parentheses in this passage exemplify Castiglione's 'disgracing'?

Description

One of the particular skills for a poet was that of description. Descriptive parts of a poem, it was commonly held, ought to function like pictures. Horace's dictum *'ut pictura poesis'* (a poem [should be] like a picture) was widely repeated: Sidney said 'poesie . . . is an art of imitation . . . a representing, counterfeiting, or figuring forth – to speak metaphorically, a speaking picture – with this end, to teach and delight.'[30] However, as we have already seen in the passage from Lanyer, the Renaissance desire for rhetorical vividness (*enargeia*)[31] did not generate descriptions that accord with our sense of what constitutes 'realism'. Moreover, many descriptions contain figures of speech: similes and metaphors, for example. Given that metaphors combine two elements, adduce 'abstract similarities between things materially different',[32] it is impossible for us to 'see' them in our mind's eye. Instead, even as we experience them, we may be invited to inspect the cultural patterns that make the assertion of similarity in dissimilarity possible.

Just as Lanyer assembled a description of place that artfully submitted chosen moral qualities to the reader, so, when describing people, authors proceeded methodically. In the love poetry of the period, as we shall see in chapter 6, there are many descriptions of women's bodies where authors list details from head to toe, following the conventions of the 'blazon' which, as in a heraldic crest, did not *show* a 'real' woman but set forth or 'ciphered' what was desirable. In other kinds of poetry, descriptions are overtly allegorized. Here is the figure that is to accompany the Knight of the Red Cross in Book 1 of Spenser's *Faerie Queene*:

> A louely Ladie rode him faire beside,
>   Vpon a lowly Asse more white then snow,
>   Yet she much whiter, but the same did hide
>   Vnder a vele, that wimpled was full low,
>   And ouer all a black stole she did throw,
>   As one that inly mourned: so was she sad,
>   And heauie sat vpon her palfrey slow:
>   Seemed in heart some hidden care she had,
> And by her in a line a milke white lambe she lad.
>
> (*Faerie Queene*, 1.1.4)

The woman, Una, is not named, and the details serve not to evoke her person but to ascribe to her the virtues of Christ who also rode upon an ass to signify his humility and who was associated with the sacrificial lamb (John 1: 29). Such a figure cannot be *seen* as a picture or *perceived* in the mind's eye but must be conceived: it is, in the language of the period, a 'conceit' that has to be *read*. (The word 'conceit' derives from the Italian *concetto* and means simply an idea or concept. It came to be applied to a fanciful or ingenious figure of speech, sometimes a much-extended metaphor of the kind enjoyed by poets like Donne and Cowley.)[33] Later, in Book 2, when Sir Guyon is approaching the Bower of Bliss, he encounters a landscape characteristic of a lost golden age:

> There the most daintie Paradise on ground,
>   It selfe doth offer to his sober eye,
>   In which all pleasures plenteously abound,
>   And none does others happinesse enuye:
>   The painted flowres, the trees vpshooting hye,
>   The dales for shade, the hilles for breathing space,
>   The trembling groues, the Christall running by;
>   And that, which all faire workes doth most aggrace,
> The art, which all that wrought, appeared in no place.
>   (*Faerie Queene*, 2.12.58)

Again, we find a description based on a list, and Spenser builds into this a paradoxical display of artfulness ('painted flowers') as well as an insistence that art must not draw attention to itself – his debt to Castiglione's notions of artistic grace is obvious.

Contemporary Criticism and Rhetoric

The study of letters was claimed to be a civilizing influence. Milton magniloquently claimed: 'These [poetic] abilities . . . are of power, beside the office of a pulpit, to inbreed and cherish in a great people the seeds of virtue and public civility, to allay perturbations of the mind, and set the affections in right tune.'[34] Indeed, Renaissance writers' interests in texts tended to centre on *effects* rather than origins: what a poem denoted to its listeners or readers, rather than what its author meant or intended. By contrast, nineteenth-century romantic critics were to centre their attentions on the origins of a discourse in a speaking or writing subject, in imaginative qualities, or in the rendering of feeling and emotion (which today might define a text as being 'literary'). Earlier theorists were more interested in the functions of language, and their understanding and practice of writing meant that the prime criterion for artistic success was fitness for purpose, or propriety, a notion to which we shall return. A poem, play or prose narrative was like a tool that had specific uses. Professional writers composed texts for patrons – such works would be judged not by evidence of authenticity, genuineness or 'sincerity', but according to criteria of art shared by a community that extended over all of Europe. Sir Philip Sidney opened his *Apology for Poetry* with a praise of the 'practice' (skill, occupation) of an esteemed Italian horseman: by implication, poets were able to train themselves and evolve a similar 'practice'.

Plays too were artefacts, and playwrights sold their texts as products to playing companies. Just as a wheelwright's shop might include a number of workers, so plays were often written in collaboration. Jointly written texts have, in a post-romantic period, been stigmatized: they cannot, it is often thought, match the 'works' of an Olympian genius but must be the stuff of mere jobbers. However, around half of the plays of the period were written collaboratively – in Henslowe's stable of writers around two-thirds.[35] For these works to enjoy the success they did, basic practices must have been shared by their authors. In general, then, 'technique' was not a *problem* to be mastered or overcome: rather, the following of systematic procedures and familiarity with forms and techniques, provided they were not too conspicuous, were regarded as enabling activities.

These techniques and the art of verbal communication centred, as we have now gathered, on the discipline of rhetoric. This was the study of discourse, spoken and written. From the time of Plato until the age of romanticism, it was an important educational discipline, a practice that raised consciousness and, indeed, fostered creativity. Ben Jonson may have claimed that Shakespeare 'wanted art' [lacked a knowledge of the techniques of writing], but we have already seen that a familiarity with rhetoric can be readily deduced from his work.

However, before proceeding further, we must note that the acquisition of rhetorical skills was not the only prerequisite for a writer. Plato considered that there was a distinction between orator and poet: while the orator had to be reasonable, the poet needed to be possessed by a kind of madness, a 'divine frenzy', a notion propounded by the Florentine neo-platonist and humanist Marsilio Ficino (1433–99).

George Chapman invoked the notion in his Dedication of Homer's *Odyssey* (1614) to the Earl of Somerset: 'for . . . says the divine philosopher [Plato], he that knocks at the gates of the Muses, *sine Musarum furore* [without the madness of the Muses], is neither to be admitted entry, nor a touch at their thresholds; his opinion of entry ridiculous, and his presumption impious.' Chapman reconciles *divinus furor* with Christian teaching by calling it 'a perfection directly infused from God'. George Puttenham too invoked 'divine instinct (the Platonics call it *furor*)', and thought that good writing came 'by excellence of nature and complexion; or by great subtlety of the spirits and wit; or by much experience and observation of the world . . . or peradventure by all or most part of them'.[36] There was, therefore, an acknowledgement of inspiration or innate talent, encapsulated in the proverb 'Poets are born but orators are made'.[37]

Poetry and oratory had been long allied. It was believed that classical rhetoric developed in law courts where speakers had to persuade their listeners of the validity of what they were saying. This is implied at the opening of one of the earliest English Renaissance rhetoric books, that by Sir Thomas Wilson: 'Rhetoric is an art to set forth, by utterance of words, matter at large, or, as Cicero doth say, it is a learned or rather an artificial declaration of the mind, in the handling of any cause called in contention, that may through reason largely be discussed.'[38] 'Persuasion' became recognized as the aim of rhetoric, indeed the purpose of very many texts. Representative testimony comes from George Puttenham: 'Utterance also and language is given by Nature to man for persuasion of others and aid of themselves.'[39]

Other Renaissance writers found themselves at the centre of the age-long debate concerning the moral effects of eloquence and writing. In 1577 John Northbrooke wrote: 'Learning and good letters to young men bringeth sobriety',[40] but for each authority who claimed that eloquence and writing could redeem and 'fashion' a gentleman, there was an antagonist who disparaged the feignings of poets and the immorality of plays, deplored the way in which profane books and plays led to depravity, and would abolish all but godly writings.

To some modern readers, rhetorical disciplines, so conspicuous in Renaissance educational practice and culture, may seem to be both irrelevant to the enjoyment of Renaissance texts and hostile to many values current in contemporary culture. The adjective 'rhetorical' is now generally a term of political or critical abuse, and the subject would seem to have gone out of fashion almost two hundred years ago. For a post-romantic sensibility, the idea of studying the craft of speaking and writing might seem to be at odds with the high valuation we place upon 'sincerity' and spontaneity. All this notwithstanding, however, some acquaintance with rhetorical theory helps readers of Renaissance texts.

Rhetoric can be purged of the two pejorative meanings that derive from modern meanings for its derivative adjective, 'rhetorical'. It does not merely designate hot air, nor is it just the arid study of rules and ornaments. It *can* be objective and not prescriptive, and can offer a conceptual framework for the description of texts. It is not simply a study of ornamentation, of figures of speech, of sound applied to sense, for example, but addresses knowledge in action, the organization of argument in discourse, and stylistic realization. Rhetoric historically included *memory* and *delivery*, the arts of the orator that derive from the kind of spoken address heard in a law court. However, rhetoric was not concerned only with formal or ceremonial discourse, high culture, and the artistic. The categories of classical rhetoric could be used to describe workaday speech, colloquial and written, as well as, of course, 'non-literary' texts.

Implicit in the awareness of both logical and rhetorical practice was a recognition that thinking cannot readily be separated from speaking and writing. Today it is often claimed (misleadingly) that a failure to communicate may be merely a failure of 'expression', that we can build up an argument in the mind and then 'put it into words' to convey it to someone else. Instead of considering thought and expression, logic and rhetoric, as two separate activities, some Renaissance authorities recognized that they were part of one complex activity. Today it is more useful to say that discourse is knowledge rather than to speak of knowledge 'in' discourse. In the Renaissance it was common to illustrate this union figuratively: a closed fist represented logic, an open palm signified rhetoric. Alexander Pope's aphorism from the eighteenth century – 'expression is the dress of thought' – is often quoted, but what is forgotten is what comes before: '[Expression] gilds all objects, but it alters none.' 'Dress' therefore means 'what makes thought visible and able to be placed or categorised'.[41]

But we do have to concede a prejudice: rhetoric has long been associated with untruth. A bad man might use the art of persuasion to goad others towards evil courses of action. We recognize this sort of thing in the *suasiones*, the persuasive monologues put into the mouths of would-be seducers. These tend to be not only effusions of loving feelings but poems that imply a response, either acceptance of an amorous invitation or engagement with the line of reasoning set out in the poem. 'Come live with me and be my love', Marlowe's invitation to his love to frolic with him in a pastoral landscape, generated sardonic rejoinders from both Donne ('The Bait') and Ralegh ('The Nymph's Reply').

Wooing occurred in public as well as in private: Marlowe's Tamburlaine acquires power not just by feats of arms but by feats of eloquence – Marlowe, unlike Shakespeare, tends not to offer on-stage battles. Any weapon might fall into bad hands, its abuse does not invalidate its use, and the Cambridge-educated Christopher Marlowe took delight in showing that skill in rhetoric, combined with political image-making, is a prerequisite for power.

Who were the authorities? In the Renaissance, as we should expect when the study of writing was the study of Latin and Greek, the works of classical rhetoricians were studied: Plato's *Gorgias*, rhetorics by Aristotle and Cicero, Quintilian's *Institutio Oratoria*, and the Pseudo-Ciceronian *Rhetorica ad Herennium*. These spawned rhetorical handbooks in English as they did in other vernacular languages of Europe, including Wilson's *Art of Rhetoric* (1553) and Puttenham's *Arte of English Poesie* (1589). Rhetoric *had* been studied in the Middle Ages – Chaucer knew Geoffroi de Vinsauf – but the humanists' revival of *litterae humaniores*, of rhetoric and eloquence, is one of the hallmarks of the Renaissance and enabled the flowering of the 'creative' work we associate with that period.

Students recognized the three kinds of oratory or writing set out by Aristotle and Quintilian: judicial (associated with the law courts), deliberative (for popular assemblies), and laudatory (or 'epideictic', sometimes used for showy praise of gods and men).[42] Among the kinds of writing exercise common at schools or universities was the preparation of a *chreia*, a discourse on the sayings or deeds of a great man.[43] In his *Art of Rhetoric*, Thomas Wilson offered 'An example of commending a noble personage', 'An example of comfort' (addressed to the Duchess of Suffolk on the death of her sons), as well as 'An Epistle to persuade a young gentleman to marriage, devised by Erasmus in the behalf of his friend.' The latter helped beget the first group of Shakespeare's sonnets addressed to an anonymous young man.

Composition

During their rhetorical training, students encountered five traditional processes or 'faculties': invention, disposition (arrangement), elocution (style), memory, and delivery. The first, 'invention', does not mean making something up out of nothing, but finding, retrieving and selecting material. In the Proem to *The Faerie Queene*, Spenser asks his muse to lay forth the contents of her 'scryne' (coffer), a figure of the virtual repository from which writers might 'invent' the matter of their texts. The first task was to assemble the facts of the case. You would then, according to Aristotle, address yourself to proofs, topics and commonplaces. When you were proving, you would first consider *ethos*, your ability to convince the audience of your own moral integrity. You might then deploy *pathos*, an emotional appeal to the audience, or *logos*, an appeal to reason by logical argument. You would also, as we have seen, have learnt schematized sets of topics – storehouses of trains of thought, or well-tried ways of stimulating thought. For example, one of the ways of praising a great man would be from the 'topic' of his place of birth – how often have we heard this today in after-dinner speeches? Thomas Wilson recommended this topic: 'The shire or town helpeth somewhat towards the increase of honour. As it is much better to be born in Paris than in Picardie, in London than in Lincoln. For that both the air is better, the people more civil, and the wealth much greater, and the men for the most part more wise.'[44] As we have seen, 'commonplaces' were originally topics that were common to many kinds of material: later the word lost its technical meaning and came to designate maxims or pithy sayings. 'All the world's a stage' is an example, an observation that could be used in both fictional and political discourses. Shakespeare used it in *As You Like It* and it is also found in 1.4 of *Freewill*, a literary tragedy devoted to theological discussion, translated into English by Henry Cheeke in 1561. (If these words are entered into an internet search engine, they will be found as titles for scholarly research sites, for educational forums, even for shopping – the commonplace survives.)

The second 'faculty', disposition, had to do with arranging the parts of a discourse and shaping its structure. Many handbooks reproduce schemas that obviously derive from practice in a court of law. A typical 'introduction' served to make hearers well disposed. Mark Antony began his address to the Roman people: 'Friends, Romans, countrymen, lend me your ears' (*Julius Caesar*, 1599, 3.2.74). Narration followed, 'an evident setting forth of all things that belong unto the [matter in hand], with a brief rehearsal grounded upon some reason',[45] followed by an outline of what was to follow (*divisio* or *partitio*), then the main part of the oration, the 'proof' (*confirmatio*), a refutation if there were opposing arguments to be dealt with, and, finally, a conclusion (*peroratio*), which might include appeals through *pathos* as well as a summing up.

Style and Decorum

Having considered what to say, the orator next considered how to say it: this process was known as *elocution*. Cicero's widely followed scheme named three basic styles: *gravis*, *mediocris*, *extenuata*. These are described in one of the most widely used rhetorical handbooks, the *Rhetorica ad Herennium*, attributed to but not in fact written by Cicero: 'The grand style consists of a smooth and ornate arrangement of impressive words. The middle style consists of words of a lower, yet not of the lowest and colloquial class of words. The simple style is brought down even to the most current idiom of standard speech.'[46] According to the principle of *decorum*, you fitted your words and style to your subject matter, to the situation or, if you were creating a fictive character, to the person speaking. You also could fashion yourself as a gentleman by adopting the style and dialect of the oligarchy in the south-east of the country.

In a play of about 1565 performed by boy players, the author, Richard Edwards, set out in the Prologue the way in which decorum served as a means of characterization:

> In comedies the greatest skill is this, rightly to touch
> All things to the quick; and eke to frame each person so
> That by his common talk you may his nature rightly know;
> A roister ought not preach, that were too strange to hear,
> But as from virtue he doth swerve, so ought his words appear;
> The old man is sober, the young man rash, the lover triumphing in
>   joys,
> The matron grave, the harlot wild and full of wanton toys;
> Which all in one course they no wise do agree:
> So correspondent to their kind their speeches ought to be.

Two points emerge from all of this. First, style does not designate what is merely ornamental, and, second, 'rhetorical' is not a word to be applied only to high style. If you use the colloquial, you are employing a style: it is not valid to label Macbeth's verse as 'rhetorical' and the prose of his Porter as 'unrhetorical'.

Awareness of decorum, of the proper relation between style and content, also created a subject for wit, parody and humour. John Marston artfully creates a kind of pastiche in what his dedication calls a 'seriously fantastical' text for boy players, *Antonio and Mellida* (c.1599). In the dialogue we find a distinctive technique: the excess of the diction suggests that the topics and figures of heroic drama are both taken up and disowned:

> PIERO   Victorious Fortune, with triumphant hand
>   Hurleth my glory 'bout this ball of earth,
>   Whilst the Venetian Duke is heavèd up
>   On wings of fair success to overlook
>   The low-cast ruins of his enemies;
>   To see myself adored and Genoa quake,
>   My fate is firmer then mischance can shake.
> FELICHE   Stand, the ground trembleth.
> PIERO   Ha? An earthquake?
> BALURDO   Oh, I smell a sound.
> FELICHE   Piero, stay, for I descry a fume,
>   Creeping from out the bosom of the deep,
>   The breath of darkness, fatal when 'tis whist [kept quiet]
>   In greatness' stomach: this same smoke, called pride,
>   Take heed she'll lift thee to improvidence,
>   And break thy neck from steep security.   (1.1.37–50)

Dialogue and Dialectic

One of the most common rhetorical exercises was the preparation of debates for and against a certain person or position, the skill of arguing *in utramque partem*. Students also took part in plays and the enactment of dialogues like those in Erasmus' *Colloquia* (1522–33), a collection of playlets with titles like 'The Shipwreck', 'Exorcism' and 'A Pilgrimage for Religion's Sake'. These taught children to express themselves in a lively style of Latin (but also inculcated a sceptical attitude towards some of the practices of Catholicism that were to be attacked by reformers). This particular rhetorical skill, combined with traditions of school and academic playing, encouraged the flowering of drama – drama grows from conflict or debate. This is important both historically and critically because for a long time there was a tendency to present Renaissance drama as moral, if not moralistic, supportive of the 'order' desired by those in authority. If we remind ourselves of these rhetorical structures, the rules of this play of mind,[47] we may be more able to see how Renaissance drama was deliberative or even interrogative of the causes and institutions of the period. In the case of a play like Marlowe's *Dr Faustus* (c.1592), meaning might be created more by the pitch and toss of arguments over whether there were or ought to be limits to human knowledge than by the play's resolution.

Dialectical mental skill was also basic to the advancement of learning: a French moralist philosopher spoke of 'Dialectic or logic, which is to learn the truth of all things by disputation.'[48] 'Disputation' created a pattern for many literary texts. Dialectical structure, the pattern of Plato's philosophical dialogues, was to be found in courtesy books like Castiglione's *Book of the Courtier*, to a degree in Sir Thomas More's *Utopia* (1516), in Spenser's *View of the Present State of Ireland* (written in 1596), as well as in debate poems such as Marvell's 'A Dialogue between the Resolved Soul and Created Pleasure'. Other poems, Donne's poems of seduction, for example, may be profitably imagined not just as monologues but as dialogues with the contesting voice suppressed, perhaps to be heard in the consciousness of the listener or reader. This is a device for irony: the poems do not 'express' a sensibility but enact or describe one.

Figures of Speech, Metre and Rhythm

To modern readers of Renaissance verse, its most prominent stylistic technique is the deployment of figures of speech to move or delight its audience. In his *Rhetoric*, Aristotle had noted that 'good style' must deploy clear and appropriate language, but might also use unfamiliar or foreign words that audiences or readers might find striking (*Rhetoric*, 1404b). Sir John Harington quoted a Latin tag that was deployed countless times: 'as Horace sayth, *Omne tulit punctum qui miscuit utile dulci*, he that can mingle the sweet and the wholesome, the pleasant and the profitable, he is indeed an absolute good writer.'[49] Puttenham considered that 'our writing and speeches public ought to be figurative.'[50]

Figures of speech were conventionally divided into two categories: 'schemes' in which the conventional order of words is adjusted, and 'tropes' where sense is turned or altered. The first sonnet of Sir Philip Sidney's *Astrophil and Stella* (1591), a poem about the writing of verse, provides convenient examples:

> Loving in truth, and fain in verse my love to show,
> That she (dear she) might take some pleasure of my pain:
> Pleasure might cause her read, reading might make her know,
> Knowledge might pity win, and pity grace obtain,
>
> I sought fit words to paint the blackest face of woe,
> Studying inventions fine, her wits to entertain:
> Oft turning others' leaves to see if thence would flow
> Some fresh and fruitful showers upon my sunburnt brain.
>
> But words came halting forth, wanting Invention's stay,
> Invention, Nature's child, fled step-dame Study's blows,
> And others' feet seemed but strangers in my way.
>
> Thus, great with child to speak and helpless in my throws,
> Biting my truant pen, beating myself for spite,
> 'Fool', said my muse to me, 'look in thy heart and write.'

The first line uses two patterns of repetition: *parison*, the even balancing of phrases, and *isocolon*, the use of similarly structured elements within the phrases. The first quatrain is built around *climax* (the Greek word for 'ladder') or 'gradation' which sets out words in increasing order of importance, culminating in 'grace', the lady's favour or, perhaps in this context, the gift of her body. Climax combines with a kind of *anadiplosis*, the repetition of the last word in a phrase at the beginning of the next ('read . . . reading', 'know . . . knowledge'). These are all 'schemes'.

Tropes in Sidney's poem include metaphors (using words to 'paint', for example), *paronomasia* or puns (on 'feet'), and personification. The poem also attends to decorum ('fit words' for a woeful speech) and alludes to the rhetorical faculty of invention. This is important in that it is tempting to take the poem as a rejection of all rhetorical practices, an injunction to speak sincerely or 'from the heart'. But what Sidney is saying is that he should avoid the fanciful schemes and tropes he has just set forth with such skill, and *seek out figures* that are associated with the joys and pains of love: 'art' and method cannot be avoided.

The poem thus demonstrates that verse of this kind cannot be adequately explained with reference to 'expressive' language. Like so many of the period's texts, the use of language is self-reflexive or heuristic: the act of writing creates definition even as it proceeds, and is an instrument of investigation (the meaning of 'heuristic'). Thinking and feeling do not come before speaking and writing but are all parts of one activity. (The German philosopher Martin Heidegger famously pointed out that 'language speaks'.) Poets of the Renaissance sometimes resemble sculptors, working with and against the grain of their material, the words and figures that they have 'invented'. Moreover, some demonstrate how, when the subject of their texts is personal, about themselves, the self is either infinitely recessive or constituted only in language: in Sonnet 58 of the same sequence, Sidney described how 'In piercing phrases late / The anatomy of all my woes I wrate.' Anatomizing the structures of a poem and the self that 'created' it are one and the same activity. To put this another way, Sidney's figure of anatomy reveals paradoxically that what is within is identical with what is performed, or that, in an instance like this, 'inwardness' may not exist in any meaningful sense.

Students also spent a lot of time committing to memory other figures of speech: irony, hyperbole, anaphora, and so on. A favourite figure for sonneteers, one used profusely by Petrarch, was oxymoron, the combination of contradictory terms:

> Some lovers speak when they their muses entertain
> Of hopes begot by fear, of wot not what desires:
> Of force of heavenly beams, infusing hellish pain,
> Of *living deaths, dear wounds, fair storms,* and *freezing fires.*
> (Sidney, *Astrophil and Stella,* 6.1–4)

In his gloss to 'Januarie' in Spenser's *Shepheardes Calender,* 'E. K.' (the author himself?) cheerfully pointed out, presumably without pedantic intention, not only that the poem was imitating Virgil but that the lines

'I love thilke lass, (alas, why do I love?) / And am forlorn, (alas why am I lorn?)' contained 'a pretty *epanorthosis* [a figure in which a word is recalled, in order to substitute a more correct or stronger term], and withal a *paronomasia* or playing with the word, where he sayth, 'I love thilke lass, (alas etc.)''. Such a poem is concerned not just with the expression of 'meaning' or 'feelings' but also with instilling the pleasure of art. Even if the kind of arid memorizing of which E. K.'s note is a token has given rhetoric a bad name, most speakers even now use figures of speech frequently, even if they do not remember their names.

The centrality of figures of speech in rhetorical composition and the fact that these change the meaning of individual words (as do metaphors) constantly draw the attention of writers and readers to the substantiveness of discourse. Words serve not only as vehicles for thought but also as instruments to interrogate thought. Ben Jonson, in imitation of the ancient metaphor of *silva* (a wood or woodland) for a collection of works similar in kind, called a group of his poems 'The Forest' (published in *Epigrams*, 1616); this was followed by *Underwoods* (1640); and *Timber, or Discoveries Made upon Men and Matter* (1641), a combination commonplace book and working notebook. The titles of these three texts serve to remind their readers of verbal materiality.

Romantic critics tended to forget the 'thinginess' of words, the topic of a conversation between the nineteenth-century poet Mallarmé and the painter Degas:

DEGAS What a business! My whole day gone on a blasted sonnet, without getting an inch further . . . and it isn't ideas I'm short of . . . I'm full of them, I've got too many . . .
MALLARMÉ But Degas, you can't make a poem with ideas – you make it with *words*![51]

Thinking of words as substantive entities means that we can refer to them as ideologically shaped or imprinted: much modern criticism rests on a study of interpretative metaphors which might help us understand cultural changes.

In drama, a conspicuous scheme is the deployment of *stichomythia*, a device found in classical Greek drama and which uses some of the schemes of repetition found in the Sidney sonnet. This is dialogue in alternate lines, used in disputes, and characterized by antithesis or the taking up of the opponent's words. In *Richard III* (1592–3),

Shakespeare uses it for the perilous wooing game played by Richard of Gloucester with the Lady Anne:

LADY ANNE   I would I knew thy heart.
RICHARD   'Tis figured in my tongue.
LADY ANNE   I fear me both are false.
RICHARD   Then never man was true.
LADY ANNE   Well, well, put up your sword.
RICHARD   Say then my peace is made.
LADY ANNE   That shalt thou know hereafter.
RICHARD   But shall I live in hope?
LADY ANNE   All men, I hope, live so.
RICHARD   Vouchsafe to wear this ring.
LADY ANNE   To take is not to give.

(*Richard III*, 1.2.180–90)

This resembles devices that were coming to be used in opera: pleasure for the audience comes as much from form as from content and it may not be appropriate to ask whether Lady Anne's acquiescence is 'realistic'.

Just as the use of figures wrests words from their normal meanings, poets often played the spoken *rhythm* of verse phrases against the normative *metrical patterns* they had established, or played clause and sentence against the lines and stanzas they had created. The actual pattern of stressed and unstressed syllables in the opening stanza of Donne's 'A Valediction of Weeping' digresses almost as far as is possible from regularity:

>   Let me pour forth
> My tears before thy face, whilst I stay here;
> For thy face coins them, and thy stamp they bear,
> And by this mintage they are something worth:
>   For thus they be
>   Pregnant of thee;
> Fruits of much grief they are, emblems of more.
> When a tear falls, that thou falls which it bore:
> So thou and I are nothing then, when on a divers shore.

There is a contest here between rhythm and metre, creating a sense of singularity that, in the context, creates a 'personality' for the speaker. Yet again we encounter an example of 'naturalness' created by art.

Syntax and Style

Those figures *parison* and *isocolon* that we encountered in the Sidney sonnet were the basis of the distinctive style ('euphuism') developed by John Lyly in his plays, and particularly in his prose romance, *Euphues, The Anatomy of Wit* (1587).[52] Here is its opening:

> There dwelt in Athens a young gentleman of great patrimony, and of so comely a personage that it was doubted whether he were more bound to Nature for the lineaments of his person, or to Fortune for the increase of his possessions. But Nature impatient of comparisons, and as it were disdaining a companion or copartner in her working, added to this comeliness of his body such a sharp capacity of mind, that not only she proved Fortune counterfeit, but was half of that opinion that she herself was only current. This young gallant, of more wit than wealth, and yet of more wealth than wisdom, seeing himself inferior to none in pleasant conceits, thought himself superior to all in honest conditions, insomuch that he deemed himself so apt to all things, that he gave himself almost to nothing but practising of those things commonly which are incident to these sharp wits, fine phrases, smooth quipping, merry taunting, using jesting without mean, and abusing mirth without measure. As therefore the sweetest rose hath his prickle, the finest velvet his brack [flaw], the fairest flower his bran, so the sharpest wit hath his wanton will, and the holiest head his wicked way . . .

Although a dazzling display of copiousness, *Euphues*, like Sidney's sonnet sequence, is scarcely a book to read for its story. Rather, it invites the reader to savour its texture – it begins with dedicatory epistles 'To the ladies and gentlewomen of England' and 'To the gentlemen readers'. Does it, however, depend entirely upon ostentation and the creation of a coterie readership? Is it a kind of early modern kitsch? No – as we may see by analysing one of the things said about Euphues who, 'seeing himself inferior to none in pleasant conceits, thought himself superior to all in honest conditions [qualities or character]'. The patterned speech acts as a kind of defamiliarization: it invites us to ponder the relationship between wit and polished manners, on the one hand, and moral worth, on the other. That part of the sentence is ironical, showing a distinction between the narrator's evaluation of Euphues and Euphues' evaluation of himself.

Another kind of high-profile prose technique is to be found in the imitation of the syntax of Cicero, who combined copiousness with suspense, keeping his intention suppressed by leaving the main verb of the sentence until its 'period' or end. A bravura periodic sentence comes from Richard Hooker's *Of the Laws of Ecclesiastical Polity* (1593–7) where the author demonstrates the necessity of political order by drawing an analogy with the natural order. Natural law, he argues, devolves from the divine law obeyed by angels, and human law, discernible by the light of reason applied to the book of nature, has as its purpose the preservation of order:

> Now if Nature should intermit her course and leave altogether, though it were but for awhile, the observation of her own laws; if those principal and mother elements of the world, whereof all things in this lower world are made, should lose the qualities which now they have; if the frame of that heavenly arch erected over our heads should loosen and dissolve itself; if celestial spheres should forget their wonted motions, and by irregular volubility turn themselves any way as it might happen; if the prince of the lights of heaven which now as a giant doth run his unwearied course, should, as it were through a languishing faintness, begin to stand and to rest himself; if the moon should wander from her beaten way, the times and seasons of the year blend themselves by disordered and confused mixture, the winds breathe out their last gasp, the clouds yield no rain, the earth be defeated of heavenly influence, the fruits of the earth pine away as children at the withered breasts of their mother no longer able to yield them relief – what would become of man himself, whom these things now do all serve?[53]

An ingenious reader might note that Hooker's technique deconstructs his intention in that the gendering of Nature, a figure standing for constancy and order, creates that deity as feminine, which, according to the customary values of the day, was associated not with permanence but with inconsistency (like the moon), wantonness and disorder.

Towards the end of the sixteenth century, there was a revolt against this kind of Ciceronian copiousness and cadence. Francis Bacon identified one of the 'distempers' of learning:

> men began to hunt more after words than matter; more after the choiceness of the phrase, and the round and clean composition of the sentence, and the sweet falling of the clauses, and the varying and illustration of

their works with tropes and figures, than after the weight of matter, worth of subject, soundness of argument, life of invention, or depth of judgment . . . In sum, the whole inclination . . . was rather towards copy than weight.[54]

Instead of Cicero, men modelled their styles on Seneca and Tacitus. Writing should be economical, pithy and sententious, although we still find balance and parallelism, as in the opening of Francis Bacon's essay 'Of Revenge' (1625):

> Revenge is a kind of wild justice, which the more man's nature runs to, the more ought law to weed it out. For, as for the first wrong, it doth but offend the law, but the revenge of that wrong putteth the law out of office. Certainly, in taken revenge a man is but even with his enemy, but in passing it over he is superior: for it is a prince's part to pardon.

For Bacon, this aphoristic style was a challenge to the mind against complacency and prejudice. It represented 'a knowledge broken' and invited 'men to enquire further':[55] a perfect example of an awareness shared by the Renaissance and the present age, of the union of form and content. The overall point is that years of rhetorical practice made audiences particularly aware of the way in which words might work upon them, and conscious of the methods of language and discourse.

CHAPTER 2

Reading, Publication, Performance

The Advent of Printing

About 1476 William Caxton started to publish from his Westminster printing house the first books produced in England using moveable type.[1] His output of more than seventy books over fourteen years included the major works of Geoffrey Chaucer and Sir Thomas Malory as well as some twenty translations of his own from French, Dutch and Latin.

How do we categorize the effects of the advent of printing? Was there a shift from a script culture to a print culture, and did this become a defining feature of the period? Did printed books become commodities, stripped of the totemic associations of hand-copied volumes? Did printing foster the critical interpretation of texts, diminishing the authority of the written word? Did printing develop a 'republic of letters', the dissemination of knowledge across cultures previously separate or antagonistic? Was printing a civilizing and democratizing force? Was it central both to the development of Renaissance humanism and to religious reformation? Did it hasten the decay of local speech and local identities and, by gradually imposing order on spelling, usage, dialect and sociolect, help to create one nation? Did it cause an 'information revolution' analogous to the recent global availability of digitized texts? A commendation from a sermon by John Donne might encourage us to venture a tentative 'yes' to most of these questions:

> Printing, by which the learning of the whole world is communicable to one another, and our minds and our inventions, our wits and composi-

tions may trade and have commerce together, and we may participate of one another's understandings as well as of our clothes and wines and oils and other merchandise.[2]

However, the complexities of the relationships between politics, religion and the evolution of a vernacular literature often make it difficult to distinguish causes from effects.

During the first two decades of Elizabeth's reign (1558–78), approximately 3,584 printed titles appeared; in the first two decades of James's reign (1603–23), the number was about 9,971, an increase of 278 per cent.[3] However, production remained tightly controlled: the Worshipful Company of Stationers, a craft guild with medieval origins, had acquired a charter from Mary Tudor in 1557 which gave them a monopoly on the production, publication and sale of printed materials. The creation of this cartel also enabled the number of printing presses to be strictly limited. Moreover, printing presses were not widely disseminated: book production and retailing (including over 80 per cent of the titles numbered above) were concentrated almost entirely in London until late in the seventeenth century. This convergence of trade interests with those of the crown prevented the Celtic literatures of Wales, Scotland and Ireland being stimulated, as literature in English was, by the development of printing. Moreover, British 'stationers' (as these printer–publishers were called) took a long time to attain the eminence of their colleagues in continental Europe[4] and England remained a net importer of books until the beginning of the eighteenth century.

Recreational Reading and 'Little Books'

This rapid increase in the number of books published is evidence of both a market for knowledge from both home and abroad and of increased reading for pleasure. We must, of course, remember that people who had been formally educated owned books in Latin or Greek with very few titles in English.[5] Moreover, although the necessary technology for printing emerged quickly enough, methods of distribution took longer to become established: few books (except texts used in schools) can have been readily available in the provinces. This is a primary reason for not regarding the market for recreational texts as an early form of modern consumerism. Most recreational reading, we surmise, must have been 'intensive' rather than 'extensive'; that is, individuals read and re-read a small number of texts, often scriptural. In her youth, Lady Jane Grey, who was to become queen briefly in 1553, escaped from 'sharp and severe parents' to a copy of Plato's *Phaedo* in Greek, in which she took 'as much delight as some gentleman would read a merry tale in Bocase [Boccaccio]'.[6]

Much reading would have been communal, convivial and 'public'. Reading aloud to the household from the Bible was ubiquitous. Recreational reading might comprise elements of personation or the singing of ballads, a contrast with modern habits of private consumption, particularly the serial reading of novels. Many artisans sang at their work: 'Better to be sung than to be read, to the tune of "Bonny Nell"', instructed one verse composed at Nottingham in 1617.[7] 'Bonny Nell' is lost but it is alluded to in Thomas Robinson's often reprinted anti-recusant and scabrous pamphlet, *The Anatomy of the English Nunnery at Lisbon in Portugal* (1622): 'at sundry times playing upon their instruments [masturbating (?)] for their father's [their confessor, Joseph Foster's] recreation, they sing him ribaldrous songs and jigs, as that of "Bonny Nell", and such other obscene and scurrilous ballads as would make a chaste ear to glow at the hearing of them.' Robinson goes on: 'Then, after supper it is usual for him to read a little of [Shakespeare's] *Venus and Adonis*, the *Jests* of George Peele, or some such scurrilous book.'[8]

It seems that few people had the skill to read silently, a skill that had evolved only gradually in the Middle Ages. Reading aloud may have increased the propagation of a book's contents, and genial readings of printed texts must have given people something to talk about, paradoxically stimulating elements of oral culture. Reading aloud was a socializing activity in both aristocratic and bourgeois households. There are obvious dangers, therefore, of creating a rigid distinction between oral and literate cultures.

Cultural shifts would eventually lead to the development of the novel, the form today's readers most associate with private or extensive reading. In the meantime, a staple diet of recreational reading was the prose romance – Sir Philip Sidney's *Arcadia* is the key example – but texts like this, as we have seen, were savoured for their style and reiteration of familiar narrative tropes rather than devoured quickly for their story. There is little suspense in romances. (It is significant that, like much verse of the period, the *Arcadia* was first published in manuscript form: Sidney had ten or so scribal copies made for members of his circle and it was printed only well after his death.) Other forms of sixteenth-century prose fiction included cony-catching pamphlets, which described criminal subcultures. Later, somewhat more domesticated fiction emerged: the stories in the weaver Thomas Deloney's *The Gentle Craft* (c.1598) portray romanticized lives of clothiers, shoemakers and weavers, and the book was often reprinted through the seventeenth century. On the title page of its second part, it is described as 'a most merry and pleasant history, not altogether unprofitable nor any way hurtful: very fit to pass away the tediousness of the long winter evenings'. The next century saw the appearance of 'character-books' built up from short prose sketches of social and moral types (Joseph Hall's *Characters of Virtues and Vices* of 1608 is the earliest).

John Taylor the 'water poet', a river-rower on the Thames, produced in the 1620s and 1630s some two hundred satirical pamphlets, jest-books, reports and travel narratives, but a large market for prose fictions that dealt with contemporary life and emotional relationships had yet to emerge. As for drama, texts of single plays did appear in print and were used occasionally for amateur performances, but print runs were small, seldom exceeding the number of spectators at a single amphitheatre playhouse performance.[9] In 1611, Sir Thomas Bodley, the founder of Oxford's Bodleian Library, who had just agreed with the Stationers' Company that they should send him a copy of each book they published, wrote that plays, like almanacs and proclamations, were 'idle books and riff-raffs', and noted that he intended to 'have none but such as are singular'.[10]

Recreational material also included a variety of 'little books'[11] and ephemeral material, many suitable for reading aloud to those who were unlettered: ballads, books of jests, woodcuts, and what were to become known as 'chapbooks' (essentially story-books, sold by itinerant 'chapmen', and containing tales, romances and folkloric 'histories' based on the forms of oral culture). Ballads, often illustrated with woodcuts, could cost as little as one penny, chapbooks as much as six pence. (Large books, depending upon how they were bound, could cost several guineas.) A London mercer, Robert Laneham, visiting Kenilworth in July 1575 at the time of a visit by the Queen, met an extraordinary Coventry mason there known as Captain Cox. Cox had a remarkable collection of such books, including *King Arthur's Book, Huon of Bordeaux,* and *The Four Sons of Aymon* (a translation by Caxton of one of the French romances of the Charlemagne cycle). He had poems including Spenser's *The Shepheardes Calender*, Copland's 'Gillian of Brainsford's testament', a poem describing how an old alewife bequeaths a fart to the people she satirizes, and 'The tunning of Elynour Rumming' (1521), a verse narrative by John Skelton of a drinking bout by country gossips at a Surrey inn. He owned *The Hundred Merry Tales*, first published in 1526 and alluded to in *Much Ado about Nothing* (1598), some plays, and 'a bunch of ballads and songs, all ancient' including 'Broom, broom on hill', 'Hey ding a ding', and 'Bony lass upon a green'. Cox seemed, by repeated reading, to have conned many of these by heart: Laneham marvelled that 'at afternoons [he could] talk as much without book as any inn-holder betwixt Brainford and Bagshot.'[12]

Ballads were also copied by hand or pasted up on walls, sometimes in houses, sometimes in public as libels or lampoons, these often chronicling sexual misdemeanours. We see ballads being touted in Jonson's *Bartholomew Fair* (1614); one of its characters, Bartholomew Cokes, an 'esquire of Harrow', exclaims to his sister: 'Do you remember the ballads over the nursery-chimney at home o' my own pasting up? There be brave pictures' (3.5.49–50). Other ballad titles indicate more topical import: 'A ballad entitled Northumberland news, / Wherein you may see what rebels do Use' (1569/70), 'God doth bless this realm for the receiving of strangers being persecuted for the gospel, though some do repine at that' (c.1570), 'A declaration of the death of John Lewes, a most detestable and obstinate heretic, burned at Norwich, the 17th day of September, 1583' (1583), 'Anything for a quiet life; or the married man's bondage to a curst wife' (c.1625), 'A description of a strange (and miraculous) fish, cast upon the sands . . . in the County Palatine of Chester . . . the certainty whereof is here related concerning the said most monstrous fish' (1636).[13] There was also a stock of godly ballads: 'Hark, man, what I thy God shall speak' (1582), 'Good Lord, what a wicked world' (1586), and 'When fair Jerusalem did stand' (1586).[14]

Texts sold by chapmen were supplemented by almanacs (of which Cox owned three). These contained medical and farming advice as well as astrological tables and chronologies of world history. Chapmen also sold metrical psalms as well as a large number of other godly texts, ABC books ('absies') and primers, and, from the 1620s, 'corantoes', later called news-books or news-letters. A character in Brome's *The*

Court Beggar (c.1640) reports, 'I . . . stood . . . at the coranto-shop to read the last great news.'

We should not, however, assume that these small books represent or define a distinct variety of 'popular' literature: scholars generated almanacs, and ballads were enjoyed by the gentry as well as by ploughmen. Sir Philip Sidney famously wrote: 'I must confess my own barbarousness. I never heard the old song of Percy and Douglas that I found not my heart moved more than with a trumpet; and yet it is sung but by some blind crowder [Welsh fiddler], with no rougher voice than rude style.'[15] The story of the mortal duel between Percy and Douglas is told in the ballad of 'Chevy-Chase', one of the most popular poems of the period. Sidney's confession indicates that reading practices were not a function of rank or social status.[16]

Publication for Reformation and Counter-Reformation

Erasmus of Rotterdam, whose scholarship and writings powered both Renaissance humanism and the first reform movements, exploited his ability to reach a wide audience through the press. The availability of a much larger number of titles increased the size of libraries – to read widely it was no longer necessary to be a wandering scholar. Larger libraries facilitated the Erasmian task of applying comparative philological methods to both classical texts and Christian scriptures. There was also a body of printed Counter-Reformation texts.[17]

The increase in book publication also manifests a desire to use the press as an instrument for ideological purposes. Secular politicians made use of the press for state and nation creation: a *Great Book of Statutes*, which recorded all statutes made in parliaments from the beginning of the reign of Edward III, translated from legal French, was printed and revised regularly during the latter part of the reign of Henry VIII. The content of school books was often designed to inculcate Christian precepts and obedience to authority, and Lord Burghley commissioned Christopher Saxton to engrave maps of the English and Welsh counties which appeared between 1574 and 1579, a demonstration of the nation's curiosity and pride in itself. Shakespeare records a fear of the power of the printed word among the unlettered when, in *2 Henry VI* (c.1590), he has the rebel Jack Cade accuse the Lord Say of having 'caused printing to be used' (4.7.30–1). In contrast, printing was positively welcomed by Protestant reformers – about half of Elizabethan book production consisted of Bibles and religious works, and these helped make many of the waves within Reformation and subsequently Counter-Reformation cultures.

Protestantism was a religion of the Book and of the Word: members of reformed groups met in 'conventicles', whose forms of catechizing and worship, based on Bible study, were anathema to the established church.[18] Although Tyndale's New Testament in 1526 and Miles Coverdale's complete Bible in 1535 were not the first publications of these works in a European vernacular, the ready availability of these texts created an instrument whereby Scripture, as apprehended by groups and individuals, could be posed against the authority of the church.[19] Parts of Tyndale's translation were passed down through later versions, the most important of which was the scholarly 'Geneva Bible' of 1560 which went through over 120 editions before the 'King James Bible' or 'Authorized Version' was published in 1611. Numerous phrases of Tyndale and of Archbishop Cranmer's *Book of Common Prayer*, first published under Edward VI in 1549, the year after which all worship had to be performed in English, passed thereby into the language.

In order to widen access to Scripture yet further, the Bible was translated into Welsh in 1581, and an Irish Gaelic New Testament was published in Dublin in 1603. This translation was also used, rather unsuccessfully, in Scotland. 'The fact that in Scotland the Bible was never printed in that version of English known as Lallans reduced the standing of Scots as a literary language.'[20] In a prefatory epistle to a collection of religious tracts, John Foxe wrote: 'We have great cause to give thanks to the high providence of almighty God for the excellent art of printing, most happily of late found out and now commonly practised everywhere, to the singular benefit of Christ's church.' He contended that the fact that 'the art of printing was not yet invented' had allowed the works of previous generations of reformers, including the Lollards, to be destroyed.[21]

The most important instrument for the forging of a Protestant identity was the largest book yet published in England: Foxe's *Acts and Monuments*, popularly known as 'Foxe's Book of Martyrs', a massive work of over two million words (see chapter 4). In contrast, one of the strangest forms of publication is represented by a pair of minute books, about 3 by 2.5 centimetres in size, and sometimes bound together: *Verbum Sempiternum* and *Salvator Mundi*, both printed in 1614, and republished seven times before 1700. These reductions of the Old and New Testaments into rhyming couplets (one per page) written by the indefatigable John Taylor must have been designed as a (lady's?) novelty item for a chapman's bag. Here is Taylor's version of St Paul's Epistle to the Romans, boiled down to eight lines and encapsulating a bold endorsement of Luther's doctrine of justification by faith:

> The apostle Paul from Corinth writes to Rome
> To strength their faith and tell them Christ is come;
> He shows how high and low, both Jew and Greek,
> Are one with God, who faithfully him seek.
> He tells how sin in mortal bodies lurks,
> How we are saved by faith and not by works.
> In loving terms the people he doth move
> To faith, to hope, to charity and love.

An edition of 1627 ends with a prayer for Charles I that perfectly reveals the union of politics and religion. Its total lack of poetic merit shows how, by making himself a celebrity, Taylor, a sculler turned rhymer, could market really very shoddy goods:

> Good God almighty, in compassion tender,
> Preserve and keep King Charles, Thy faith's defender;
> Thy glory make his honour still increase,
> In peace, in wars, and in eternal peace.
>
> Amen

In 1560, compilers of the Geneva Bible printed Joshua 1: 8 on its penultimate page as a kind of valediction: 'Let not this book of the law depart out of thy mouth, but meditate therein day and night, that thou mayest observe and do according to all that is written therein: so shalt thou make thy way prosperous [successful], and then thou shalt succeed.' This agenda for reading says it all, and its practice penetrated deep into the consciousness of princes, merchants, and boys that drove the plough[22] throughout the nations of Britain.

Literacy and Male and Female Readership

Literacy rates in the period are extremely difficult to measure since reading and writing were taught separately, and skill in reading was more common than skill in writing. This means that documents that show that individuals could not sign their names but only inscribe their marks do not necessarily reveal that these people could not read. Nor should we equate, as tends to happen today, literacy levels with 'intelligence', wisdom or some ability to shape life according to reasoned choices. There are accounts of 'illiterate' individuals possessed of prodigious memories for what they had heard read out.[23] This was an age when knowledge and learning were transmitted by both the spoken and the written word: attendance at sermons and religious 'lectures' by preachers supported by local parishes was ubiquitous. The poet John Donne was also renowned for his sermons: the rhetorical cadences, combination of biblical citation and local imagery, and examples of nice reasoning in something like the following extract (first published in 1630) provide a verbal diet as rich as anything available in print and bring the scriptural text to life in a way no mere reading could do:

PSALM 89: 48. WHAT MAN IS HE THAT LIVETH, AND SHALL NOT SEE DEATH? At first, God gave the judgement of death upon man, when he should transgress, absolutely, *Morte morieris*, thou shalt surely die. The woman in her dialogue with the serpent, she mollifies it, *Ne fortè moriamur*, perchance, if we eat, we may die; and then the Devil is as peremptory on the other side, *Nequaquam moriemini*, do what you will, surely you shall not die. And now God in this text comes to His reply, *Quis est homo*, shall they not die? Give me but one instance, but one exception to this rule, *What man is he that liveth, and shall not see death?* Let no man, no woman, no devil offer a *Ne fortè* (perchance we may die), much less a *Nequaquam* (surely we shall not die), except he be provided of an answer to this question, except he can give an instance against this general, except he can produce that man's name and history that hath lived, and shall not see death. We are all conceived in close prison; in our mothers' wombs, we are close prisoners all; when we are born, we are born but to the liberty of the house; prisoners still, though within larger walls; and then all our life is but a going out to the place of execution, to death. Now was there ever any man seen to sleep in the cart, between Newgate and Tyburn? Between the prison and the place of execution, does any man sleep? And we sleep all the way; from the womb to the grave we are never thoroughly awake; but pass on with such dreams and imaginations as these: 'I may live as well as another, and why should I die rather than another? But awake, and tell me, says this text, *Quis homo?* Who is that other that thou talkest of? What man is he that liveth, and shall not see death?'[24]

The market for printed sermons indicates how pervasive was the appetite for wisdom derived from preaching and lectures. Pictures and engravings were also used in printed books as vehicles for religious propaganda; plays served not just as entertainment but also as ways of imparting the skills of oratory and raising consciousness of social and political issues. John Bale wrote morality plays in the 1530s to inculcate Protestant doctrines, and morality plays continued to be written and performed throughout the life of Shakespeare. As Roger Chartier concluded, 'Literacy rates do not give an accurate measure of familiarity with the written word.'[25]

Widely accepted figures for literacy in England derive from the work of David Cressy: he estimated that 70 per cent of men were illiterate on the eve of the Civil War and that about 90 per cent of women and almost all labourers were illiterate.[26] However, there is quite a lot of evidence that educated women were readers of literature.[27] As we might expect, literacy rates were massively higher among the nobility, gentry, clergy and some yeomen, and were higher in towns than in the country. They were also higher when success in trade depended upon record-keeping: among certain groups of artisans and distributive traders.[28] The Merchant Tailors famously founded their own grammar school in 1561 primarily for the benefit of their own sons.

Book learning was quickly recognized as a means to power and an emblem of status or privilege: knowledge gleaned from books confers power on Marlowe's Faustus and Shakespeare's Prospero. If convicted robbers and murderers could read a 'neck-verse' (usually the beginning of the fifty-first psalm printed in Latin), they could plead 'benefit of clergy' and escape the gallows. In Shakespeare's *2 Henry VI*, the Clerk of Chartham is executed by rebels led by Jack Cade simply because he can 'write and read' (4.2.78) – the same phrase is used of two candidates chosen to be constable in *Much Ado about Nothing* (3.3.11).

Prejudices Against Reading

Books may have been proliferating and literacy rates creeping up, but there were deep-running prejudices, often utilitarian, against book learning. Although Francis Bacon in his essay 'Of Studies' could write 'Reading maketh a full man; conference [giving counsel, conversation] a ready man; and writing an exact man', others argued for the primacy of the active over the contemplative life. The great Italian humanists of the fifteenth century, and scholars in northern Europe like Erasmus who initiated the Reformation, were accorded fame and respect, but in England during the sixteenth century men renowned for their learning were few, most being theologians rather than scholars. Although there were some famous schoolmasters, the stock figure of the pedant who appears in prose fiction and in drama suggests a widespread devaluation of learning. Richard Pace, one of Henry VIII's secretaries, reported the outburst of an English gentleman at a banquet: 'I swear by God's body I'd rather that my son should hang than study letters. For it becomes the sons of gentlemen to blow the horn nicely, to hunt skilfully, and elegantly carry and train a hawk. But the study of letters should be left to the sons of rustics.'[29]

Somewhat later, there appeared a proliferation of courtesy books inspired by Castiglione's *Book of the Courtier* (translated into English in 1561). These often argued that any learning that was not ornamental to the individual was inimical to courtliness.[30] The beginning of the seventeenth century saw the emergence of the cult of virtuosi, men of wealth who disdained to put learning to use but sought, in Francis Bacon's words, to

> entertain their minds with variety and delight . . . as if there were sought in knowledge a couch whereupon to rest a searching and restless spirit; or a terrace for a wandering and variable mind to walk up and down with a fair prospect . . . and not a rich storehouse for the glory of the Creator and the relief of man's estate.[31]

Robert Burton's long 'Digression of the Misery of Scholars' in his *Anatomy of Melancholy*[32] reminds us of widespread contempt for the learned.

Overall, England's social structure, shaped as it was by a hierarchy of birth and landed wealth, made it difficult for men to rise by their learning alone. Marlowe showed the precarious social position of one of Edward II's minions:

> My name is Baldock, and my gentry
> I fetched from Oxford, not from heraldry.   (2.2.242–3)

Although most noblemen were instructed in the liberal arts, the humanist programme of formal education based on the study of classical texts became increasingly out of touch with the interests of both noble and entrepreneurial groups: the City did not find that Latin and Greek helped with the building of ships or the negotiation of business. 'The use, not the reading, of books produces prudent men' (*Usus libri, non lectio prudentes facit*) is the title of an emblem (see chapter 7) by Geoffrey Whitney in his *Choice of Emblems* (1586).

Reading and Interpretation

In a famous letter to Can Grande, Vicar-General of Verona, the great Italian poet Dante Alighieri (1265–1321) had set out a method – it derived from the Church Fathers – for the explication of biblical texts. They are polysemous (of more senses than one), he argued, and might be systematically explored on four levels: the literal, the moral, the allegorical and the anagogical (having to do with the spiritual meaning of the whole work).[33] The method was commended by Tyndale in *The Obedience of a Christian Man*,[34] John Donne in his sermons,[35] and by Sir John Harington:

> Perseus, son of Jupiter, is feigned by the poets to have slain Gorgon and, after that conquest achieved, to have flown up to heaven. The *historical* [i.e. literal] sense is this: Perseus the son of Jupiter . . . slew Gorgon, a tyrant in that country (Gorgon in Greek signifieth earth), and was for his virtuous parts exalted by men up unto heaven. *Morally* it signifieth this much, Perseus a wise man, son of Jupiter endowed with virtue from above, slayeth sin and vice, a thing base and earthly, signified by Gorgon, and so mounteth up to the sky of virtue. It signifies in one kind of *allegory* thus much: the mind of man being gotten by God, and so the child of God killing and vanquishing the earthliness of this gorgonical nature, ascendeth up to the understanding of heavenly things, of high things, of eternal things. In which contemplation consisteth the perfection

of man: this is the natural allegory, because man, one of the chief works of nature. It hath also *a more high and heavenly allegory*, that the heavenly Nature, daughter of Jupiter, procuring with her continual motion corruption and mortality in the inferior bodies, severed itself at last from these earthly bodies and flew up on high, and there remaineth for ever. It hath also another theological allegory: that the angelical Nature, daughter of the most high God, the creator of all things, killing and overcoming all bodily substance signified by Gorgon, ascended into heaven.[36]

Methods of biblical exegesis were, however, not suited to the reading and enjoyment of secular literature, although they could, as Harington's argument demonstrates, serve as a defence for the survival of pagan gods. Conversely, allegory remained an important mode of writing, making the poet, as Sir Philip Sidney said, 'the right popular philosopher',[37] and inviting, in the case of Jonson's *Sejanus* (1605) and *Eastward Ho* (1605), unwelcome 'applications' of the personalities of dramatic characters to contemporaries.[38]

Manuscript

Although printing rapidly became increasingly important, circulation in manuscript (with certain texts commercially copied) remained the preferred method of publication for many texts up to about the end of the seventeenth century. In some cases, this may represent a reaction by a variety of elites to the democratization of print. Sidney's *Arcadia* began its life in manuscript for the pleasure of coteries. John Taylor compared printed books to whores, his comparison built around notions of commonness and deception:

> So stationers their old cast [discarded] books can grace,
> And by their titles paint afresh their face.[39]

In *The Winter's Tale* Shakespeare satirizes naïve belief in the authority of print: the country wench Mopsa says, 'I love a ballad in print alife [dearly], for then we are sure they are true' (4.4.258–9).

The period's lyric poems, which we encounter in print and perhaps assume to be records of uniquely private experiences or effusions, usually became known first after being copied onto single sheets or into manuscript books. In Jonson's *Every Man in his Humour* (1598), the pockets of Matteo, a would-be gentleman lover, are stuffed with copies of poems. Poems might then be copied into commonplace books and passed down through families. Others circulated within coteries and around institutions: the court, Oxbridge colleges, the Inns of Court. Their 'meaning' derives as much from their function within these interpretative communities as from their authors' feelings or emotions. Indeed, commonplace books, containing, as many did, texts by a multitude of writers, tended to occlude any authorial presence. Within such communities, a love poem in manuscript by Donne might be read not as an emotional effusion but as a bravura stylistic exercise. This might be a corrective to the Petrarchisms that had become stale through recycling in the sonnet sequences that had abounded after the publication of 'Tottel's Miscellany', or an exploration of the limits of sexual outspokenness or religious extravagance. Poems that were intended as a gift for a patron might have been read differently when they were offered to a wider readership, although Shakespeare had Malvolio describe the nature of a 'true sonnet': 'Please one, and please all' (*Twelfth Night* [1601], 3.4.22). We realize that a full account of any text, whether printed or written, must take account of its material form and not just its content. Authors do not write *books* but *texts*, and texts are not merely sources for ideas and images but are 'carriers of relationships'.[40] Given that the ownership of dramatic texts rested with companies rather than dramatists, recent scholarship has considered appropriate aspects of plays more in relation to other play texts owned by the company than to other 'works' by the same author.

In hand-written form, poems might be bound up with letters, miscellanies of short prose texts like Bacon's essays, or with recipes and medical notes. Some longer manuscripts contain a collection of a single author's works; others resemble a gathering of dried flowers or an individual's compilation CD, the pattern of arrangement depending upon the chances of circulation and personal fancy. Many manuscripts contain 'answer poems' which either record a particular occasion or perhaps the compiler's reflection upon a familiar text. Shorter poems might be engraved on windows and on plates, mugs and trenchers for the table, or circulated as libels or ballads around particular communities.[41]

Manuscripts were sometimes prepared for presentation to a patron, a survival of the pre-printing era when 'literature' could be written for a single individual or to please the tastes of a small coterie. (The assumption that the 'presence' of its author is more authentic in a hand-written note than in one that has been typed or word-processed remains with us today.) Although verse by women appeared in print only rarely before the later seventeenth century, their poems circulated more freely in manuscript: concentration on printed material belies the amount of literary production by women. Indeed, the poet Margaret Cavendish, Duchess of Newcastle (1624–74), not only gestures towards an actual distrust of the effect of printing but counters a general prejudice against verse of the kind she wrote:

> But be it bad or good it is my own,
> Unless in printing 'tis a changeling grown.
> Which sure I have no reason for to doubt:
> It hath the same mark, when I put it out.
> But be it fair, or brown, or black, or wild,
> I still must own it, 'cause it is my child.
> And should my neighbours say 'tis a dull block,
> 'Tis honestly begot, of harmless stock.
> By motion in my brain 'twas formed and bred,
> By my industrious study it was fed.
> And by my busy pen was clothed – though plain
> The garments be, yet are they without stain.
> But be it ne'er so plain, not rich, and gay,
> Fantastical 'tis dressed, the world will say.
> The world thinks all is fine that's in the fashion,
> Though it be old if fashioned with translation.[42]

Other manuscripts contain recusant verse – the poetry of Catholics – songs from the old religion, accounts of Catholic martyrdom to counterbalance the descriptions of Protestant martyrs in Foxe, or devotional material that it would have been impossible to have licensed for printing in multiple copies. Contrariwise, there are collections of anti-Catholic verse.[43] Manuscripts prepared within male coteries often included satirical, scurrilous and misogynistic verse that would also have been impossible to print. An example is 'The censure of the parliament fart', describing an indiscretion by Henry Ludlow MP on 11 March 1607 during a debate on the Act of Union. It was probably by John Hoskyns, was circulated widely in a multitude of versions, and mentioned by

Ben Jonson in *The Alchemist* (1610). Dozens of MPs are named in this exercise in scurrility. It ends thus:

'Here silence', quoth Bond,[44] though all words be wind,
Yet I must mislike of these motions behind.'
Upriseth the speaker, that noble Ephestian [native of the country]
And saith, 'Gentlemen, I'll put it to th'question.'
The question being made, the yeas did it lose
For the major part went clear with the noes [nose].
But all at last said it was most fit
The fart as a traitor to the Tower commit;
Where, as they say, it remains to this hour,
Yet not close prisoner, but at large in the Tower.[45]

Political verse – and indeed manuscript circulation generally – proliferated during the political turmoil of the seventeenth century, with
examples of both Puritan and anti-parliament compilations extant.
Here is the beginning and end of 'The Commons' petition of long-
afflicted England, to the Chief Chancellor of Heaven . . .', seemingly
composed about 1612 and eventually printed in 1642:

If bleeding souls, dejected hearts, find grace,
Thou All-Disposer, turn not back Thy face
From us Thy supplicants; thrice three suns have worn
Their summer suits since we began to mourn:
Egypt's ten plagues we have endured thrice-told
Since blest Eliza was with saints enrolled . . .

The caterpillar hangs on every tree,
Lousy promoters, monopoly-mongers,
A crew of upstart rascals, whose fierce hungers
Can ne'er be satisfied; a sort of slaves
Far more unsatiate than are whores or graves,
And do more mischief than Egyptian flies
That with their buzzing blind the people's eyes.
Yet at the last God hath us comfort sent
In the bright sunshine of our parliament,
Which may dispel the misty fogs of error
And turn our cloudy day into fair weather.
The last petition we most humbly crave
Is, they one heart, one mind may have.[46]

And here is the refrain of 'The distracted puritan' by Bishop Richard Corbett (1582–1635), printed in *Poetica Stromata* (1648) after his death. It went to the tune of 'Tom o' Bedlam', a tune both for poems of madness and for libels:

> Boldly I preach, hate a cross, hate a surplice,
>   Mitres, copes, and rochets [bishops' vestments]:
> Come hear me pray nine times a day,
>   And fill your heads with crotchets.

These methods of publication might lead us to reconsider our categorization of much early modern poetry. First, manuscript publication, through error and emendation on the part of the copyists, generates variant readings of particular poems. The poem in Jonson's *Volpone* (1606) that begins 'Come, my Celia, let us prove, / While we can, the sports of love' (3.7.165–6), begins, in an aristocratic miscellany of 1642, 'Come, sweet mistress'.[47] The implication is that the owner of the manuscript may have converted it for purposes of his own. Sometimes compilers of manuscripts conferred their own titles upon particular poems. Some extant manuscripts contain corrections or re-writing in the hands of the poems' authors, but this raises the critical question of whether there are 'authentic' texts of these poems. If we are concerned with the intention of their authors, we may be uncertain as to when these intentions were realized: when the poem was first composed or when it was emended in form, or perhaps re-written in part so that it could be used for a different occasion. As has been said of jazz, there are tunes but no tune: in the case of many poems we might wish to consider a plurality of texts that were clearly read in a variety of contexts rather than one particular definitive or 'authentic' text. Poems that we might take to be personal could be engendered as much by social occasion, often by annual festivity. All of this clouds the divisions between the personal and the social: a love poem, which it is tempting to take as the heart-felt outpouring of a poet who is now one of the age's celebrities, may well have been written as a five-finger exercise in a particular style for the delight of friends, as an imitation which gained its effect by the pleasure members of a coterie might take from its allusions (thus confirming their identity as an elite group), or even for the use of a patron.[48]

Professional Authorship

Authors sought a role for themselves in antique models: both Samuel
Daniel and Ben Jonson, imitating the titles of collections of ancient
writings, published collected editions of their '*Works*' in 1601 and 1616
respectively. In the case of Jonson, his title was greeted with some
scoffing, the title being a translation of the Latin *opera* which, it was felt,
ought to be reserved for graver matter. Rachel Speght sought to justify
her temerity as a woman in writing by citing classical exempla and
authorities. The following comes from *Morality's Memorandum* (1621), an
allegorical dream vision in which she pleads for education for women:

> Cleobulina and Demophila
> With Telesilla as historians tell
> (Whose fame doth live, though they have long been dead)
> Did all of them in poetry excel.
> A Roman matron that Cornelia hight
> An eloquent and learned style did write.
>
> ('The Dream', 139–46)

However, unlike their continental counterparts, British stationers were
not in the habit of undertaking large and carefully prepared editions
of substantial scholarly or literary works. Nor were they prepared to
pay more than small amounts for the texts produced by authors. After
a work had been printed, authors owned no copyright or legal title to
their intellectual property – the word 'copyright' did not enter the language until 1735. The 'privilege' in respect of the text, the sole right
of printing or publishing it, was invested in the stationer rather than the
author, and was maintained by the 'Register' of the Stationers' Company in which the names of works to be published were supposed to
be inscribed for the benefit of their guildsman owners. (In reality,
many books and pamphlets were published without authority in order
to save the registration fees.)

Printing enabled dramatists to reach an audience of readers as well
as an audience of spectators. Although, as we have seen, print runs
were small, 'By the time of [Shakespeare's] death, over forty editions
of his plays had reached print, and three – *Richard II* (1595), *Richard
III*, and *1 Henry IV* (1596–7) – had been published in five or more
editions.'[49] This would seem to disprove the long-cherished myth that
Shakespeare was not particularly concerned to see his works in print.

Many of his texts are simply too long to be performed uncut, but decisions to print probably came from his companies and he did not, as Jonson did, affirm his right to sell texts to the bookseller and attend himself to the correction of proofs. Jonson depended not only upon the market for printed drama but also upon patronage, and dedicated some of his plays and masques to notable members of the court.[50]

There is, in fact, some evidence of prejudice against performance. The somewhat enigmatic epistle prefixed to a quarto version of Shakespeare's *Troilus and Cressida* (written about 1602) seems to boast that the play has never been performed, never been 'clapper-clawed with the palms of the vulgar'. John Marston felt he had to apologize for the printing 'of the entrances and music' in the text of his tragedy of *Sophonisba* (1606) 'as it was presented by youths, and after the fashion of the private stage'.[51] This implies that he thought that the play was best apprehended as a dramatic poem that was vulgarized by the full descriptions of the material elements of production: elaborate entrances by characters bearing emblematic properties and music provided by a range of instruments. In contrast, the epistle to Thomas Heywood's tragedy *The Rape of Lucrece* (1638) notes: 'Because we would not that any man's expectation should be deceived in the ample printing of this book, lo, gentle reader, we have inserted these few songs, which were added by the stranger that lately acted Valerius his part.'

Successful dramatists could live by their profession, if they produced copious amounts of material, by selling their texts to theatrical entrepreneurs like Philip Henslowe, or, as Shakespeare did, by becoming sharers (shareholders) in the theatrical companies with which they were associated. But the financial reward that came to authors who worked in other genres continued to derive from income from their patrons rather than the sale of their printed texts – another factor that maintained the habit of generating manuscript versions well after print was thoroughly established. That said, almost all printed books from the period begin with a flattering and sometimes quite lengthy dedication, almost always a plea for financial favour.

Censorship

The royal charter given to the Stationers' Company not only created a monopoly but, through systems of licensing, provided a basic legal instrument for the control of everything that appeared in print. The Warden of the Company was supposed to scrutinize every manuscript and issue an ordinance for it, but agents of the crown supplemented this self-censorship by the trade. From 1566 a court known as the High Commission attempted to control books imported into England.[52]

In 1599 there were two famous actions against printed material. The first was the suppression of John Hayward's *Life and Reign of Henry IV*, which had been dedicated to the Earl of Essex and which elaborated upon the deposition of Richard II, a story that obviously made the Queen blench for fear that Essex would take on the role of Bullingbrook. The narrative, set out in the 1577 edition of Holinshed's *Chronicles*, had been censored from the 1587 edition. In the same year, the Archbishop of Canterbury and the Bishop of London issued a decree forbidding the printing of satires and epigrams, and any plays, particularly English history plays, that had not been 'allowed' by the Privy Council. About eight extremely miscellaneous texts, some satirical, some purportedly obscene, including a copy of Marlowe's translation of Ovid's *Amores*, issued in a volume with Sir John Davies's *Epigrams*, were duly and ritually burned. The episode is exceptional and suggests a flaring of ecclesiastical temper rather than a developed system of control.

As for 'publication' in forms other than print, in 1559 a proclamation, one of the first acts after Elizabeth became queen, had instructed those concerned with the licensing of plays to 'permit none to be played wherein either matters of religion or of the governance of the estate of the Commonweal shall be handled . . . being no meet matters to be written . . . upon but by men of authority, learning, and wisdom, nor to be handled before any audience but of grave and discreet persons'.[53] In fact, very few plays were refused a licence and when, from the end of the 1580s, English and Roman history plays were being openly performed, the gist of the proclamation was repeated in a Privy Council order of 1589.[54] This suggests that although, from 1580, the power to censor drama had been delegated to a court official, the Master of the Revels, his task may have been more to act as an intermediary between plays and court than as a modern censor. Sir Henry Herbert, Master of the Revels from 1623 to 1642 and, after the Restoration, from 1660 to 1673, actually licensed Middleton's *Game at Chess* in 1624, seemingly a conspicuous act of non-censorship, even though the play disparaged the forging of an alliance between England and Spain through the marriage of Prince Charles to the Spanish Infanta.[55]

There is only intermittent evidence that various individuals with powers of censorship required changes in scripts used by the playing companies: 'among the 2,000 plays composed between 1590 and 1642, there is evidence of censorship being exercised on only about thirty occasions, and few of these were directly political interventions.'[56] This suggests that authors and playing companies were given to self-censorship, that the theatre was not perceived as an important threat to the political and social order, or simply that, as in so many fields of endeavour, the reach of the Tudor and Stuart regimes exceeded their grasp.

Censorship, therefore, was a hit-and-miss affair, and the evidence that supposedly seditious passages were not *printed* in particular editions of plays, as with the case of the deposition scene of Shakespeare's *Richard II*, does not mean that the missing lines were suppressed in *performance*. The playbook was one thing, performance another. After having allowed James Shirley's *The Ball* (it was licensed on 16 November 1632), the Master of the Revels, Sir Henry Herbert, went to an early performance:

> There was diverse personated so naturally, both of lords and other of the court, that I took it ill and would have forbidden the play, but that Beeston [the actor-manager of the Cockpit in Drury Lane] promised many things which I found fault withal should be left out, and that he would not suffer it to be done by the poet any more, who deserves to be punished; and the first that offends in this kind, of poets or players, shall be sure of public punishment.[57]

What offended Herbert was calumny rather than any kind of ideological critique. Equally, the Act to Restrain the Abuses of the Players of 1606 was not always efficacious. It was supposed to purge the stage of oaths and blasphemy and in fact caused more interventions than did girds at politicians, but there are examples of the asseverations of the old religion, 'Zounds' ('by God's wounds') and 'marry' (by the [virgin] Mary'), in printed texts that obviously derive from theatrical manuscripts.

The 'Publication' of Drama

As we have already seen, 'publication' involved not just the production of books. Just as verse was often read in manuscript rather than printed form, so theatrical productions generally derived from non-printed texts. Playwrights sold their plays to playing companies who then produced three kinds of derivative manuscript. First, a 'book', a regularized transcription of what on one occasion was referred to as the author's 'foul papers' (his first complete draft), which seems to have been the controlling document for a performance. It served the company's 'book-holder' who combined the roles of stage-manager and prompt. Second, a 'plot' which, mounted on card, was kept in the tiring house and which listed the players required for each scene; and, third, the 'parts', long rolls of paper from which players conned their own lines – only the cues at the end of other players' speeches were written out. As the copying process progressed, changes or mistakes appeared. Moreover, the quality of the production of many printed playbooks was often poor and obviously conferred little prestige upon their authors. The process of printing often compounded what we can infer to have been prior difficulties in the manuscripts that were used as copy for the compositors. Modern editors need to intervene frequently, not only to regularize spelling, punctuation, stage directions and so on to make them fully accessible to contemporary readers, but also to correct manifest errors. Often, however, the processes of textual transmission created cruces that are never fully solvable.

The final stage of 'publication' was the enlivening of the lines by the voices and gestures of the players – and there are many complaints from playwrights about the ways in which players changed the play by altering words or creating attitude by their stage actions. At the end of his career, Ben Jonson, always an astringent critic of actors, and one who valued words above stage action and spectacle, warned his Blackfriars' audience in the Prologue to *The Staple of News* (1631) of the dangers of being seduced by the pleasures of the eye:

> For your own sakes, not his, he bade me say,
> Would you were come to hear, not see, a play.
> Though we his actors must provide for those
> Who are our guests here in the way of shows,
> The maker hath not so. He'd have you wise
> Much rather by your ears than by your eyes.

However, when the play was revived for a performance before Charles I at court in 1626, Jonson softened his admonition:

A work not smelling of the lamp, tonight,
　But fitted for your Majesty's disport,
　And writ to the meridian of your court,
We bring, and hope it may produce delight:
The rather being offered as a rite
　To scholars, that can judge and fair report
　The sense they hear, above the vulgar sort
Of nutcrackers, that only come for sight.

George Chapman, in a commendatory epistle to Jonson's *Sejanus*, praised the author and actors together for

Performing such a lively evidence
In thy narrations, that thy hearers still
Thou turn'st to thy spectators; and the sense
That thy spectators have of good and ill,
Thou subject'st [lay before] jointly to thy readers' souls.

This suggests two things: first, that the wiser sort saw theatre as providing serious matter, something other than mere entertainment. In an age when literacy rates were much lower than they are today, theatrical performances, like sermons, had an educational function, serving as a way of publishing history and politics, as well as the lessons in morality, which, in the hope of sober citizens, were delivered from the stage. Secondly, *seeing* plays on the stage was another form of *reading*, of fairly complex decoding. In *Henry V* (1598–9), Fluellen says 'There is figures in all things' (4.7.27): dramatic structures, notably sub-plots, plays-within-plays, inset masques and so on, retained patterns of allegory and typology which presupposed active and sophisticated hearers, able to understand the implicit comparisons and contrasts that supplemented their enjoyment of the unfolding narrative.

Not that all drama was didactic or *representational*, creating stage images of historical events or imaginary narratives. Pleasure in the playhouses often came from the *presentational* skills of players trained in physical and verbal techniques (tongue-twisters or feats of memory, for example), clowns, dancers or musicians. Evidence comes from the insets/inductions that show players discussing their art:[58]

MESSENGER　Your honour's players, hearing your amendment,
　Are come to play a pleasant comedy . . .

SLY Marry, I will let them play it. Is not a comonty
  A Christmas gambol or a tumbling trick?
BARTHOLOMEW No, my good lord, it is more pleasing stuff.
SLY   What, household stuff?
BARTHOLOMEW   It is a kind of history.
  (Shakespeare, *The Taming of the Shrew*, 1591, Ind. 2.125–36)

SIMON Some talk of things of state, of puling stuff;
  There's nothing in a play to a clown, if he
  Have the grace to hit on't; that's the thing indeed;
  The king shows well, but he sets off the king.
                  (Middleton, *Hengist King of Kent, or*
                The Mayor of Queenborough, 1618, 5.1)

Clowns seem to have enjoyed improvising and also interacting with their audiences. Hamlet may have decried clowns who spoke more than was set down for them, but the practice was common. Some memorial texts contain traces of improvisations – it was known as 'gag'. Generating the widest range of response was a prime ambition for playing companies. Here is another passage from *Hengist*:

SIMON Now, sir, are you comedians?
2 PLAYER We are, sir, comedians, tragic-comedians, comi-tragedians, pastorists, humorists, satirists; we have them, sir, from the hug to the smile, from the smile to the laugh, from the laugh to the handkerchief.
(5.1)

That notwithstanding, the existence of a system of censorship indicates that playing often had to do with graver matters than simply the generation of emotional response.

Most performances took place in the London amphitheatre or 'public' playhouses and later in indoor or 'private' playhouses. There were, however, times when the companies were on tour in the provinces, often because the plague had closed their London bases. As we saw, a certain amount of verse that might seem to us to be 'personal' in nature was actually occasional, written for special groups and often produced for particular seasons within the Christian calendar. This was even truer of drama. The leading patrons of the playing companies came to include Elizabeth I, who lent her name to the Queen's Men, a company that flourished from 1583 to 1594 before the Lord Admiral's

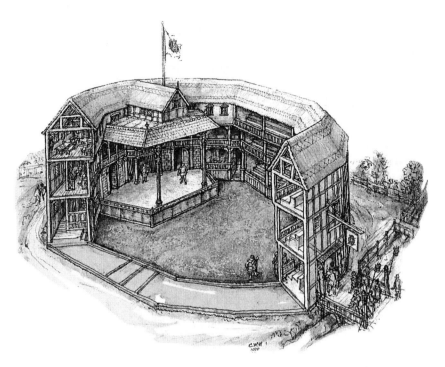

FIGURE 1 'Reconstructed view of the Rose theatre, Phase II', from Julian Bowsher, *The Rose Theatre: An Archaeological Discovery* (London: Museum of London, 1998), p. 80.

Men rose to greater prominence, and later James I, who took over the patronage of Shakespeare's company, the Lord Chamberlain's Men, who became the King's Men in the year of the king's accession. For these princes, there were command performances at court for the important seasons of revelry, Shrovetide (the carnival time before Lent), Christmas, Hocktide (shortly after Easter) and Michaelmas (29 September), which divided the year between winter and summer. In *2 Henry IV* (1597–8), Justice Silence sings part of a wassail (drinking) song, ''Tis merry in hall when beards wag all / And welcome merry Shrovetide. Be merry, be merry' (5.3.29–30).

Plays at court were arranged by the Master of the Revels, the same official to whom all manuscripts proposed for performance were sent to be 'seen and allowed'. Occasional plays could be designed to enact elaborate compliments, as with Peele's *Arraignment of Paris* (1581) where the play is resolved by having Paris give to the chief spectator, the Queen herself, a golden apple, possession of which had been contested by Juno, Venus and Pallas [Athena] who appear 'within' the action. Plays were also performed by the professional companies in the halls of the great, the Inns of Court, sometimes in guildhalls or town squares as part of civic festivities.

It is clear, therefore, that many plays, now 'literary' classics, were originally related to forms of knock-about clowning and juggling contained within jigs or 'interludes', as well as to ritual or occasional entertainments, such as pageants and masques, which do not fit easily into modern categories of 'literature' – verbally rich products generated by the genius of a single author. Moreover, it is helpful to remember that, as in the Middle Ages, plays were often included in categories of 'sports' or 'games'. We forget that the word 'play' can designate both a literary artefact and sportive or imaginative activity. A Robin Hood play, printed between 1553 and 1569, has on its title-page: 'Robin Hood and the Friar. Here beginneth the play of Robin Hood, very proper to be played in *May Games*'. Scene 2 opens with the entrance of the actor who is to take the part of Friar Tuck: as in a modern pantomime, he introduces himself, his role in the action, and the martial skills he will have to deploy. In such a part there is more of the performative than the personative:

> FRIAR TUCK   *Deus hic! Deus hic!* God be here!
> Is not this a holy word for a frere?
> God save all this company!
> But am not I a jolly friar?
> For I can shoot both far and near,
> And handle the sword and buckler.

Here, as in most comedies, characters need not be possessed of what is expected by modern spectators, individuated or 'rounded' personalities – the metaphor is singularly inappropriate in a playhouse – with whom they might 'identify'. That metaphor implies a passive relationship to the dramatic action viewed from a single perspective. Theatrical experience in the early modern period, when there was no proscenium arch to separate the world of the play from the world of the spectators, was more of a collaborative activity in which author, players and audience were working together, taking part in the same 'sports' – the word 'sport' occurs twelve times in *A Midsummer Night's Dream*.

In his 'Epistle to the Readers' in the Beaumont and Fletcher Folio of 1647, the dramatist James Shirley describes a double process of 'identification' and 'alienation':

> how you may here find passions raised to that excellent pitch, and by such insinuating degrees, that you shall not but consent and go along with them, finding yourself at last grown sensibly the very same person you read; and then stand admiring the subtle tracks of your engagement.

Playwrights enjoyed reminding the audience of the conventions of the action, the rules of the theatrical game, and this 'meta-theatrical' awareness was undoubtedly a source of pleasure.

Playgoers, therefore, when enjoying the structured patterns of language and physical action that were offered in the playhouses, were involved in a kind of 'reading' of the performance that is analogous to the experience of modern spectators at, say, a game of football. If we remember this, we may wish to abandon attempts to determine the kinds of 'realism' to be found in early modern playhouses or to work out whether audiences 'believed in' elements of the action. As modern semiologists point out, everything that is presented to a theatrical audience is a sign and, as Bertolt Brecht thought, a player is not so much a personator as a demonstrator, as much concerned with delineating the externals of his role as projecting the inwardness of a highly individuated character. This means that the player's task is to render the type, to act with attitude, or, where appropriate, to maintain, in the terms of a common trope, earnestness in jest. Shakespeare had a merry time delineating the mechanicals in *A Midsummer Night's Dream*: they believed that physical illusion was necessary for theatrical realization and that audiences would take dramatic characters 'for real'.

The patterns of many plays resemble games or sports: some, for example, are structured around contests. In comedies, there is often a conflict between youth and age; in *Love's Labour's Lost* the contest is between learning and love that, at the conclusion of the play, is figured in a musical *débat* between Owl and Cuckoo who are emblematic of winter and spring. In morality plays and romances, right strives against wrong or good with evil. Many critics, following Hegel, believe that some great tragedies involve contests between two incompatible values that are both 'right'. Then we might argue that the conventions of play-making resemble the rules of games. Plays are shaped by conventions, and the principle of decorum entailed rules or conventions of speech for love scenes, distinctive huffing styles for heroes or tyrants. Conventions for plot are seldom spelt out with such bravura relish of excess as they are in *The Revenger's Tragedy* (1606). We hear Vindice proclaim: 'When the bad bleeds, then is the tragedy good' (3.5.205).

Biblical injunctions against men donning female attire meant that boys or young men played women's parts, and many texts complicate the games of cross-dressing by having female characters played by boys disguise themselves as males.[59] Lots of games involve 'dressing up': so does theatre. Tamburlaine's lines as he invests himself with the emblems of power turned into a catchphrase:

> Lie here, ye weeds that I disdain to wear!
> This complete armour and this curtle-axe [cutlass]
> Are adjuncts more befitting Tamburlaine.
> (*1 Tamburlaine*, c.1587, 1.2.41–3)

The child-like lines in fact pack a political punch, suggesting that it might be merely external signs rather than anointing with consecrated oil that can make a king. Conversely, after Shakespeare's Richard II has ritually disinvested himself of his regalia and Bullingbrook has taken the crown from him, the new king's gravity is stripped from him when he finds himself playing the lead in a farcical interlude, written in comic couplets, wherein the Duke and Duchess of York plead respectively for the death and life of their son, Aumerle, who has been plotting against the new regime:

> Our scene is altered from a serious thing,
> And now changed to 'The Beggar and the King'.
> (*Richard II*, 5.3.77–8)

This is a reference to a ballad about King Cophetua and the beggar maid.[60] The scene had begun with Bullingbrook asking for news of his own unruly son, Prince Hal (later Henry V). Bullingbrook had moved to occupy the throne with assurance, forming tactical alliances, getting rid of Richard's minions, men he calls the 'caterpillars of the common-wealth' (2.3.165), who had been feeding on the garden of England.

Now he is revealed as just another father, unable to control the energies of his son. He is just a player king, monarchizing in a stage-play world.

To conclude: full comprehension of the kinds of text described in this chapter demands attention to their conditions of production as well as their content. The liveliness and invention of the period's best literature may make it seem easily accessible, but it is always useful to defamiliarize works that have hardened into classics by some consideration of the forms and pressures of that foreign country, early modern England.

---- CHAPTER 3 ----

Forms Ancient
and Modern

Contemporaries Debate 'Renaissance'

Labels we bestow on periods or literary texts all too often define
or restrict the questions we ask of them. Particular problems derive
from the packaging of the literature and culture of sixteenth- and
seventeenth-century England in 'Renaissance' wrappers. The notion
of 'rebirth' – the metaphorical meaning of 'renaissance' – implies the
renewal of traditions of art that had become moribund or designates
a moment of revolutionary achievement, in this case the swift emergence of literary ideals from renewed and intense study and imitation
of classical texts and forms.

The word 'Renaissance', however, did not enter the English language
until the age of Ruskin in the nineteenth century. Even in the early
modern period the notion of renewal was problematic. In his *Observations in the Art of English Poesie* (1602), the poet and composer Thomas
Campion, arguing for the abolition of rhyme, set out a straightforward
claim for cultural rejuvenation:

> Learning, after the declining of the Roman Empire and the pollution of
> their language through the conquest of the barbarians, lay most piti-
> fully deformed till the time of Erasmus, Reuchlin [a German humanist
> who revived Hebrew studies], [and] Sir Thomas More . . . who brought
> the Latin tongue again to light, redeeming it with much labour out of
> the hands of the illiterate monks and friars.[1]

To this, the poet Samuel Daniel's *Defence of Rhyme* (1603) offered a
prompt retort, disputing a 'renaissance' within a specific period. Daniel

celebrates Petrarch and Boccaccio, and narrates how, some two hundred years before the time of Erasmus, Greek had begun to be taught in Venice again after a gap of seven hundred years, so

> transporting Philosophy beaten by the Turk out of Greece into Christendom. Hereupon came that mighty confluence of learning in these parts, which returning, as it were *per postliminium* [through its own home], and here meeting then with the new invented stamp of printing, spread itself indeed in a more universal sort than the world ever heretofore had it.[2]

In both authors we encounter the familiar paradox that, in the Renaissance, modernity entailed the veneration of antiquity.

Yes, in sixteenth-century England there was brilliant achievement and, yes, there was formal experiment, but we should not expect to find radical breaks with the past that are definable in any but the widest terms. Many conventions of the period – the mingling of jest and earnest in the theatre, for example – are features of medieval dramaturgy, and traditions of allegorical thinking, which for centuries had imbued so much art and biblical interpretation, did not disappear with the reconfiguration of tragedy in Senecan moulds, the writing of historical epics for the stage (witness Shakespeare's history plays), or the writing of new kinds of verse, like that of John Donne, seemingly written to the moment and rooted in experience. The influential *Mirror for Magistrates*, first published in 1559, was a compilation of moral tales concerning the falls of great Englishmen who, it was asserted, were punished by God for their abuse of office. Put together by William Baldwin and others, it is a 'medieval' text that influenced 'modern' texts: it continues a project of narrating the falls of great men and women (the *De Casibus* tradition) started in the fourteenth century by Boccaccio. (In 1494 John Lydgate had translated Boccaccio's work as *The Fall of Princes*.) The topic occurs in the epilogue to John Ford's *Perkin Warbeck* (1633), although, significantly, the emphasis is placed upon institutional failure rather than, as in most medieval versions of the theme, divine will or the turning of Dame Fortune's wheel:

> Here has appeared, though in a several fashion,
> The threats of majesty, the strength of passion,

> Hopes of an empire, changes of fortunes; all
> What can to theatres [spectacles] of greatness fall [befall],
> Proving their weak foundations.

The passage is also meta-theatrical, reminding the audience that they are in both a playhouse and a stage-play world. An 'English Renaissance', therefore, may encompass some but not all the *cultural movements* of the age that includes Sir Thomas More and John Milton, but it is almost impossible to use the notion adequately to define the *period*.

Nor does 'Renaissance' imply the supplanting of venerated English writers. The critical edition of the English poet Geoffrey Chaucer's works by William Thynne in 1532 was as significant a cultural event as the outburst of interest in the Roman historian Tacitus around 1590. Sixty-six years later, in an epistle to Thomas Speght's edition of Chaucer of 1598, Francis Beaumont praised

> Chaucer's device of his Canterbury pilgrimage [which] is merely [entirely] his own, without following the example of any that ever write before him. His drift is to touch all sorts of men, and to discover all vices of that age, and that he doth in such sort as he never fails to hit his every mark he levels at.

Beaumont defended Chaucer against charges that his language was old-fashioned or full of 'incivility' (indecency), and praised him for, in *Troilus and Criseyde*, 'excellently imitating Homer and Virgil and borrowing often of them, and of Horace also'. His remarks on Chaucer's innovation and imitation, moral intention, diction, and observation of decorum define or allude to what was commonly desired in Renaissance texts, but his praise of Chaucer indicates that he does not recognize the kinds of division between 'medieval' and 'renaissance' to which we are accustomed. Spenser, in the February eclogue of *The Shepheardes Calender*, gave Chaucer the designation Tityrus, a name Virgil had invented for himself. George Puttenham, writing about the best authors of satire, listed 'Lucilius, Juvenal, and Persius among the Latins, and with us he that wrote the book called *Piers Ploughman*',[3] even though William Langland (c.1332–1400) had used an abandoned alliterative form of verse that was distinctive of both Old and Middle English poetry.

We must also remember 'Reformation' influences. Plays concerning saints' lives could no longer be performed in post-Reformation England, and in the 1530s John Bale used morality play forms as vehicles for fierce Protestant propaganda. In about 1553 William Baldwin produced a bravura prose satire entitled *Beware the Cat*, which incorporates a multiplicity of medieval genres. The informing allegory involves a regiment of predatory cats in Ireland, reincarnations of witches and led by Grimalkin, whose monstrous appetites and murderous behaviour stand for the villainous tricks or 'shifts' of what was then called papistry.[4]

Nor, in England, did new forms generally emerge *directly* from pioneering re-engagement with classical literature. Much self-consciously innovative writing was indebted to models developed in Italy and France where literary coteries had taken up humanist studies rather earlier than in England. The fashion for writing sonnet sequences in England was inspired by translations from the Italian poet Francesco Petrarch (arguably a 'medieval' figure in that his death antedates that of Chaucer by thirty-six years) and to a lesser degree by the writings of the group of French poets known as 'La Pléiade' led by Pierre de Ronsard (1524–85). Comedies like *Twelfth Night* and *Much Ado about Nothing* had as their principal sources Italian comedies of mistaken identity and cross-wooing. These had mutated into prose tales collected in 1554 by Matteo Bandello (*Novelle*). In France, François de Belleforest assembled a similar collection in 1569, the *Histoires tragiques*, which included tales from Danish history by Saxo Grammaticus (lived about 1200), and which is a source for *Hamlet*.

As in continental Europe, however, in order to define a 'renaissance', we might consider not just pioneering formal literary texts but innovative groups and critical coteries, for example at Oxbridge colleges, wealthy households, the Inns of Court, or court circles where humanist ideals produced literary activity. Henry VIII constituted his court as a centre of magnificence: he wrote poems and music himself, and presided over revels during which new kinds of dramatic fare, including the interludes of John Heywood, were performed. It was in the king's interest to 'medievalize' the past, to foment a cultural revolution to consolidate the new political order established by his break from Rome.[5] The households of Sir Thomas More and Archbishop Morton (died 1500), whom More had tended as a page and where Henry Medwall, another author of interludes, served as chaplain, were also important centres of patronage and literary innovation. In the context of court culture, the elaborate and very expensive court masques (see below), which drew heavily upon classical mythology and exhibited the newest literary, design and musical skills, and which were performed before James I and his son Charles I, are further signs of Renaissance 'modernity'.

A New Criticism

One group of texts in which we do find new emphases comprises those devoted to the criticism of texts. Medieval 'arts of poetry' tended to be rhetorics, and in that period rhetorics tended to concentrate on verbal styles and *textures*, concentrating on the hierarchy of styles and verbal patterning examined in chapter 1.[6] By contrast, critical books in the sixteenth century give extended treatment to *structures*, to genres. (The word 'genre', however, was not imported from France until late in the eighteenth century: contemporaries used the words 'form' or 'kind'.) 'E. K.', who contributed a gloss to Spenser's *The Shepheardes Calender* (probably to make it look like an edition of a classical poem), praised the poet: 'For what in most English writers used to be loose and, as it were ungirt, in this author is well framed and strongly trussed up together.'[7] It could be argued that the decision of John Heminge and Henry Condell in 1623 to arrange Shakespeare's works in their folio edition according to genre registered the establishment of the awareness of genre in England: Ben Jonson had printed his plays in chronological order in his *Works* of 1616.

In England we can see how this concern with and for genre was emerging by comparing the passages in which Sir Thomas Elyot, one of Henry VIII's officials, wrote about poetry in his *Book Named the Governor* (1530) with the discussion of literary forms in George Puttenham's *Art of English Poesie* (1589) and Sir Philip Sidney's *Defence of Poesie* (1595, but written a decade earlier). Elyot discussed classical literature as a quarry for knowledge and wisdom, a gallery of portraits of life and manners: 'What ploughman knoweth so much of husbandry as . . . is expressed [in Virgil's *Eclogues*]? Who, delighting in good horses, shall not be thereto more enflamed, reading of the breeding, choosing, and keeping of them? In the declaration [explanation] whereof Virgil leaveth far behind him all breeders, hackneymen, and scorsers [horse-traders]' (I. x). Sidney, however, looked not only at ancient texts but also at plays and poems being written in his own times, and measured them against classical norms. He praised *Gorboduc*, a political tragedy written for a coterie audience at the Inner Temple in 1562, for conforming to Aristotelian models, and censured theatrical romance narratives from the popular stage because they violated what came to be called the 'unities' of time and place. We also find authors of the period invoking ancient cultural patterns in defence of contemporary prejudices. Sir John Harington defended drama and theatre against those moralists who, in the sixteenth century, would have had the playhouses plucked down: 'witness the huge theatres, and amphi-theatres [of the ancient world], monuments of stupendous charge, made only for tragedies and comedies, the works of poets to be repres-ented on.'[8]

However, not all critics felt that classical critics had promulgated poetic laws that must be obeyed. Like Francis Bacon and Sir Walter Ralegh, Ben Jonson was not convinced that the light of learning was shut up in Aristotle's brain: 'Let Aristotle and others have their dues; but if we can make farther discoveries of truth and fitness than they, why are we envied [regarded with disapproval]? Let us beware, while we strive to add, we do not diminish or deface.'[9]

The Positive Power of Forms

To a modern sensibility, a dedicated responsiveness to classical genres might seem to place restrictions upon an author. In the case of readers, measuring texts prescriptively against generic standards ('Is this a true sonnet') can be a sterile activity, but for writers a knowledge of genre, as with a ripe knowledge of rhetorical practices, could be enabling rather than prescriptive:[10] enabling because the writing of imitations at school and university provided well-resourced training in the art of writing, and because formal constraints could breed experimentalism. Moreover, audiences would no more be bored by a procession of *good* formulaic works than audiences for genre-movies are today. The sur-prise that comes when an author modulates a verbal register or breaks a generic mould is one source of pleasure, but so is the satisfaction that comes from having expectations fulfilled – or delicately tweaked. Even if genre, strictly defined, evolved into mode – as with, say, the fantastical plays of John Marston that turned tragedy into a series of theatrical turns – the constraints and stimulations survived.

Coleridge offered some challenging remarks when he compared the resolutions of Shakespeare's plays with those of Jonson (who often resolved his theatrical intrigues with a twist in the plot or the unexpected introduction of a new character): 'As the feeling with which we startle at a shooting star, compared with that of watching the sunrise at the pre-established moment, such and so low is [the] surprise [of Jonson] compared with expectation [aroused by the patterns of Shakespeare's dramatic actions].'[11] This, of course, is not always true. Graham Bradshaw observed: 'Where *Lear* refuses to finish like a fiction, *The Winter's Tale* pointedly reminds us that it is a fiction.'[12] But it is obvious that writers of the period delighted in drawing the attention of their audiences to the verbal or narrative structures they deployed, and often the effect of these depended upon an apprehension of generic patterning shared by author and audience.

We might consider that reflections upon genre can interfere with our unique apprehension of an artefact (witness Polonius's pedantic taxonomy of the kinds of drama, 'tragical-comical-historical-pastoral'), but texts that were written in imitation of antique models or that contained patterns of allusion could bind authors and knowledgeable readers together as they shared the expectations and pleasures of what has come to be called 'textuality'. Generic conventions and the verbal modes associated with them are instruments of communication as well as classification. The wiser sort at performances of Thomas Kyd's *Spanish Tragedy* (c.1587) would have recognized 'Seneca' as soon as the Ghost of Don Andrea, accompanied by a personification of Revenge, entered at the beginning of the play:

ANDREA When this eternal substance of my soul
Did live imprisoned in my wanton flesh,
Each in their function serving other's need,
I was a courtier in the Spanish court.

In turn, these lines were parodied in later plays, including Beaumont's *The Knight of the Burning Pestle* (1607):

RAFE When I was mortal, this my costive [constipated] corpse
Did lap up figs and raisins in the Strand. (5.284–5)

Sometimes insets (dumbshows and plays-within-plays, for example) or framing devices (inductions, prologues and epilogues) served to foreground the familiar fictive patterns surrounding or embedded within them.[13] This happens in George Peele's *Old Wife's Tale* (1593) where the action of the play starts as a story told by an old woman encountered by three pages lost in a forest. Their names, Antic, Frolic and Fantastic, define the tone for the romantic play of love and adventure that ensues. Then her tale becomes dramatized, narration turns to representation. In Sir Thomas More's prose tale of *Utopia* (1516) the description of the ideal community is put into the mouth of a traveller, Raphael Hythloday, which means that the praises of publicly owned property and divorce, for example, might have been intended as ironic fictions: they are explored not asserted, both owned and disowned by More.

On occasion, formal allusion might generate witty counter-genres like the anti-pastoral sequences and scenes in which Rosalind supplants the role of the male hero in Shakespeare's *As You Like It*. Other writers rejected categorization: in the Prologue to his court play *Endymion* (1588) John Lyly had claimed: 'We present neither comedy, nor tragedy, nor story [history], nor anything.' Sometimes dramatists portrayed theatrical contentions between personifications of the genres: examples are found in the anonymous *A Warning for Fair Women* (1589) and Thomas Randolph's *The Muses' Looking-Glass* (1630). Devices like these, which drew attention to theatrical art, could create multiple perspectives upon the matter in hand or, by the importation of extra-literary forms such as a fool's comic interruption of a narrative, carnivalize[14] the text or representation of it. Forms or topics characteristic of one genre – the Petrarchan hyperboles and oxymorons often found in sonnets, for example – could be imported into another: many passages from *A Midsummer Night's Dream* and *Romeo and Juliet* (1595) provide examples. Conversely, John Donne imported techniques for deliberative self-presentation from the playhouses into his love poems and satires.

These justifications of the creative power of forms notwithstanding, there remain acres of undistinguished composition from the period. Thomas Carew, in his elegy upon the death of Donne, saw the great poet as a fiercely energetic gardener, making way for what was fresh and vigorous:

The Muses' garden with pedantic weeds
O'erspread was purged by thee; the lazy seeds
Of servile imitation thrown away
And fresh invention planted.   (25–8)

Making it New

Two texts that do proclaim a fresh start or 'renaissance' are Edmund
Spenser's set of pastoral poems, *The Shepheardes Calender* (1579), and
Christopher Marlowe's *1 Tamburlaine* (c.1587). *'Pastor'* is the Latin
word for shepherd; Puttenham was to describe the form of pastoral
and eclogue thus: 'There were . . . others who . . . in base and humble
style by manner of dialogue uttered the private and meanest sort of
men, as shepherds, haywards [herders of cattle], and such like: such
was among the Greeks Theocritus, and Virgil among the Latins. Their
poems were named eclogues or shepherdly talk.'[15] Spenser's pastoral
poems, in which fine sentiments and sometimes pointed social criticism emerge from the mouths of rustics, are prefixed by an epistle and
a 'general argument' (by 'E. K.') which set out the genealogy of Latin
eclogues. These prefaces also invoke a hierarchy of genres and praise
Spenser's decorous ability to match style to subject, singling out his
archaisms (here words taken from Chaucer and Lydgate) as being
especially fitting to this new exercise in an ancient mode:

> No less, I think, deserveth his wittiness in devising, his pithiness in
> uttering, his complaints of love so lovely, his discourses of pleasure so
> pleasantly, his pastoral rudeness, his moral wiseness, his due observing
> of decorum everywhere, in personages, in seasons, in matter, in speech,
> and generally in all seemly simplicity of handling his matter and fram-
> ing his words: the which of many things which in him be strange, I
> know will seem the strangest, the words themselves being so ancient,
> the knitting of them so short and intricate, and the whole period [gram-
> matical language] and compass of speech so delightsome for the round-
> ness and so grave for the strangeness.[16]

In this critical encomium, the preciosity of the repetitive forms, balanced phrases, and plays upon words themselves proclaim a union of
the artistic with the academic.

1 Tamburlaine is a heroic play that is also a kind of anti-pastoral in that its hero translates himself from a Scythian shepherd into an emperor. Marlowe begins with a prologue that also sets out an artistic agenda:

> From jigging veins of rhyming mother wits
> And such conceits as clownage keeps in pay,
> We'll lead you to the stately tent of war
> Where you shall hear the Scythian Tamburlaine
> Threat'ning the world with high astounding terms
> And scourging kingdoms with his conquering sword;
> View but his picture in this tragic glass,
> And then applaud his fortunes as you please.

The lines summon up two bonded principles: generic hierarchy and decorum. Classical writers, including Plato and Horace, had established not only presentational varieties (narrative, dramatic, lyric) but also hierarchical degrees of genre. Subsequently, in his Florentine lectures, the humanist scholar Benedetto Varchi (1503–65) distinguished eight genres: heroic, tragic, comic, lyric, elegiac, satiric, pastoral, and epigrammatic.[17] In the *Tamburlaine* prologue, Marlowe, having scaled the heights of the heroic and tragic, looks down disparagingly upon lesser writers, exhausted on the lower slopes of literature and damned by their addiction to vernacular traditions of rhyming (later, as we have seen, to be defended by Samuel Daniel). In similar vein, E. K. wrote: 'I scorn and spew out the rakehelly [rascally] rout of our ragged rhymers' ['Epistle'], and Milton wrote a note against rhyme that is prefixed to *Paradise Lost*. As Marlowe was writing *Tamburlaine* as a 'tragedy' or heroical play, he thought it fitting to adorn his diction with magniloquence, with 'high astounding terms' that raised his play above popular forms of verse and theatre.

Although what Marlowe called 'mother' genres, like the ballad, remained popular and were enjoyed by gentlemen and ploughmen alike, it became fashionable to decry them.[18] Having completed his humanist education by standing upon 'Parnassus' bi-cleft top', Michael Drayton confesses that he has no time for lesser forms:

> I scorned your ballad yet, though it were done
> And had for finis William Elderton.
>   ('Of Poets and Poesie', 41–2)

(William Elderton wrote journalistic ballads: he may have died in 1592 having been choirmaster to Eton and then Westminster School.) Drayton goes on in this poem to write a catalogue of what he took to be the most important English writers of the past two hundred years: again it is notable that the canon he thus establishes begins with Chaucer, confirming that many contemporaries did not recognize a 'renaissance' after medieval barbarism.

Decorum

Decorum, the code of appropriateness, may be the most important principle of the literary art of the English Renaissance – as well as of the visual arts and architecture. What Sir Henry Wotton wrote about architecture could, with appropriate adjustment, be applied to literature:

> Truth (as we metaphorically take it in this art) is a just and natural proportion in every part of the determined figure. Grace is a certain free disposition in the whole draft, answerable to that unaffected frankness of fashion in a living body, man or woman, which doth animate beauty where it is and supply it where it is not.[19]

Matching style to subject and choosing subjects to suit occasions and contexts were both basic to an artist's intention and essential for success, and their contemporaries castigated many writers for failing to do this. In the opening to his *Ars Poetica*, Horace maintained that consistency was necessary for unity, and that each subject or theme must be represented by proper diction, metre, form and tone. Quintilian argued in his *Institutio Oratoria* that everything the orator says, his diction, his gestures, and his appearance must match his subject, the occasion, his audience, and his relation with it (I. v. 1). In 1602, for the philosophical poet John Davies of Hereford, decorum was even a manifestation of the divine:

> By nought so much as by His providence
> Is God discerned; which all must needs discern
> That hath a human soul and common sense;
> For common sense, the outward'st sense intern,
> At the first sight that principle doth learn [teach]:
> For if through the effects we see their cause,

Then may we plainly see whose nature's stern [terrible in aspect],
By that *decorum* we see in her laws,
Namely this power that land and ocean awes.

(*Mirum in Modum*, 2297–305)

To a defence of satire (see below), Edward Guilpin prefixed a sonnet that combines notions of proper or genteel conduct (projecting the feminine as an emblem of the sexually incontinent) with matters of stylistic appropriateness:

Some dainty ear, like a wax-rubbed city room,
Will haply blame my Muse for this salt rheum,
Thinking her lewd and too unmaidenly,
For dancing this jig so lasciviously:
But better thoughts, more discreet, will excuse
This quick coranto of my merry Muse,
And say she keeps *decorum* to the times,
To women's loose gowns suiting her loose rhymes:
But I, who best her humorous pleasance know,
Say that this mad wench when she jesteth so
Is honester than many a sullen one,
Which being more silent thinks worse being alone:
Then my quick-sprighted lass can speak: for who
Knows not the old said saw of the still [quiet] sow.

(From *Skialetheia*, 1598)

A 'still sow', which eats and does not talk, is an emblem of selfishness: social decorum encourages more outgoingness.

The Hierarchy: Epic, Epyllion and Popular Heroics

Classical epics, which occupied the highest place on the literary hierarchy, were widely studied by humanist scholars and eventually translated into English: the first English text of Homer, part of the *Iliad*, was translated out of French by Arthur Hall in 1581 into lumbering fourteeners. This is the opening:

I thee beseech, O goddess mild, the hateful hate to plain
Whereby Achilles was so wrong and grew in such disdain

That thousands of the Greekish dukes, in hard and heavy plight,
To Pluto's court did yield their souls and gaping lay upright [supine],
Those senseless trunks, of burial void, by them erst gaily borne,
By ravening curs, and carrion fouls, in pieces to be torn.

Hall's *Iliad* had been preceded by a translation of the *Aeneid* by Gavin Douglas (1513, but printed only in 1553), and by translations of Ovid's *Metamorphoses*, a collection of verse narratives that contains epic elements, by Caxton in 1480 (again from French) and by Arthur Golding in 1565–7.

Sir John Harington praised Homer and 'heroical poesy, that with her sweet stateliness doth erect the mind and lift it up to the consideration of the highest matters: and allureth them, that of themselves would otherwise loath them, to take and swallow and digest the wholesome precepts of philosophy, and many times even of the true divinity.' But, he wrote, 'as Sir Philip Sidney confesseth, Cupido is crept even into the heroical poems.'[20] He was referring to Italian imitations of ancient epics that incorporated romance material, notably Ludovico Ariosto's *Orlando Furioso* (1516) and Torquato Tasso's more Virgilian *Gerusalemme Liberata* (1581), which deals with the capture of Jerusalem during the First Crusade. These were translated into English by Sir John Harington in 1591 and Edward Fairfax (*Godfrey of Bulloigne, or the Recovery of Jerusalem*) in 1600. Both poems affirm their allegiance to Virgil by opening with variations of the first line of the *Aeneid*: '*Arma virumque cano*', 'I sing of arms and the man.'

Orlando Furioso, usefully classed as a chivalric epic, in turn provided one of the models for Spenser's *Faerie Queene*, which turned into heroic verse Arthurian legends of the sort that had been set out in prose in Sir Thomas Malory's *Le Morte Darthur* (1485), another of the books published by Caxton. In a prefatory letter to Sir Walter Ralegh, Spenser's first point is that his poem is not simply a narrative but 'a continued allegory or dark conceit . . . coloured with an historical fiction', the purpose of which 'is to fashion a gentleman or noble person in virtuous and gentle discipline'. Spenser also declares his allegiance to Homer, Virgil, Ariosto and Tasso as well as his intention to write twelve books, each based on one of the Aristotelian moral virtues. His Faerie Queene is, of course, 'the most excellent and glorious person of our sovereign the Queen', who is also figured in the persons of Belphoebe and Cynthia. Spenser's subject, however, is as

FIGURE 2 'Ruggiero fells an upstart falconer with his magic shield',
illustration to Book 8 of Ludovico Ariosto, *Orlando Furioso in English
Heroical Verse*, trans. Sir John Harington (London, 1591), p. 56, London,
British Library.

historical and political as it is moral. Book 1, assigned to Holiness, is an allegory of the contention between the reformed English church (figured in Una) and the Church of Rome (Duessa).

More overtly historical-political epics were to come from Samuel Daniel (*The Civil Wars between the two Houses of Lancaster and York*, 1595–1601), from John Milton in *Paradise Lost* (1667), and Abraham Cowley in his fragmentary *Poem upon the Late Civil War* (published only in 1679, twelve years after his death). Milton and Cowley used classical epic forms to explore the historical circumstances of the seventeenth century as Daniel had done to explore the Wars of the Roses. Like the Italian writers, Daniel begins with a genuflection to the first line of the *Aeneid*. Before he turns to the tragedy of Adam and Eve embedded within the epic, Milton offers a strangely noble portrait of Satan. Here is Satan exclaiming at the sight of the fallen Beelzebub, perhaps the devil's Cromwell, a passage in which Milton fuses allusions to both Isaiah (14:12) and to the *Aeneid* (2.274) as well as to the course of recent English history:

> If thou beest he; But O how fall'n! how changed
> From him, who in the happy realms of light
> Clothed with transcendent brightness didst out-shine
> Myriads though bright: if he whom mutual league,
> United thoughts and counsels, equal hope
> And hazard in the glorious enterprise,
> Joined with me once, now misery hath joined
> In equal ruin: into what pit thou seest
> From what height fall'n, so much the stronger proved
> He with his thunder: and till then who knew
> The force of those dire arms? Yet not for those,
> Nor what the potent victor in his rage
> Can else inflict, do I repent or change,
> Though changed in outward lustre; that fixèd mind
> And high disdain, from sense of injured merit,
> That with the mightiest raised me to contend,
> And to the fierce contention brought along
> Innumerable force of spirits armed
> That durst dislike his reign, and me preferring,
> His utmost power with adverse power opposed
> In dubious [uncertain] battle on the plains of heav'n,
> And shook his throne. What though the field be lost?
> All is not lost; the unconquerable will,

And study of revenge, immortal hate,
And courage never to submit or yield:
And what is else not to be overcome?

(*Paradise Lost*, 1.84–109)

Cowley produced a piece of royalist propaganda that exemplifies the period's distinctive mixture of history and allegory, all set in a quickly sketched Spenserian landscape:

On two fair hills both armies next are seen,
The affrighted valley sighs and sweats between;
Here angels did with fair expectance stay
And wished good things to a king as mild as they;
There fiends with hunger waiting did abide,
And cursèd both but spurrèd on the guilty side.
Here stood Religion, her looks gently sage,
Aged, but much more comely for her age!
There Schism, old hag, though seeming young appears,
As snakes by casting skins renew their years;
Undecent rags of several dyes she wore
And in her hand torn liturgies she bore.
Here Loyalty an humble cross displayed,
And still as Charles passed by she bowed and prayed.
Sedition there her crimson banner spreads,
Shakes all her hands and roars with all her heads.
Her knotty hairs were with dire serpents twist,
And every serpent at each other hissed.
Here stood white Truth and her own host does bless,
Clad with those arms of proof, her nakedness.
There Perjuries like cannons roar aloud,
And Lies flew thick, like cannon's smoky cloud.

(*Poem upon the Late Civil War*, 207–28)

One distinctive heroic form was the epyllion, a miniature epic, imitated from poems by Theocritus and Ovid. The name for this genre was revived only in the nineteenth century – some term these poems 'verse romances' – and many late sixteenth-century dramatists and wits, Lodge, Shakespeare, Marlowe, Beaumont and Marston among them, produced examples of the genre. They were often erotic: an example can be found in the description of Leander's naked body in Marlowe's *Hero and Leander* (1593). The poem opens knowingly with a description of Hero:

The outside of her garments were of lawn,
The lining purple silk, with gilt stars drawn,
Her wide sleeves green, and bordered with a grove,
Where Venus in her naked glory strove
To please the careless and disdainful eyes
Of proud Adonis that before her lies.
Her kirtle [skirt] blue, whereon was many a stain
Made with the blood of wretched lovers slain.
Upon her head she ware a myrtle wreath,
From whence her veil reached to the ground beneath.
Her veil was artificial flowers and leaves
Whose workmanship both man and beast deceives.
Many would praise the sweet smell as she past,
When 'twas the odour which her breath forth cast.
And there, for honey, bees have sought in vain,
And beat from thence, have lighted there again.
About her neck hung chains of pebble stone
Which, lightened by her neck, like diamonds shone.
She wore no gloves, for neither sun nor wind
Would burn or parch her hands, but to her mind,
Or warm or cool them, for they took delight
To play upon those hands, they were so white.
Buskins of shells all silvered usèd she,
And branched with blushing coral to the knee;
Where sparrows perched, of hollow pearl and gold,
Such as the world would wonder to behold:
Those with sweet water oft her handmaid fills
Which, as she went [walked], would chirrup through the bills.
Some say for her the fairest Cupid pined,
And looking in her face, was strooken blind.
But this is true, so like was one the other,
As he imagined Hero was his mother.

(Hero and Leander, sestiad I, 15–46)

The mixture of allusions to the Greek deities with grotesquery, and of magniloquent description with bathos (the blood-stained kirtle and the swarming bees), along with the final feminine rhyme, suggest that Marlowe was knowingly writing a pastiche, at once committing himself to the conventions of the genre and exposing their quaint or archaic properties. In drama, we could look to John Marston's fantastical plays *Antonio and Mellida* (1599) and *Antonio's Revenge* (1600) whose excessive stylistic devices suggest a fascination with and disdain for contemporary heroic writing.

Tragedies

Medieval tragedies, as we have seen, depicted the fall of a great person from high degree. Often this was ascribed simply to the remorseless turning of Fortune's wheel. By the time of Shakespeare, however, tragedies had been written in imitation of the ancients that concentrated on passion, revenge and the spilling of blood. Classical influence on English Renaissance tragedy did not come directly from the great Greek tragedians, Aeschylus, Euripides and Sophocles, but from the writings of Lucius Annaeus Seneca (4BC–AD65) who, like the Greeks some five hundred years before, used mythological figures. In these texts, Stoic sentiments (Seneca also wrote a series of moral essays or epistles), uttered by a chorus or incorporated within declamatory set speeches, are set against lurid episodes which often involve supernatural figures. All of these devices enabled dramatists to explore inner experience, an individual's response to the moment.

From 1566, while he was an undergraduate at Cambridge, John Studley (?1545–?90) published a set of translations from Seneca: *Hippolyta, Medea, Agamemnon* and *Hercules Octaeus*. Seneca's texts seem to have been designed for play-reading rather than public theatrical performance and tend towards the declamatory. Here is the Nurse, in rhyming fourteeners, suggesting to Deianira in *Hercules Octaeus* that she punish her husband Hercules by the use of magic:

> It is almost a common guise that wedded wives do haunt
> Their husbands' hearts by magic art and witchcraft to enchant,
> In winter cold I charmèd have the woods, to make them sprout.
> And forced the thunder dint [roll] recoil, that hath bin bolting out.
> With walt'ring [rolling] surges I have shook the seas amid the calm.
> I smoothèd have the wrestling waves, and laid down every walm [billow].
> The dry ground gapèd hath like gulfs, and out new springs have gushed,
> The roaring rocks have quaking stirred, and none thereat hath pushed.
> Hell['s] gloomy gates I have brast [burst] ope, where grisly ghosts all hushed
> Have stood and, answering at my charm, the goblins grim have scowled.
> The threefold-headed hound of hell with barking throats hath howled.
> Thus both the seas, the land, the heavens, and hell bow at my beck.

Noonday to midnight, to and fro turns at my charming check [attack].
At my enchantment every thing declines from nature's law.
Our charm shall make his stomach stoop, and bring him more in awe.[21]

In the 'Pyramus and Thisbe' play in *A Midsummer Night's Dream*, Shakespeare parodied this huffing style.

Mary Sidney, Countess of Pembroke (1561–1621) wrote a more modulated imitation in her *The Tragedy of Antony* (1595). Here is part of a Chorus that is close to Seneca's *Agamemnon*, although the play as a whole, written for a private performance, is a translation of Robert Garnier's *Marc Antoine* (1592) into English blank verse:

Lament we our mishaps,
   Drown we with tears our woe:
   For lamentable haps
   Lamented easy grow:
   And much less torment bring
   Than when they first did spring.

We want [lack] that woeful song
   Wherewith wood-music's queen
   Doth ease her woes, among
   Fresh springtime's bushes green,
   On pleasant branch alone
   Renewing ancient moan.

We want that moanful sound
   That prattling Procne makes
   On fields of Thracian ground
   Or streams of Thracian lakes,
   To empt her breast of pain
   For Itys by her slain.[22]

Around the second decade of the seventeenth century, tragedies came to deal increasingly not just with the miseries attendant upon political change but also with clashes between intense sexual desires and the social order.[23]

By the time of Shakespeare it is often hard to distinguish tragedies from the history plays that were produced in some numbers after the defeat of the Spanish Armada. Early editions ascribe them indiscriminately to either or both genres. Marlowe and Shakespeare drew upon patterns of medieval morality and used the chronicles of Hall and Holinshed as sources for both 'history' and 'tragedy'. History plays constituted an important English dramatic genre that did not figure in neo-classical lists. What may be important is that both these genres have important political resonances, addressing themselves, for example, to contests between goodness and greatness, to the relationship between material power and the authority that comes to an individual from office or by inheritance, or to the dilemma of a ruler whose sense of his own rights is curtailed by awareness of the duties he owes to his subjects. They depict not just the fall of one man but the catastrophes that befall a group or state. (The notion of a 'tragic hero' is anachronistic: the word 'hero' was not used in English in this sense until a hundred years after Shakespeare.)

In Norton and Sackville's *Gorboduc*, material from the English chroniclers is moulded into a Senecan five-act structure divided by choruses. Like *King Lear* (1605–6), it deals with the fatal consequences of dividing a kingdom between two rulers. Each act is preceded by a dumbshow. The first enacts the theme:

> *First the music of violins began to play, during which came in upon the stage six wild men clothed in leaves. Of whom the first bare in his neck a fagot of small sticks, which they all both severally and together assayed with all their strengths to break, but it could not be broken by them. At the length one of them plucked out one of the sticks and brake it: and the rest plucking out all the other sticks, one after an other did easily break, the same being severed which, being conjoined, they had before attempted in vain. After they had this done, they departed the stage, and the music ceased. Hereby was signified that a state knit in unity doth continue strong against all force. But being divided, is easily destroyed. As befell upon Duke Gorboduc dividing his land to his two sons which he before held in monarchy, and upon the dissension of the brethren to whom it was divided.*

Not only did dramatists match high styles to high subjects, but decorum advocated the depiction of noble personages in tragedy and commoners in comedy. Thomas Kyd invoked the convention:

BALTHAZAR   Hieronimo, methinks a comedy were better.
HIERONIMO   A comedy?
  Fie, comedies are fit for common wits:
  But to present a kingly troop withal

Give me a stately-written tragedy,
Tragedia cothurnata, fitting kings,
Containing matter and not common things.
                    (*The Spanish Tragedy*, 4.1.155–60)

Cothurnata means 'buskined', referring to the half-boots worn by tragic actors in the ancient world. Comic actors wore low-heeled slippers (*socci*), to which Milton alluded when, in 'L'Allegro' (1631) he wrote:

Then to the well-trod stage anon,
If Jonson's learnèd sock be on,
Or sweetest Shakespeare, Fancy's child,
Warble his native wood-notes wild.   (131–4)

There are many thundering tragedies of state concerned with the fates of monarchs and life at court, and in the early seventeenth century there was a demand for citizen comedy (see chapter 5), the intrigues of which generally depicted the triumph of love over material values. However, alongside these specimens of decorous orthodoxy there is a small but significant number of domestic tragedies (the anonymous *Arden of Faversham* (c.1591) and Thomas Heywood's *A Woman Killed with Kindness* (1603) and a large number of romantic comedies (including almost all of Shakespeare's) peopled by nobles accompanied by their comic servants.

Audiences, however, according to many apologetic or sheepish prologues, seem to have enjoyed mixtures: 'lamentable tragedy mixed full of pleasant mirth'.[24] Nathaniel Woodes in this prologue to his *The Conflict of Conscience* (c.1572) is representative:

And though the history of itself be too-too dolorous,
And would constrain a man with tears of blood his cheeks to wet,
Yet to refresh the minds of them that be the auditors,
Our author intermixèd hath, in places fit and meet,
Some honest mirth, yet always 'ware decorum to exceed.

A decade or so later, John Lyly, in the Prologue to *Midas* (1589), justified this mingling by claiming that it represented what Dr Johnson was to call 'the real state of sublunary nature': 'All cometh to this pass that what heretofore hath been served in several dishes for a feast, is now minced in a charger [platter] for a gallimaufry [meal made of scraps]. If we present a mingle-mangle, our fault is to be excused because the whole world is become an hodge-podge.'

Not only were the dramatic registers mingled, but it is often the case that, as in Middleton's comedies, characters switch from prose to blank verse to rhyming couplets within a single scene, or dramatists insert lyric passages, sometimes actual songs. In some ways these were like arias in a modern opera, having as their primary function neither the advance of the plot nor the development of character, but the demonstration of skill and the kindling of audience pleasure. This interpenetration of genres, the self-conscious use of multiple forms and generic registers to create a plurality of perspectives upon the subject, has been related to 'novelization', the dialogic co-presence of generic languages within a work, used to link it more closely to the complexities of life.[25]

It has become a cliché to designate inset scenes for clowns and fools, particularly those in Shakespeare's tragedies and history plays, as 'comic relief'. If we do, we must be aware that the notion implies an audience who did not have time for serious matter, which may not have always been the case. George Bernard Shaw usefully refined the notion when he referred to 'the Shakespearian-Dickensian consolation of *laughter at mischief*, accurately called comic relief'.[26] Moreover, the mischief in such scenes often consists not simply of knockabout but of jibes and jests, from clowns and professional fools alike, at the expense of authority figures. Tragedies and histories were not always supportive of the hegemonic order: in the contention between Tragedy and Comedy in 1.3 of Thomas Randolph's *The Muses' Looking-Glass* it is Satire who is the attendant of Tragedy while Mime follows Comedy.

This kind of embedded reflection is common in texts of the period, as is the presence of plays-within-plays like 'Pyramus and Thisbe' in *A Midsummer Night's Dream*, another meta-theatrical convention that reveals the element of self-consciousness in the dramaturgy of the period. In yet another device of this kind, the Induction Ben Jonson wrote for the opening of *Bartholomew Fair*, the Book-holder drew up 'articles of agreement' (line 64) with his audience, defining the rules of the theatrical game in which they were both involved. Pedantic Ben Jonson was right: such a relationship has to exist, and it is specific to the medium.

We must distinguish plays with inset humorous scenes only loosely connected with the plot, from plays in which matters serious and comic are laced together, plays that came be called 'tragicomedies'. Battista Guarini established this mixed genre in Italy, and his dramatic pastoral *Il pastor fido* (1590) was imitated and translated all over Europe. John Fletcher wrote an English version (*The Faithful Shepherdess*) around 1608 and prefixed a lengthy epistle that takes up some of the points set out in Guarini's defence of charges (in his *Compendio della poesia tragicomica* of 1601) that his play violated Aristotelian rules for dramatic structure:

> It is a pastoral tragicomedy, which the people seeing when it was played, having ever had a singular gift in defining, concluded to be a play of country hired shepherds in grey cloaks, with curtailed dogs in strings, sometimes laughing together, and sometimes killing one another; and, missing Whitsun-ales, cream, wassail, and morris-dances, began to be angry. In their error I would not have you fall, lest you incur their censure. Understand, therefore, a pastoral to be a representation of shepherds and shepherdesses with their actions and passions, which must be such as may agree with their natures, at least not exceeding former fictions and vulgar traditions; they are not to be adorned with any art but such improper ones as nature is said to bestow, as singing and poetry; or such as experience may teach them, as the virtues of herbs and fountains, the ordinary course of the sun, moon, and stars, and such like. But you are ever to remember shepherds to be such as all the ancient poets, and modern, of understanding, have received them: that is, the owners of flocks, and not hirelings. A tragicomedy is not so called in respect of mirth and killing, but in respect it wants deaths, which is enough to make it no tragedy, yet brings some near it, which is enough to make it no comedy, which must be a representation of familiar people, with such kind of trouble as no life be questioned; so that a god is as lawful in this as in a tragedy, and mean people as in a comedy.

Both Jonson and Shakespeare seem to have known of and to have taken up the patterns Guarini had instituted.[27]

Comedy

As with tragedy, English Renaissance comedy had roots in both native traditions and classical models. In medieval plays, both those that served to narrate scriptural stories ('mysteries') and didactic allegories ('moralities'), serious matter had been larded with comedy, often performed by clowns who took the parts of devils and their attendant 'vices'. Moral interludes written at the beginning of the sixteenth century and performed at banquets in great houses and at court also contained elements of clownery and knockabout. As late as 1626 Ben Jonson revealed that he was happy to cut new theatrical costumes from old dramatic patterns:

> MIRTH   . . . How like you the Vice i' the play?
> EXPECTATION   Which is he?
> MIRTH   Three or four: old Covetousness, the sordid Pennyboy, the Money-bawd, who is a flesh-bawd too, they say.
> TATTLE   But here is never a fiend to carry him away. Besides, he has never a wooden dagger! I'd not give a rush for a Vice that has not a wooden dagger to snap at everybody he meets.
> MIRTH   That was the old way, gossip, when Iniquity came in like Hocus-Pocus [a stock figure of a conjurer] in a juggler's jerkin with false skirts, like the Knave of Clubs. But now they are attired like men and women o' the time, the Vices male and female: Prodigality like a young heir, and his Mistress Money (whose favours he scatters like counters) pranked up like a prime lady, the Infanta of the Mines.
>
> (Act 2, Intermean)

In Marlowe's *Dr Faustus* Robin is designated as a clown. He is the servant of Faustus's servant Wagner and is, as a punishment, driven up and down the stage by two devils (scene 4): in Shakespeare's *1 Henry IV* one of Falstaff's attributes is a 'dagger of lath' (2.4.116), a stage property of the morality play Vice. However, writers of comedy (especially Ben Jonson) were equally aware of classical models, both the satirical 'Old Comedy' associated with Aristophanes and the 'New Comedy' written by the Greek dramatist Menander, the plays of whom are now lost but known through the Latin imitations of Plautus and Terence.[28]

Old Comedy contained little in the way of plot: plays are composed out of episodes thematically linked and peopled by stock characters. Plays like Jonson's 'humour' comedies are more interesting for their variety than for their stories. Indeed, Jonson celebrated comedy for showing:

so many and various affections of the mind. There shall the spectator see some insulting with joy, others fretting with melancholy, raging with anger, mad with love, boiling with avarice, undone with riot, tortured with expectation, consumed with fear; no perturbation in common life but the orator finds example of it in the scene.[29]

New Comedy, by contrast, is built upon intrigue: there is usually a young and attractive 'hero' accompanied by a wily servant or slave. Together, they win a girl (and often her fortune) from under the nose of her father or of unsuitable suitors, who often form part of a group of stock characters: the pedant, the pantaloon, the quack doctor, the lawyer. The hero stands for new life and vitality, and his values often expose the hypocrisy of grasping or lusty age. This pattern was the basis of both the printed *commedia erudita* and the improvised *commedia dell'arte* that flourished in Italy in the sixteenth century, the forms of which were taken up by English playwrights in the age of Shakespeare. It was particularly suited to city values, given that the hero often stood for energy and enterprise, gulling corrupted or dilapidated representatives of decaying social orders.

This can create moral ambiguity in performance, yet comedy was defended for its moral function. In the dedication of *Volpone* Jonson wrote that it was the 'office of a comic poet to imitate justice', although the dénouement of *The Alchemist* results in great but undeserved wealth for a character whose name 'Lovewit' reveals that he has triumphed simply by outwitting the rogues of the play and not as a reward for restoring a moral order. In an earlier play, *The Poetaster* (1601) Jonson gives a good summary of the stock characters whipped by the satirical dramatists of the time:

> the tongue of the oracle never twanged truer. Your courtier cannot kiss his mistress' slippers in quiet for 'em, nor your white innocent gallant pawn his revelling suit to make his punk a supper. An honest decayed commander cannot skelder [live by begging], cheat, nor be seen in a bawdy house, but he shall be straight in one of their wormwood comedies.

In the playhouses, however, comedy would not have appeared as a strictly formalized genre. In performances, comedies included song, instrumental music, dance, as well as feats of activity: clownage, mime, exhibitions of the grotesque. In the epistle to *The Alchemist* Ben Jonson complained: 'Now the concupiscence of dances and antics so reigneth that to run away from Nature and be afraid of her is the only point of art that tickles the spectators.' ('Antics' were grotesques, clowns or monsters that could share some features with beasts.) Performances often seem to have ended with jigs, short hybrids of dance and drama, often obscene.[30]

The moral patterning of New Comedy could, of course, be reversed: the hero might be no better that he should be (an example is provided by Thomas Middleton's *A Trick to Catch the Old One* [1605]). Comedies, said Thomas Heywood, are

> pleasantly contrived with merry accidents and intermixed with apt and witty jests to present before the prince at certain times of solemnity, or else merrily fitted to the stage. And what is then the subject of this harmless mirth? Either in the shape of a clown, to show others their slovenly and unhandsome behaviour, that they may reform that simplicity in themselves, which others make their sport, lest they happen to become the like subject of general scorn to an auditory. Else it entreats of love, deriding foolish inamorates [lovers] who spend their ages, their spirits, nay themselves, in the servile and ridiculous employments of their mistresses. And these are mingled with sportful accidents, to recreate such as of themselves are wholly devoted to melancholy, which corrupts the blood, or to refresh such weary spirits as are tired with labour or study, to moderate the cares and heaviness of the mind, that they may return to their trades and faculties with more zeal and earnestness after some small soft and pleasant retirement. Sometimes they discourse of pantaloons, usurers that have unthrifty sons, which both the fathers and sons may behold to their instructions. Sometimes of courtesans, to divulge their subtleties and snares in which young men may be entangled, showing them the means to avoid them. If we present a pastoral, we show the harmless love of shepherds diversely moralized, distinguishing betwixt the craft of the city and the innocency of the sheep-cote. (*An Apology for Actors*, 1612)

Masques

In contrast with the robust mixtures of genre offered in playhouses, the court masque, a highly formalized genre, emerged at the end of the sixteenth century and flourished throughout the Stuart period.[31] Masques involved minimal story and characterization; the inordinate costs of these entertainments went on conspicuous sets, costumes, music and dance. The best poets, artists and musicians collaborated – although Ben Jonson fiercely elevated the 'soul' of the masque, its words, over its 'body', scenic display, when he came to feel that the art of Inigo Jones, the greatest architect of his day, was eclipsing his own (see his poem 'An Expostulation with Inigo Jones'). In his designs, Jones used new techniques of perspective to create a degree of illusion. Deities were chosen as part of a programme of political flattery, but masques could also instruct by praising, the audience being well aware that King James or his favourite Buckingham, for example, scarcely matched the exemplars of virtue displayed before them. The main parts were taken by courtiers (including women), although these came to be supplemented by professional players who took roles in 'anti-masques', comic or grotesque 'foils' (as Jonson called them) that embodied values opposed to those celebrated in the masque itself. In Chapman's *Masque of the Middle Temple and Lincoln's Inn*, written for the wedding of King James's daughter Elizabeth, the processional entrance included:

> baboons attired like fantastical travellers in Neapolitan suits and great ruffs, all horsed with asses and dwarf palfreys, with yellow foot-cloths, and casting cockle-demois [shells representing money?] about, in courtesy, by way of largesse; torches borne on either hand of them, lighting their state as ridiculously as the rest nobly.[32]

The genre had evolved out of mummings or disguisings: the entertainments began with the arrival of the aristocratic masquers; the action generally climaxed with the entrance of a deity or allegorical figure who resolved difference or discord; and ended when the spectacle 'dissolved' and the masquers 'took out' members of the audience to join them in the revels.

Shorter Poetic Forms

In his reports of his conversations with Ben Jonson, Drummond of Hawthornden reported: 'He cursed Petrarch for redacting [reducing] verses to sonnets; which he said were like that tyrant's bed, where some who were too short were racked, others too long cut short.'[33]

Jonson, of course, was exaggerating: not all short poems were sonnets, but particularly in the Elizabethan period they were one of the dominant forms, along, of course, with songs and airs, elegies, verse-epistles, ballads and epigrams.

Some of the poems in 'Tottel's Miscellany' (see chapter 1) were Wyatt's and Surrey's important adaptations of sonnets by Petrarch: previously these had circulated only in manuscript. The Preface celebrates a new venture for the English language and affirms the value of short poems:

> That to have well written in verse, yea and in small parcels, deserveth great praise, the works of divers Latins, Italians, and other, do prove sufficiently. That our tongue is able in that kind to do as praiseworthily as the rest, the honourable style of the noble Earl of Surrey, and the weightiness of the deep-witted Sir Thomas Wyatt the elder's verse, with several graces in sundry good English writers, do show abundantly. It resteth now, gentle reader, that thou think it not evil done to publish to the honour of the English tongue, and for profit of the studious of English eloquence, those works which the ungentle hoarders up of such treasure have heretofore envied thee. And for this point, good reader, thine own profit and pleasure, in these presently, and in more hereafter, shall answer for my defence. If perhaps some mislike the stateliness of style removed from the rude skill of common ears, I ask help of the learned to defend their learned friends, the authors of this work; and I exhort the unlearned, by reading to learn to be more skilful, and to purge that swine-like grossness, that maketh the sweet marjoram not to smell to their delight.[34]

Although 'sonnet', from the Italian word for a 'little song', continued to be used as a synonym for 'song', Petrarch's fourteen-line verses established a prototype that was to be much emulated. English sonnets were generally decasyllabic and often, as in Petrarch, were comprised of two sections: the first eight lines (the octave) and the last six (the sestet). A *volta* between the octave and sestet marked a 'turn' of thought or modal transition, often from narrative to reflection. The sonnets of Wyatt and Shakespeare, however, tend to comprise three quatrains followed by a closing or summarizing couplet. Elizabethan sonneteers were prolific – like Petrarch, who had written sequences of songs and sonnets devoted to the life and death of his 'Madonna Laura'. Petrarch liked to pun on the name of his beloved – '*L'aura*' could mean 'the breeze' in Italian – and the names chosen by his English followers indicate that they are as much concerned with exploring symbolic structures of love as with describing or generating sensuous feelings about a particular person. Sidney's poems were written to 'Stella', Greville's sequence was entitled 'Caelica', and Shakespeare played on his own name 'Will'. Consequently, it is probably better to approach these 'sequences' not as stories or depictions of states of mind but explorations and inter-rogations of poetic conventions and the languages of love.

Sir Thomas Wyatt and the Earl of Surrey both published translations of Petrarch's Sonnet 140 from the sequence *In vita di Madonna Laura*:

> *Amor, che nel penser mio vive e regna*
>   *E 'l suo seggio maggior nel mio cor tene,*
>   *Tal or armato ne la fronte vène,*
>   *Ivi si loca, et ivi pon sua insegna.*
> *Quella ch'amare et sofferir ne 'nsegna*
>   *E vòl che 'l gran desio, l'accesa spene,*
>   *Ragion, vergogna et reverenza affrene,*
>   *Di nostro ardir fra se stessa si sdegna.*
> *Onde Amor paventoso fugge al core*
>   *Lasciando ogni sua impresa, et piange, et trema;*
>   *Ivi s'asconde, et non appar piú fòre.*
> *Che poss'io far, temendo il mio signore,*
>   *Se non star seco infin a l'ora extrema?*
>   *Ché bel fin fa chi ben amando more.*

Wyatt's version is one of a group of translations from Petrarch. It comes early in the Egerton manuscript, the most important manuscript collection of his poems, and was also printed in 'Tottel's Miscellany':

> The long love that in my thought doth harbour,
>   And in my heart doth keep his residence,
>   Into my face presseth with bold pretence
>   And there campeth, displaying his banner.
> She that me learns to love and suffer,
>   And wills that my trust and lust's negligence
>   Be reined by reason, shame, and reverence,
>   With his hardiness taketh displeasure.
> Wherewithal love to the heart's forest he fleeth,
>   Leaving his enterprise with pain and cry,
>   And there him hideth and not appeareth.

What may I do, when my master feareth,
But in the field with him to live and die?
For good is the life, ending faithfully.

Surrey's version also appeared in 'Tottel's Miscellany' (with many variant readings), under the heading 'Complaint of a Love Rebuked':

Love that doth reign and live within my thought,
And built his seat within my captive breast,
Clad in the arms wherein with me he fought,
Oft in my face he doth his banner rest.
But she that taught me love and suffer pain,
My doubtful hope and eke my hot desire
With shamefaced look to shadow and refrain,
Her smiling grace converteth straight to ire.
And coward love, then, to the heart apace
Taketh his flight, where he doth lurk and plain
His purpose lost, and dare not show his face.
For my lord's guilt thus, faultless, bide I pain;
Yet from my lord shall not my foot remove:
Sweet is the death that taketh end by love.

Wyatt used to be denigrated for not keeping metre: here irregularity gives the effect of the presence of a speaking voice, whereas Surrey takes refuge in formulaic patterning ('My doubtful hope and eke my hot desire') and often, unlike Wyatt, sacrifices vividness to an exact rhyme.

The deliberative modes and verbal complexities of sonnets meant that they were seldom set to music, although many other short poems reprinted in modern anthologies have been silently shorn of their musical settings. Songs generally voice the feelings of an individual, although a dominant Elizabethan form was the madrigal, in which lyrical verses were sung in elaborate counterpoint by an unaccompanied consort of voices. Some dealt with love; others, like those published in *The Triumphs of Oriana* (1601) and set to tunes by Thomas Morley, Thomas Weelkes and others, were vehicles for compliments to the Queen. Around the turn of the century, madrigals gave way to 'airs', songs generally for a single voice with lute accompaniment, the music of which served not just to display the complexities of the composer's art, but also to express emotion by matching the tune to the words and sentiments of the verses. Here are the words of one of the most famous songs of the period, referred to in countless texts, John Dowland's 'Lachrimae [Tears]', in a version for voice and lute with a sung base:

Flow my tears, fall from your springs;
Exiled for ever, let me mourn
Where night's black bird her sad infamy sings,
There let me live forlorn.

Down, vain lights, shine you no more,
No nights are dark enough for those
That in despair their last fortunes deplore:
Light doth but shame disclose.

Never may my woes be relieved,
Since pity is fled, and tears,
And sighs, and groans my weary days,
Of all joys have deprived.

Fro the highest spire of contentment
My fortune is thrown, and fear
And grief and pain for my deserts,
Are my hopes since hope is gone.

Hark, you shadows that in darkness dwell,
Learn to contemn light:
Happy, happy they that in hell
Feel not the world's despite.[35]

Quantitative Verse

Certain poets, as well as imitating the forms used by Greek and Latin poets, sought to experiment with converting classical metres into English. English metres are accentual, deriving from patterns of *stressed* and *unstressed* syllables; Latin metres are quantitative, based on patterns of *long* and *short* syllables. Thomas Campion, whose metrical experimentation had been anticipated by Sidney and Sir Edward Dyer (1543–1607), produced notable examples of this kind of versification:

What fair pomp have I spied of glittering ladies,
With locks sparkled abroad and rosy coronet
On their ivory brows, tracked to the dainty thighs
With robes, like Amazons, blue as violet;
With gold Aglets adorned, some in a changeable
Pale [cloak], with spang[le]s wavering, taught to be moveable.

('Canto Secundo')

Campion defended what he called 'numerous [quantitative] poesy' in his *Observations in the Art of English Poesie* (1602).

Satire

One of the stock defences of literature, and of drama in particular, was that it inculcated virtue, and one of the dominant instructive modes was satire, the scourge of vices and follies of the age. A particular feature of Renaissance satire was that it was often deliberately railing: unpolished, shaggy, savage and often erotic. This was because the word 'satire' was believed to derive from the Greek *'satyros'*, the mythological half-man, half-goat, an emblem of all that was bestial. Accordingly, Joseph Hall wrote:

The ruder satyre should go ragged and bare,
And show his rougher and his hairy hide.[36]

Perhaps for this reason, Donne's satires seem deliberately rough. Here he addresses a companion who arrives to entice him to court. After a sophistical meditation on the virtues of nakedness and an unconvincing volte-face on the grounds that his nameless friend has repented of his sins, he agrees to proceed to court where all the vices he abhors may be enjoyed:

Away thou fondling motley humorist,
Leave me, and in this standing wooden chest,
Consorted with these few books, let me lie
In prison, and here be coffined when I die;
Here are God's conduits, grave divines, and here
Nature's secretary, the philosopher,
And jolly statesmen, which teach how to tie
The sinews of a city's mystic body;

Here gathering chroniclers, and by them stand
Giddy fantastic poets of each land.
Shall I leave all this constant company
And follow, headlong, wild uncertain thee? . . .

Why should'st thou – that dost not only approve,
But in rank itchy lust, desire, and love,
The nakedness and barrenness to enjoy,
Of thy plump muddy whore, or prostitute boy –
Hate Virtue, though she be naked and bare:
At birth, and death, our bodies naked are,
And till our souls be unapparelled
Of bodies, they from bliss are banished.
Man's first blest state was naked; when by sin
He lost that, yet he was clothed but in beast's skin,
And in this coarse attire, which I now wear,
With God and with the Muses I confer.
But since thou like a contrite penitent,
Charitably warmed of thy sins, dost repent
These vanities, and giddinesses, lo
I shut my chamber door, and come, let's go.   (1–12, 37–52)

To a modern reader the extreme disjunction in a passage like this between rhythm and metre is a recognized means for creating an individual voice; to Alexander Pope in the eighteenth century the poems seemed so uncouth that Pope published *The Satires of Dr Donne Versified* (i.e. regularized).

Much satirical writing had its origins in a desire to libel or lampoon an individual, but authors commonly asserted that the objects of their scorn were general rather than particular. Middleton's epistle to *The Roaring Girl* (1611) invokes 'in such discoveries where reputation lies bleeding, a slackness of truth than fullness of slander'. A passage from 5.1 of John Day's allegorical masque *The Parliament of Bees*, written perhaps in 1607 but not published until 1641, gives a good impression of the exuberant verbal violence of the genre:

STUPRATA   A scholar speak with me? Admit him; do it;
I have business for him.
SERVANT   Business? He's a poet,
A common beadle, one that lashes crimes,
Whips one abuse, and fetches blood o' the times . . .

ILLTRISTE   Assume thy brightest flames
And dip thy pen in wormwood juice for me.
Canst write a satire? Tart authority
Do call 'em libels: canst write such a one?
POET   I can mix ink with copperas [vitriol].
ILLTRISTE   So; go on . . .
Thou hast the theory?
POET   Yes, each line must be
A cord to draw blood . . .
               A lie to dare
The stab from him it touches . . .
Such satires, as you call 'em, must lance wide
The wounds of men's corruptions; ope the side
Of vice; search deep flesh and rank cores.
A poet's ink can better cure some sores
Than surgeon's balsam.

Other writers wrote in a smoother or polished style: an example would be Ben Jonson's 'On the Famous Voyage' which satirizes contemporary London by offering a parody of Aeneas' journey to the underworld in the form of a narrative of a trip along Fleet Ditch.

As we have seen, performances of plays were often occasional, associated with seasonal revelry. One of the features of festivity outside theatres was a recurrent pattern of ritual inversion, in which a lord of misrule, a boy bishop, or a carnival prince might lord it for a day over a community, a religious institution, the court or Inns of Court. Such occasions provided opportunities for impertinency and satire. These conventions could be carried onto public stages: in 1603, Henry Crosse wrote 'there is no passion wherewith the king, the sovereign majesty of the realm, was possessed, but is amplified and openly sported with, and made a May-game to all the beholders, abusing the state royal.'[37] Milton believed that 'Satire, as it was born out of a Tragedy, so ought to resemble his parentage, to strike high, and adventure dangerously at the most eminent vices among the greatest persons.'[38]

Epigrams

Epigrams were both a learned and a popular form. The pithy and often scabrous short verses of the Latin poets Catullus and Martial, sometimes trifling, sometimes didactic, were much imitated by neo-classical poets like Jonson. Tavern walls could be the place of publication for lampooning verses chalked up by customers.[39] Donne's couplet 'On Manliness' not only scores a point but also implicitly reveals that manliness is a construction:

> Thou call'st me effeminate, for I love women's joys;
> I call not thee manly, though thou follow boys.

The grammatical language-game turns upon the pun upon 'women's': the speaker may be confessing that he enjoys what women enjoy or boasting that he enjoys women. In contrast, here is Jonson's 'Of Death':

> He that fears death, or mourns it in the just,
> Shows of the Resurrection little trust.

Romance and Prose Narrative

As we have seen, much theory derived from classic authorities, particularly Aristotle, who did not take account of what Dryden called 'the other harmony of prose' (Preface to *Fables*). However, prose narratives were much read in the period. Many were translations of romances from the Iberian peninsular – the sort of thing that was parodied in Miguel de Cervantes' *Don Quixote*, which appeared in 1605 followed by an English translation of the first part by Thomas Shelton in 1612. Romances are not novels: their plots are episodic, their settings imaginary, noble characters are set against monsters and grotesques, and their morality is based on feudal idealizations projected forward from medieval predecessors.[40] Often, as with the case of Lyly's *Euphues* (1578) and Sidney's *Arcadia* which was published in 1590 after the author's death (although it had previously circulated in manuscript), they appeal as much for the savour of their prose style as for the adventures of their heroes: the subtitle of Lyly's work is *The Anatomy of Wit*.

Romance elements remained popular in the theatre: the inferior ones were an easy target for Francis Beaumont's parodic satire, *The Knight of the Burning Pestle*, but the genre was developed by Beaumont's collaborator John Fletcher, as well as by Shakespeare himself. Yet certain authors, for example Thomas Nashe and Thomas Deloney who was a silk-weaver, probably from Norwich, did mingle elements or reportage into their settings and descriptions: there was not yet, however, a large non-coterie or non-elite readership who desired depictions of lives akin to their own set in familiar locales and written in a style that was neither overly rhetorical nor academic. The forms of late medieval prose narrative, ungalvanized by classical precedents, were still too strong to give way to this kind of modernity.

CHAPTER 4

Defining the Past

National and Political History

In 1599, the lawyer and historian Dr John Hayward quoted Cicero's definition of history, a formula that recurs in countless texts of the period: 'the witness of times, the light of truth, the life of memory, and the messenger of antiquity.'[1] But history has always had purposes wider than the collection of stories from the past, the memorializing of great men, and the depiction of significant social movements. The relationship between the disciplines of history and statecraft, between the narration of events and reflections on political conditions, was especially close in the early modern period. Specifically when, after the Reformation, the Tudors needed to reconstitute the state, they used history as a political instrument. For their project of nation-building they needed a rewritten and illustrious English history. The English monarchy had lost its territories in continental Europe and the English church had forsaken the see of Rome. The task was to construct a narrative concerning those offshore islands of Britain that had the resonance of the 'matters' of Greece and Rome that were the staple of historical studies in schools and universities.

Henry VIII laid the groundwork when he commissioned an Italian historian, Polydore Vergil (c.1470–1555), to write an *Anglica Historica*. (This was completed by 1513 but not printed until thirty or so years later.) Vergil placed monarchy at the centre of his work in that he arranged each chapter around a reign: the history of the nation was built around the history of the monarchy. This kind of history survived in the curriculum delivered to schoolchildren for hundreds of years (and was as useful to Victorian imperialists as it had been to Tudor apologists).

Obviously, Vergil's history, composed under royal patronage, was not 'objective': it was history 'with attitude', and presented the story of England as directed to an end, the unification under the Tudors of the houses of York and Lancaster, whose battles during the Wars of the Roses (1455–85) had placed England on the rack. Vergil proceeded as far as 1538, five years after the Act of Appeals and the Act of Supremacy that severed the monarchy's ties with Rome. In some respects, however, he did not serve his master well in that he questioned the existence of the legendary English hero King Arthur (who may or may not have lived in the sixth century) so, in some ways, undermining Sir Thomas Malory's great prose narrative *Le Morte Darthur*. In the 1485 Preface to William Caxton's edition of that text, the first English printer–publisher described it as 'the noble history of the Saint Grail, and of the most renowned Christian king, first and chief of the three best Christian [kings – the other two being David and Judas Maccabaeus] and worthy, King Arthur, which ought most to be remembered among us Englishmen to-fore all other Christian kings'. Polydore Vergil also demolished the myth of origin propagated in the twelfth-century *Historia Regum Britanniae* by Geoffrey of Monmouth that the British royal line descended from the grandson of Prince Aeneas of Troy, Brutus, who was supposed to have given his name to Britain.

This critical scholarship notwithstanding, fifty years later Edmund Spenser created an ambivalent inspirational figure for *The Faerie Queene*, which, significantly, can be read either as Clio, Muse of History, or Calliope, Muse of Heroic Poetry, to support his fiction that ancient documents authenticate the story of Arthur:

> Helpe then, ô holy Virgin chiefe of nine,
> Thy weaker Nouice to performe thy will,
> Lay forth out of thine euerlasting scryne [strong-box]
> The antique rolles, which there lye hidden still,
> Of Faerie knights and fairest Tanaquill [wife of the first Tarquin],
> Whom that most noble Briton Prince [Arthur] so long
> Sought through the world, and suffered so much ill,
>
> (*The Faerie Queene*, Proem, 2)

Later, he offers a vision of a third Troy (the second being Rome, founded by Romulus). The defining landmark of 'Troynouant' ('New Troy') is

London Bridge, resolutely withstanding the currents caused by its massive piers:

> There there (said *Britomart*) a fresh appeard
>   The glory of the later world to spring,
>   And *Troy* againe out of her dust was reard,
>   To sit in second seat of soueraigne king,
>   Of all the world vnder her gouerning.
>   But a third kingdome yet is to arise,
>   Out of the *Troians* scattered of-spring,
>   That in all glory and great enterprise,
> Both first and second *Troy* shall dare to equalise.
>
> It *Troynouant* is hight, that with the waues
>   Of wealthy *Thamis* washed is along,
>   Vpon whose stubborne neck, whereat he raues
>   With roring rage, and sore him selfe does throng,
>   That all men feare to tempt his billowes strong,
>   She fastned hath her foot, which standes so hy,
>   That it a wonder of the world is song
>   In forreine landes, and all which passen by,
> Beholding it from far, do thinke it threates the skye.
>   (*The Faerie Queene*, III. ix. 44–5)

This mythical topic was adapted for grimmer purpose in an account of contemporary history, probably by Dekker, to create an icon of the outbreak of plague in 1603:

> Empress of cities, Troynouant:
> When I thy lofty towers behold,
> (Whose pinnacles were tipped with gold
> Both when the sun did sit and rise,
> So lovely wert thou in his eyes),
> Now like old monuments forsaken,
> Or like tall pines by winter shaken;
> Or, seeing thee gorgeous as a bride
> Even in the height of all thy pride
> Disrobed, disgraced, and, when all nations
> Made love to thee in amorous passions,
> Now scorned of all the world alone;
> None seek thee, nor must thou seek none,

But like a prisoner must be kept
In thine own walls, till thou hast wept
Thine eyes out, to behold thy sweet
Dead children heaped about thy feet.[2]

It would, however, be a mistake to censure Polydore Vergil and the poets and chroniclers who followed him for a lack of 'objectivity': combining narrative with propaganda or imbuing it with moralization was central to the writing of most Renaissance historical endeavour. Here is a typical description of history by the German sceptic and occultist philosopher Henry Cornelius Agrippa (1486–35):

> An history is a declaration of things done, with praise or dispraise, which, as it were in a certain lively picture, doth set before our eyes the counsels, deeds, and ends of great things, the enterprises of princes, and noblemen, with the order and description of times and places. And therefore all men, for the most part, call it the mistress of life and very profitable to the framing thereof, because that, with the examples of many things, she doth partly enflame most excellent men, for the immortal glory of praise and renown, to all worthy enterprises; partly, because for fear of perpetual infamy, she letteth [prevents] all wicked and naughty men from misdoing, albeit this thing oftentimes hath chanced otherwise; and many . . . had liefer have a great than a good fame, and many men, because by their virtue they cannot be known, they will for their mischievous deeds be remembered and written in histories.[3]

A modern historian would be surprised by this definition. Agrippa sees the writing of history essentially as a high social activity, concerned with idealizing and demonizing, and with politics as much as with actions: it depicts how events were analysed and debated and freely deduces the intentions of those involved ('the counsels, deeds, and ends of great things'). The emphasis is not on scientific detachment, nor is there more than a hint of the kinds of objective analysis ('the order . . . of times and places') that are involved in most modern historical writing.

About 1613, one 'R. A.', possibly Robert Armin (1565?–1615), a player who took fools' parts in the plays of the King's Men, wrote a play called *The Valiant Welshman, or the true Chronicle History of the Life and Valiant Deeds of Caradoc the Great, King of Cambria, now called Wales.* The Epistle 'To the Ingenuous [noble] Reader' begins thus:

> As it hath been a custom of long continuance, as well in Rome the capital city as in divers other renowned cities of the world, to have the lives of princes and worthy men acted in their theatres, and especially the conquests and victories which their own princes and captains had obtained, thereby to encourage their youths to follow the steps of their ancestors; which custom even for the same purpose, is tolerated in our age, although some peevish [foolish, spiteful] people seem to dislike of it . . .

The author is registering the power of historical drama to represent political actions that might equally deserve emulation or conjure sedition.

For one of his early English histories, Shakespeare turned to Sir Thomas More who, in his *History of King Richard III* (c.1513), produced a more 'modern' kind of history than that written by Polydore Vergil, in that it concentrated on a comparatively narrow period, the reign of a single monarch. Richard III, of course, had been defeated at the Battle of Bosworth in 1485 by Henry VIII's father, Henry VII, that Henry Tudor whose badge united the white rose of York with the red rose of Lancaster. The work also contains 'orations' on sanctuaries and civil war. Not surprisingly, Richard is vilified in order to legitimate the claim to the throne of the Tudors, which was dynastic – and somewhat tenuous.

A passage vibrant with political sagacity occurs just after More has revealed how Richard, Duke of Gloucester had taken it upon himself to be king. It purports to be a homily against sedition and the interruption of the ceremonies of state. Yet, as we attend to More's prose, we discover irony – his writing is as subversive as it is admonitory:

> In a stage play, all the people know right well that he that playeth the sultan is percase [perhaps] a souter [cobbler]. Yet if one should can [know] so little good to show out of season what acquaintance he hath with him, and call him by his own name while he standeth in his majesty, one of his tormentors might hap to break his head – and worthy for the marring of the play. And so they said that these matters be king's games, as it were stage plays, and for the most part played upon scaffolds (in which poor men be but the lookers on). And they that wise be will meddle no further. For they that sometime step up and play with them, when they cannot play their parts, they disorder the play and do themself no good.[4]

The author has just demonstrated that there is no doubt about whether or not a bishop is a bishop, but with kings it is different. He asks the wicked question: can even a duly anointed king, but one who can be known only in his kingly role as an actor, be a true king? Are all kings player kings? This was a question put repeatedly in the play-houses for which Shakespeare wrote.

The Tudor historical project was consolidated and extended for about thirty years after 1548 by a set of ambitious chronicles. The first was by Edward Hall (d.1547): its title, *The Union of the Two Noble and Illustre* [Illustrious] *Families of Lancaster and York* (1548), again indicates an end-directed endeavour. Hall, like all of his generation of historians, incorporated passages from More without true acknowledgement. When he died, Richard Grafton continued his work and published his own *Chronicle at large . . . of the Affairs of England from the Creation of the World unto the First Year of Queen Elizabeth* (1568). However, John Stow's *Summary of English Chronicles* (1565) was more successful – Stow was also to write a *Survey of London* (1598), which also incorporated much historical detail. This tradition culminated in 1577 with the publication of *The Chronicles of England, Scotland, and Ireland*, originally under the direction of Raphael Holinshed who, however, like Hall, died before his work was completed. This text, in fact a collection of discrete works by various hands (including More's *Richard III*), was the prime source for dramatists, including Shakespeare, who began writing history plays and tragedies based on British history around the time of the Spanish Armada.

When it came to ancient history, one of the most significant historians – for literature – was Plutarch (AD c.48–125). He was freely translated first into French by Jacques Amyot and thence, again freely, into English by Sir Tomas North. Amyot's epistle to his readers describes Plutarch's book as:

> [a] parallelon, as much to say as a coupling or matching together, because he matcheth a Grecian with a Roman, setting down their lives each after other and comparing them together, as he found any likeness of nature, conditions, or adventures betwixt them, and examining what the one of them had better or worser, greater or lesser than the other. Which things he doth with so goodly and grave discourse everywhere, taken out of the deepest and most hidden secrets of moral and natural philosophy, with so sage precepts and fruitful instructions, with so effectual commendation of virtue and detestation of vice, with so many

goodly allegations of other authors, with so many fit comparisons, and with so many high inventions, that the book may better be called by the name of the treasury of all rare and perfect learning than by any other name.[5]

This combination of history and moralizing is typical of the period. Montaigne proclaimed that, without Amyot's book, French authors would not have been able to speak and write. Shakespeare used North's version as the principal source for his Roman history plays.

Biblical History

In many ways, the Bible was the most important historical source in the period, many of its books being narratives that were essentially parables, examples of how to behave, or chronicles that set forth the manifest destiny of the elect nation of Israel. Biblical scholarship or exegesis had for centuries included the discipline of what came to be called 'typology', which often consisted of identifying common 'types' or 'figures' in the Old and New Testaments. So Isaac, almost sacrificed by his father Abraham is, according to the heading to Genesis 22 in the Geneva Bible, 'a figure of Christ'.

In Shakespeare's *Henry V*, the credulous Welshman Fluellen is, unbeknown to himself, doing typology as he draws out a comparison between Alexander of Macedon and Harry of Monmouth (Henry V):

> There is a river in Macedon, and there is also moreover a river at Monmouth. It is called Wye at Monmouth, but it is out of my prains what is the name of the other river – but 'tis all one, 'tis alike as my fingers is to my fingers, and there is salmons in both. If you mark Alexander's life well, Harry of Monmouth's life is come after it indifferent well. For there is figures in all things.   (4.7.21–6)

It follows from this that when we read, say, a Shakespearean 'history' play we should neither pore over the texts for errors nor assume that Shakespeare was seeking, *pace* Agrippa, to give an accurate 'picture' of the past. Rather, past events were read as figural representations of present realities – which is why history was such 'dangerous matter'.

The most important propagandist history for the consolidation of English national identity is enshrined in the massive (over two million words) compendium of tales of Protestant martyrs: the *Acts and Monuments* of John Foxe, popularly known as 'Foxe's Book of Martyrs', which appeared in two Latin editions (1554, 1559) and then in four English editions during Foxe's lifetime (1563, 1570, 1576 and 1583).[6] Foxe's aim was to weave together accounts of the martyrs of the primitive church with those of the sixteenth century, particularly the three hundred burned at the stake during the reign of Mary Tudor (1553–8) when Roman Catholicism was briefly restored to England.

The militant anti-Catholicism in this book was fundamental to the emergence of an English nation and an insular identity: Foxe considered that the English had superseded the Jews as an 'elect nation'. He prophesied that a Christian emperor would defend the reformed Protestants, slaying the papal antichrist and inaugurating a new millennium that would see the return of Christ. In the sixteenth century, churches were ordered to have copies of 'The Book of Martyrs' alongside the Bible, available for pubic perusal, and the book continued to be revised through the seventeenth century. More recently, emphasis has been placed on the fact that Foxe was a true researcher and that his writings were as accurate as his sources, all noted in the margins of his book, would permit.[7]

Politic History

For generations, it was a critical commonplace to claim that, under the influence of the chroniclers, Shakespeare saw his task as being to propagate 'the Tudor myth [which] presented a scheme fundamentally religious, by which events evolve under a law of justice and under the ruling of God's providence, and of which Elizabeth's England was the acknowledged outcome'.[8] It is all too easy to disregard the way in which religious concerns informed almost every kind of discourse in early modern England, but this sort of reading is tendentious. It involves reading the plays in the order of the kings' reigns rather than with regard to their order of composition. The fact that *Richard II*, which depicts the deposition and murder of an anointed king, comes first if the plays are shuffled in this manner does not mean that Shakespeare thought that there was a causal connection between the events of that play and those that he had written before, those dealing with the reigns of Henry VI and Richard III.

It is true that in *Richard II* the Bishop of Carlisle prophesies that the deposition of his king will cause England to be called 'The field of Golgotha and dead men's skulls' (4.1.133), but although his words might have the resonance of truth, the climax of the scene comes afterwards when he is immediately arrested: prophesying was recognized as a powerful tool for destabilizing a regime and was treated as a capital offence. The moment reminds us that such scenes are as much concerned with politics as with events, and that the plays are a prolonged meditation upon the nature, creation and transfer of power. We should also remind ourselves that speeches by characters who claim to understand the workings of the world, subject to Fortune or manifesting divine will, are not necessarily choric, statements of what the author believed. It may be more profitable to regard these as portraits of minds in action, of the human tendency in the face of catastrophe to seek comfort in some overarching explanation. This is a new kind of 'politic history', an art of demonstration, rather than, as history had been in the hands of medieval chroniclers, an art of interpretation. That is the 'method' of Chaucer who, in 'The Monk's Tale' followed the *Roman de la Rose*, as well as Boccaccio's accounts of the falls of biblical, classical and near contemporary figures, his *De Casibus Virorum Illustrium*:

> I wol biwaille, in manere of tragedie,
> The harm of hem that stoode in heigh degree,
> And fillen so that ther nas no remedie
> To brynge hem out of hir adversitee.
> For certein, whan that Fortune list to flee,
> Ther may no man the cours of hire withholde.
> Lat no man truste on blynd prosperitee;
> Be war by thise ensamples trewe and olde.[9]

This kind of interpretation, wrote Walter Benjamin, 'is not concerned with an accurate concatenation of definite events, but with the way these are embedded in the great inscrutable course of the world',[10] here ruled by Dame Fortune. By contrast, Shakespeare's earlier plays are a chronicle not of the workings of fortune or providence but of aristocratic factionalism. The depiction of a popular uprising in *2 Henry VI*, led by Jack Cade, although mindless and brutal, kindles an exhilarating anarchy. 'The first thing we do let's kill all the lawyers' (4.2.70) has been printed on T-shirts, sold by the Folger Shakespeare

Library in Washington, DC, and worn by people who would never countenance what is done immediately after this line has been uttered: the murder of the Clerk of Chartham simply because he can write and read.

The source of this scene is in Holinshed. The unruly commons, he wrote, put precept into practice:

> beheading all such men of law, justices, and jurors as they might catch and lay hands upon, without respect of pity, or remorse of conscience, alleging that the land could never enjoy her native and true liberty till all those sorts of people were dispatched out of the way.
>
> This talk liked well the ears of the common uplandish people, and by the less conveying the more, they purposed to burn and destroy all records, evidences, court-rolls, and other muniments, that, the remembrance of ancient matters being removed out of mind, their landlords might not have whereby to challenge any right at their hands.[11]

This is written from the point of view of orthodox morality, but it would seem that Shakespeare may have caught the tone of these sequences not from the text but from the marginal glosses. For against the first of those two paragraphs we read: 'Lawyers, justices, and jurors brought to blockam feast by the rebels.'[12] This reconstitutes the slaughter into a carnival of violence, enacted in the grisly display in which the heads of the executed Lord Say and Sir James Cromer are made to kiss at the end of their pikes (4.7.118). Against the second we read: 'The next way to extinguish right.' This deftly inverts the argument of the text; for whereas Holinshed intended his reader to understand the way in which the nobles were deprived of their rights, the second offers the example as a means for so doing.

Nor are Shakespeare's histories merely narratives, albeit ambivalent narratives. On occasion he moves from *showing* the course of events to very different theatrical modes of *telling*. Examples are 3.5 in *Richard III* when Richard of Gloucester and the Duke of Buckingham pretend to defend an imaginary castle of England. Their theatrical game seems to take in the citizens of London who are on the brink of calling for Richard to become king. In *Henry V*, we find a very full underplot, much of it filled by Pistol and his crew: Pistol steps in, after the death of Falstaff, to represent the principle of the ungovernability of England. After Henry, having received the gift of the Dauphin's tennis balls, has lit upon a *casus belli*, an excuse for going to war with France, and ordered the execution of the traitors, he leads his courtiers off-stage and to war with a cheeringly heroical speech:

> Now lords for France, the enterprise whereof
> Shall be to you, as us, like glorious.
> We doubt not of a fair and lucky war,
> Since God so graciously hath brought to light
> This dangerous treason lurking in our way
> To hinder our beginnings. We doubt not now
> But every rub is smoothèd on our way.
> Then forth, dear countrymen. Let us deliver
> Our puissance into the hand of God,
> Putting it straight in expedition.
> Cheerly to sea, the signs of war advance:
> No king of England, if not king of France.
> (*Henry V*, 2.2.178–89)

In the following scene, Pistol enters, takes leave of the Hostess, and then marches his men off the stage:

> Come, let's away. – My love, give me thy lips. [*He kisses her*]
> Look to my chattels and my movables.
> Let senses rule. The word is 'Pitch and pay'.
> Trust none, for oaths are straws, men's faiths are wafer-cakes,
> And Holdfast is the only dog, my duck.
> Therefore *caveto* [beware] be thy counsellor.
> Go, clear thy crystals. – Yokefellows in arms,
> Let us to France, like horseleeches, my boys,
> To suck, to suck, the very blood to suck!   (2.4.39–47)

His fustian blank verse exposes the king's heroics as a kind of jingoism, the royal rhetoric as a cover-up of the realities of war. Glory may derive not from chivalric action but from the acquisition of 'chattels' and tenacious fighting as grim as that evinced by a fierce hunting dog with its teeth in its prey. May the launching of the expeditionary force to France be read not as the restoration of English magnificence, but as a way of enacting Bullingbrook's deathbed injunction to his son to 'busy giddy minds / With foreign quarrels' (*2 Henry IV*, 4.3.341–2)? Modern directors have marked the parallel between the two sequences by quoting the gesture, having courtiers and riff-raff use the same exit from the stage.[13]

Shakespeare, we see, is as much concerned with historiography, with comparing competing readings of key events in English history: was Cade's revolt just a bloody uprising or did it contain the elements of revolution, a moment when the will of the people, enflamed by longstanding grievances, was hijacked by a grandee seeing an opportunity to pursue his own ends? (Cade was the creature of the ambitious Duke of York.) But Shakespeare was as much concerned with procedure as with process, with form as with content, with the way in which forms of theatre can enact their own strategies, the way in which drama turns to meta-drama and becomes a demonstration of theatricality in the behaviour of the actors on the stage of the world. The complexity of his method anticipates what Linda Hutcheon described as a key mode of postmodernism, 'historiographic meta-fiction'[14] – 'historiographic' because Shakespeare unpicks the ideological assumptions that underlie his narratives, and 'meta-fictional' because he exposes his own representational techniques.

Polydore Vergil was not the only Italian humanist whose writings founded a tradition of English history writing. English scholars soon became aware of the work of the Florentine Niccolò Machiavelli (1469– 1527) whose *Florentine History* (1525) was preceded by the works that made him notorious, *The Prince* and his *Discourses on the First Ten Books of Livy* (1513). Although *The Prince* was not published in English until 1640, it was known and discussed by intellectuals and writers throughout the sixteen century, including William Thomas (d.1554), a clerk of the Privy Council and tutor to Edward VI, Christopher Marlowe, Nicholas Breton, Sir Walter Ralegh and Francis Bacon.

It used to be thought, however, that 'Secretary Machiavel, a politic not much affected to any religion',[15] was known in England only through anti-Florentine propaganda originating in France while Marie de Médicis was regent. The prime text here is Innocent Gentillet's *Discours . . . Contre-Machiavel* (1576). Gentillet refashioned Machiavelli as a kind of bogeyman who was to be incarnated in a string of stage 'Machiavels' or satanic 'politicians', originating with Lorenzo in Thomas Kyd's *The Spanish Tragedy*. In Jonson's *Volpone*, the English traveller Sir Politic Wouldbe is too foolish to achieve the power of a true Italianate rogue.

However, even though 'Machevil', the Prologue to *The Jew of Malta* (1589), may have emerged through a trapdoor onto the stage of the Rose playhouse from the cellarage, the place of origin of stage devils, his lines reveal that Marlowe may have been mocking this myth of Machiavelli:

> Albeit the world think Machiavel is dead,
> Yet was his soul but flown beyond the Alps
> And, now the Guise is dead, is come from France
> To view this land and frolic with his friends.
> To some perhaps my name is odious:
> But such as love me guard me from their tongues,
> And let them know that I am Machiavel,
> And weigh not men and therefore not men's words:
> Admired I am of those that hate me most.
> Though some speak openly against my books,
> Yet will they read me, and thereby attain
> To Peter's chair [the papal throne], and, when they cast me off,
> Are poisoned by my climbing followers.
> I count religion but a childish toy
> And hold there is no sin but ignorance.
> Birds of the air will tell of murders past!
> I am ashamed to hear such fooleries.
> Many will talk of title to a crown:
> What right had Caesar to the empire?
> Might first made kings, and laws were then most sure
> When, like the Draco's, they were writ in blood.
> Hence comes it that a strong-built citadel
> Commands much more than letters can import:
> Which maxim, had Phalaris observed,
> H'had never bellowed in a brazen bull
> Of great ones' envy. O' [by] the poor petty wits
> Let me be envied and not pitied!
> But whither am I bound? I come not, I,
> To read a lecture here in Britain,
> But to present the tragedy of a Jew,
> Who smiles to see how full his bags are crammed,
> Which money was not got without my means.
> I crave but this: grace him as he deserves,
> And let him not be entertained the worse
> Because he favours me.

It is easy to assume that Machevil is a figure of Barabas, the diabolic central character who, totally without scruple, sets out to murder all who withstand him. (Barabas takes his name from the murderer whom Pilate released instead of Christ.) Later he boasts of going about poisoning wells (2.3.177). The irony is that Barabas meets his end, in a boiling cauldron, as a result of a 'Machiavellian' trick played by the 'good' Christian Governor of Malta, Ferneze, and in certain modern productions of the play the actor playing Machiavel has been doubled with Ferneze. Particular details of the speech, however – the references to the punitive legal codes of the Athenian law-giver Draco and the 'strong-built citadel' – indicate that Marlowe understood the true nature of Machiavelli. The Florentine's aim was, above all, what is now called 'demystification'. He rejected imaginary republics of the sort that Plato had created. As Francis Bacon put it, 'We are much beholden to Machiavel and others, that write what men do and not what they ought to do.'[16]

A second wave of secularizing historiography, also characterized by a quizzical attitude to authority, occurred just before Marlowe went up to Corpus Christi College in Cambridge, about the time that Gabriel Harvey noted that in that university town: 'You cannot step into a scholar's study but (ten to one) you shall lightly find open either Bodin *De Republica* or Le Roy's exposition upon Aristotle's *Politics* or some other like French or Italian politic discourse.'[17] No exact dating is possible, but there is common ground occupied by, say, Kyd's *Spanish Tragedy*, Shakespeare's Henry VI trilogy, and Marlowe's *The Massacre at Paris*. We could call it the moment of politic history and locate it about the time of the composition of Marlowe's translation of Lucan's *Pharsalia* and the publication of Sir Henry Savile's translation of Tacitus' *Histories* in 1591[18] with an epistle that, according to Jonson, was written by the Earl of Essex himself.[19]

But Tacitean matter – it is not just a question of style – can be discerned earlier. Publius Cornelius Tacitus (AD c.55–117) delighted in exposing the hypocrisy of courtiers: his target was absolutism and its handmaid, theatricality. His tone was sardonic and his characters could be theatricalized and fantastical. In Book 1 we find a marvellous sentence on one Percennius, leader of the revolt in Pannonia, 'who had been sometimes a ringleader of factious companions on stages and theatres, afterward a common soldier, an impudent and saucy prater, well practised in disturbing assemblies, to show favour unto such actors as he favoured'.[20]

In his epic poem, the *Pharsalia*, Marcus Annaeus Lucanus (i.e. 'Lucan', AD 39–65) had taken a very sceptical view of Julius Caesar's imperial ambitions, and Tacitus' view of history was likewise quizzical and secular: his emperors were, unlike some of Shakespeare's monarchs, scarcely possessed of a mystic as well as a natural body, and his great themes were ancient liberty,[21] and what his translator, almost certainly invoking *Tamburlaine*, called 'higher aspiring minds',[22] and modern servitude.[23] In the epistle he wrote:

> In these four books . . . thou shalt see all the miseries of a torn and declining state: the empire usurped, the princes murdered, the people wavering, the soldiers tumultuous, nothing unlawful to him that hath power, and nothing so unsafe as to be securely innocent . . . If thou dost detest their anarchy, acknowledge our own happy government, and thank God for her, under whom England enjoys as many benefits as ever Rome did suffer miseries under the greatest tyrant.

Here Roman history is obviously a mirror for English politics, but sometimes the connection was only implicit. Implications or 'applications' of this kind caused Ben Jonson to get into trouble by writing Tacitean history plays in the next century and during the next reign. In the 'Argument' to his *Sejanus*, performed in 1603, we read:

> Sejanus labours to marry Livia [Tiberius' daughter-in-law], and worketh with all his engine [cunning] to remove Tiberius from the knowledge of public business with allurements of a quiet and retired life; the latter of which Tiberius (out of a proneness to lust and a desire to hide those unnatural pleasures which he could not so publicly practise) embraceth . . . [until] when Sejanus least looketh and is most secure, with pretext of doing him an unwonted honour in the Senate, he trains him from his guards; and, with a long doubtful letter, in one day, hath him suspected, accused, condemned, and torn in pieces by the rage of the people.
>
> This do we advance as a mark of terror to all traitors and treasons; to show how just the heavens are in pouring and thundering down a weighty vengeance of their unnatural intents, even to the worst princes: much more to those for guard of whose piety and virtue are in continual watch, and God himself miraculously working.

After he had been investigated by the Privy Council and, possibly, in the aftermath of the Gunpowder Plot of 5 November 1605, Jonson may well have been ordered to add the second paragraph, printed in larger type in the first edition of the play and completely at odds with the politic reading of Roman history set out just before. He dropped it in the collected edition of his *Works*.

Six years earlier, Dr John Hayward had been imprisoned for dedicating his *First Part of the Life and Reign of King Henry IV* to the Earl of Essex, who in that year fell from grace and was executed. Hayward's totally secular arguments scathingly conclude that Richard II had brought his deposition upon himself by imprudent conduct, and present Henry Bullingbrook as a heroic saviour of the kingdom. Hayward also imitated the sententiousness of Tacitus. In a long speech that he put into the mouth of the Archbishop of Canterbury, he offered an account of life under Richard II:

> Our ancestors lived in the highest pitch and perfection of liberty, but we of servility, being in the nature not of subjects but of abjects and flat slaves: not to one intractable prince only but to many proud and disdainful favourites, not always the same but every new, and no sooner have we satisfied some but fresh hungry masters are straightways set upon us, who have more endamaged us by extortions and bribes than the enemy hath done by the sword.[24]

Queen Elizabeth had famously said 'I am Richard II', and Hayward, whose interrogation by the Attorney General, Sir Edward Coke, focused on this speech,[25] had to remain in prison until the accession of King James.

Towards the end of the reign of Elizabeth, Sir Henry Wotton (1568–1639), ambassador to Venice, wrote an ambitious set of observations upon the history of the previous two or three centuries entitled *The State of Christendom* (the work was not published until 1667). Wotton, too, was essentially a politic historian. The title page states that he gives 'a perfect and exact discovery of many political intrigues and secret mysteries of state practised in most of the courts of Europe'. The work is galvanized by his assumption that most evils emanated from Spain, but his acute Machiavellian observation is deployed to create a powerful Erasmian indictment of contemporary warmongering:

> Of the princes [rulers], their designs, and their means, I will deliver unto you my opinion in general and in particular. Generally, you see, I consider that by the competencies, pretensions, titles, quarrels, and debates of all these princes, the general estate of Christendom is greatly weakened, and the strength of the common adversary daily increased.

That all these realms and dominions are either molested by continual wars within the very bowels and poor inward parts of the same; or grieved with intolerable charges in sending out men and munition with other things necessary to the said wars; that their subjects are greatly impoverished by reason of these charges, and their hearts sorely oppressed with grief and anguish because of these troubles. Lastly, that some of these princes fain would and cannot, others can and will not, redress these enormities.[26]

Wotton's 'common adversary' is the devil, but this incarnation of evil is brought into being by political action, and wars, contrary to many contemporary polemics, were fought not in the interests of divine justice but of secular ambitions.

It is, of course, a fallacy to imagine that providential history was eclipsed by secularizing texts that derived from Italian or classical sources. Imprisoned in the Tower of London by King James for his fiercely anti-Spanish policies from 1603 to 1616, Sir Walter Ralegh wrote an immense *History of the World*, published, its first edition anonymously, in 1614. In 1592 charges of 'atheism' had been laid against him: at this time the word could be used against sceptical rationalists or anyone who grounded the existence of God on rational argument rather than faith. However, the charges could be taken to designate godlessness (see chapter 7). Perhaps in order to restore his reputation, in the *History* Ralegh looked for truth in the workings of God's providence and insisted on the contingency of all human knowledge, purpose and action. Ralegh's history grew out of theology and, like medieval historians, he felt that he had to write universal history rather than the limited histories that More, Bacon and other contemporaries advocated.[27] Although his unfinished work does, in fact, comprise two limited histories, it begins with the Creation, which is dealt with not so much as an historical event but as a theological fact to use against Aristotle who denied creation (*nihil ex nihilo fit* [nothing is made of nothing]) and implied the necessity of natural events.

In *The Advancement of Learning* Bacon had noted that the history of providence 'containeth that excellent correspondence which is between God's revealed will and his secret will'.[28] Ralegh, too, placed history on the frontiers of knowledge, although he never formulated his conviction unhedged with qualifications or contradictions. This was because for Ralegh history was the *summa* of human knowledge, comprising divine, natural and human wisdom. It was both the supreme manifestation of divine providence, a tableau of revealed truth, and an exaltation of man, a triumph over time:

> True it is that among other benefits, for which it hath been honoured, in this one it triumpheth over all human knowledge, that it hath given us life in our understanding, since the world itself had life and beginning, even to this day: yea, it hath triumphed over time, which, beside it, nothing but eternity hath triumphed over; for it hath carried our knowledge over the vast and devouring space of so many thousands of years, and given so fair and piercing eyes to our mind that we plainly behold now, as if we had lived then, that great world, *magni Dei sapiens opus*, 'the wise work', saith Hermes, 'of a great God', as it was then when but new to itself.[29]

Given these premises, Ralegh's task was to deduce the divine plan from human authorities.

Although Ralegh often says that no one can conceive or express the manner in which God works in his creatures,[30] he notes that all historians agree on the existence of a supreme power: ' "All these men's opinions", saith Lactantius, "though uncertain, come to this, that they agree upon one Providence; whether the same be nature, or light, or reason, or understanding, or destiny, or divine ordinance; that it is the same which we call God." '[31] Having confronted his authorities one with another, Ralegh compounds his deduction with a declaration of faith – an argument typical of his scepticism: 'so, after all the searches that human capacity hath, and after all philosophical contemplation and curiosity, in the necessity of this infinite power, all the reason of man ends and dissolves itself.'[32] Often, however, Ralegh does not carry precept into practice, for despite his assertion that man cannot understand God's workings, his Preface is a confident explanation of how providence has guided the fortunes of the royal houses of England, France and Spain.

It followed from the assertion of the providential nature of the historical process that truth was to be sought first in revelation:

> Wherefore it being the end and scope of all history, to teach by example of times past such wisdom as may guide our actions, we should not marvel though the chronicles of the kings of Juda and Israel, being written by men inspired with the Spirit of God, instruct us chiefly in that which is most requisite for us to know, as the means to attain unto

true felicity both here and hereafter, propounding examples which illustrate this infallible rule, *The fear of the Lord is the beginning of wisdom.*[33]

Ralegh's task, therefore, was to correlate scriptural narrative with the accounts of later historians and the conjectures of biblical commentators. Although his attempts to reconcile and rationalize his sources can be seen as a form of textual criticism and the necessary prerequisite for the writing of objective history, we find that the first three books of *The History*, which cover the period of the Old Testament, are a laborious proof of the necessary truth of scripture. To do this, the author had to demonstrate how the events in the Old Testament could be explained rationally and how the Hebrew chronologies were mathematically accurate in order to refute such atheistic opinions (like that attributed to Marlowe) as that there were men before Adam. As Jean Leclercq pointed out, this preoccupation with studying the Old Testament as if it were an historical document is foreign to the Middle Ages.[34]

Accordingly Ralegh, probably with the help of Thomas Harriot, among whose papers are to be found lists of Old Testament dates,[35] made careful investigation into questions like the geographical location of Eden and the cubic capacity of Noah's Ark, as well as meticulously collating chronicles and chronologies. Usually Ralegh finds a 'natural' solution that satisfies him from scriptural data alone, rejecting the conflicting evidence of commentators, but he often asserts that a supernatural power intervened, as in Noah's flood,[36] or is forced to argue for the longevity of the patriarchs or the existence of giants. Where details are missing from the scriptures, they can be filled out with the aid of reason 'to make . . . good those things which authority alone, without further circumstance, ought to have confirmed in every man's belief.'[37] The scriptures contain the truth, even if our bedimmed faculties cannot at once perceive it.

The following argument is brought against the assembler of scriptural commentaries, Benedict Pererius (1535–1610), from whom Ralegh drew more of his citations than he acknowledged. Pererius thought 'it was either unlikely or impossible that Egypt should be peopled within 100 or 200 years after Adam'. Ralegh begins:

> Now seeing the scriptures are silent herein, and that it is no point of our saving belief, it is lawful for every man to be guided in this and the

like questions by the best reason, circumstance, and likelihood; and herein, as in the rest, I protest that I do not gainsay any man's opinion out of any crossing or cavilling humour; for I think it is the part of every Christian, rather to reconcile differences, where there is possibility of union, than, out of forward subtlety and prejudiced resolvedness, to maintain factions needless, and dangerous contentions.[38]

But despite his insistence on the unimportance of the question, Ralegh devotes six pages to the argument that are more tightly tied to scriptural data than to 'the best reason, circumstance, and likelihood':

> Now it may be gathered that Nimrod came into the valley of Shinaar with so many multitudes as sufficed to build the city and tower of Babel; and that to this increase there was given but 130 years by Berosus [a native historian of Babylonia who lived around 300 BC], and after to the account of the scriptures (reckoning . . . by the birth of Arphaxad, Selah, Heber, and Phaleg) but 101 years; I see no cause to doubt but that in the infancy of the first age, when the bodies of men were most perfect, even within 130 years, the same, if not a greater, number might be increased; and so within seventy years after, (that is by such time as the world had stood 200 years) as well Assyria, Syria, and Egypt might be possessed [inhabited] before the flood, as they were within the same or less time after it.[39]

Ralegh often, of course, had to rely on secondary sources, and also consulted the Platonic writers Philo and Plotinus, as well as mystical texts associated with Orpheus and Hermes, along with many other pagan writers. He even repeated the opinion that Homer 'had read over all the books of Moses'.[40] His sceptical treatment of classical authorities gives shrewder results in his history of the classical world where he was not tied to scriptural veracity. A good example is Book 5, chapter 3 where he reprehends the lack of disinterestedness in those national historians of both sides who falsified the truth about the Battle of Cannae (216 BC) when the Romans were crushed by the Carthaginians under Hannibal.

One of the chief arguments a Protestant apologist had to counter was that of the allegorists, both medieval scriptural commentators and classical writers. In Book 1, chapter 3, in a section entitled 'That there was a true local paradise eastward in the country of Eden', Ralegh attacks the Vulgate translation which renders Genesis 2: 8: 'And the

Lord God planted a paradise of pleasure from the beginning.'[41] The vagueness of the Vulgate rendering had drawn forth a number of allegorical and counter-allegorical interpretations. As Ralegh attacks the commentaries with literal common sense, he quotes Jerome himself against the allegorists, and goes on:

> Furthermore, by the continuation and order of the story, is the place made more manifest. For God gave Adam free liberty to eat of every tree of the garden (the tree of knowledge excepted), which trees Moses in the ninth verse saith that they were good to eat; meaning the fruit which they bare. Besides, God left all beasts to Adam to be named, which he had formerly made; and these beasts were neither in the third heaven, nor near the circle of the moon, nor beasts in the imagination; for if all these things were enigmatical or mystical, the same might also be said of the creation of all things.[42]

When, on the other hand, it is a question of pagan sources, we find that Ralegh, like Chapman and Bacon, was interested in finding a deeper truth beneath the surface of the fable, since he asserted that classical legends were perverse plagiarisms of divine truth:

> the Greeks and other more ancient nations, by fabulous inventions and by breaking into parts the story of the creation, and by delivering it over in a mystical sense, wrapping it up mixed with other their own trumpery, have sought to obscure the truth thereof; and have hoped, that after-ages, being thereby brought into many doubts, might receive those intermixed discourses of God and nature for the invention of poets and philosophers, and not as anything borrowed or stolen out of the books of God.[43]

Ralegh's explanation of the divinity of the pagan gods is euhemeristic – he believed that they were originally mortals.[44] He cites Lactantius, to whom we owe the preservation of some fragments of Euhemerus, when he identifies the gods with biblical personages: 'Now as Cain was the first Jupiter . . . so were Jubal, Tubal, and Tubalcain [Genesis 4: 22] (inventors of pastorage, smith's craft, and music) the same which were called by the ancient profane writers, Mercurius, Vulcan, and Apollo.'[45] But despite his dislike of obscure scriptural commentary, Ralegh does not exclude Old Testament typology from his work, and even resorts to allegorizing himself when he cannot find a biblical equivalent for a classical figure, or, as in his account of St George, one which he finds difficult to believe.[46]

If we read only the duller and more pedantic sections of *The History of the World*, the proof of scriptural veracity might seem to be the informing intention of the book. Yet, like almost all Renaissance historians, Ralegh valued historical investigation not so much in connection with the search for objective truth as for the lessons it provided and the manifestation of divine wisdom that could be extracted from it. The bald catalogue of divine retribution visited upon wicked English monarchs in the Preface, undoubtedly written to curry favour with King James, is perhaps an unfortunate example, and often we admire Ralegh most when his religious sense is defeated by the intractability of his material and is transmuted into triumphant assertion or irrational comprehension. Providence could not always be perceived – and Ralegh gave up trying sometimes and turned to the political studies of Machiavelli.[47] Yet he usually asserted its workings, even if he could not understand them and, confident in its general influence on human endeavours, he felt free to make 'poetical addition' to 'mere historical truth', to 'beautify the face of his subject'[48] by composing speeches for heroical princes. Belief in providence in fact allowed his eloquence a greater scope than commitment to objectivity would have done, for not only could incidentals be neglected where convenient, but the history of men would be written as the history of God.

CHAPTER 5

Designing the Present

Forging State and Nation

The Tudors had quickly to forge new historical narratives in order to legitimate their tenuous dynastic hold on the throne of England. Similarly, during the first English Reformation, new forms of government and nation had to be brought into being. Henry VIII's Act of Appeals (1533) was in effect England's Declaration of Independence from the papal see. Its proclamation that 'this realm of England is an empire' announced not only a break from Rome but also a new kind of national identity. There was to be no 'restraint or provocation [appeal] to any foreign princes or potentates':[1] the new English state owed allegiance to no other power, particularly not to the papacy. Political independence was bolstered by geography: England was (part of) what Shakespeare's John of Gaunt called 'this blessed plot' (*Richard II*, 2.1.50) and the English became, in the words of the Victorian patriotic poet Sir Henry Newbolt, 'an island race'. There were, accordingly, new projects not only for historians but also for what Donne in his 'First Satire' was to call 'jolly statesmen [experts in government] which teach how to tie / The sinews of a city's mystic body' (ll. 7–8).

To consolidate their authority, monarchs looked to their images in the visual and literary arts, and in both worked to establish an iconic status for themselves. Henry VIII adopted a commanding stance for his portrait by Holbein, and Elizabeth in many of her portraits appears more as a goddess than a woman. In several Tudor plays and in Jacobean court masques a figure of the monarch or an appropriate allegorized princely virtue takes the role of the *deus ex machina*, the god who had descended from a crane onto the stage to resolve the plot in the theatres of the ancient world. (Queen Elizabeth plays this role in John Madden's film of 1998, *Shakespeare in Love*.) Monarchs played similar roles in non-theatrical revels and rituals: Elizabeth staged herself to the eyes of her subjects at ritualized tilts or jousting matches every year on the anniversary of her succession.[2] The progresses that took her and her successor James I around the kingdom were dazzling representations of power that were performed in allegorized spaces, brought into being by devices such as triumphal arches or symbolic castles. Tudor and Stuart courts were so obviously theatres of power that we may be tempted to describe Renaissance England as a 'theatocracy', the designation Plato disparagingly applied to the Athens of his time (*Laws*, 701).

Like Plato, Renaissance students of politics liked to categorize different kinds of governance: Machiavelli began *The Prince* (1513) with a comparative assessment of kinds of rule, an implicit invitation to lay down political foundations for new institutions. He demonstrated, to the consternation of the powers that be, that political change could be instigated from below as well as from above. We see so many characters thinking tactically about structures of power in histories and tragedies by authors like Shakespeare and Chapman that it is tempting to re-categorize theatrical 'histories' as 'political plays'. It is characteristic of the period, however, that most new designs for state and nation derived from classical and biblical models. Although there were no political uprisings strong enough to unsettle the English monarch until the Civil War, republicanism was much discussed – inevitably, given the subject's prominence in the Roman history that everyone studied. The 'Argument', probably by Shakespeare, prefixed to his *The Rape of Lucrece* (1593–4), reads the narrative as a political text that endorses a change of government 'from kings to consuls'. In Webster's *Duchess of Malfi* (c.1614) Bosola balefully soliloquizes:

> A politician is the devil's quilted anvil:
> He fashions all sins on him, and the blows
> Are never heard. (3.3.323–5)

The demonization reveals how dangerous any dream of ideological change in the status quo was held to be: many 'evil' characters in court plays from the time of Kyd's *Spanish Tragedy* (c.1587) had been, like

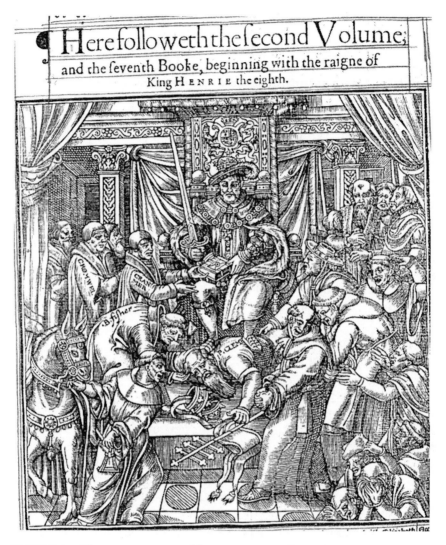

FIGURE 3 'The pope suppressed by Henry VIII', illustration to John Foxe, *Acts and Monuments* (London, 1570 edn), sig. 3B2ʳ, London, British Library.

Bosola, branded as 'politicians'. Alternative models for government also derived from comparisons of what was familiar with what was new. Paradoxically, however, ancient parables of government also informed the descriptions of the 'New World' across the Atlantic with its 'virgin' lands or 'barbarous' cultures. As we shall see, myths of lands ruled by

Amazons or of a Golden Age percolate into many discovery narratives. These, however, were often not only mythically but materially inspired, since the tussle with Spain for the gold of the Americas impelled most of the voyages of discovery. Gold figured as both the object of travellers' quests and as a metonym for the massive cultural changes of the period.

Jonson supplied a figure of magic, of the transmutation of base metals into gold, to shape his demonstration of the way new wealth might overthrow customary social forms in *The Alchemist* (1610). Sir Epicure Mammon boasts to Surly that what he takes to be his untold new wealth has created a new world that fatuously yokes together a fabled site of riches from Biblical Arabia with the Americas:

> Come on, sir. Now you set your foot on shore
> In *novo orbe* [a new world]: here's the rich Peru,
> And there within, sir, are the golden mines,
> Great Solomon's Ophir! He was sailing to't
> Three years, but we have reached it in ten months!   (2.1.1–5)

In the Stuart period, Philip Massinger was to devote much theatrical time to an anatomy of the fear of the aristocracy that their 'blood' might be adulterated by the marriage of their male progeny to the daughters of citizens with 'new money'.

English Reformations later in the sixteenth century also developed political reform: in 1547, during the reign of Edward VI, a *Book of Homilies* appeared. This was a set of authorized sermons for the reformed Church of England; it was republished with additions in 1561–2, and was regularly reprinted until the reign of Charles I. A preface in the 1547 edition commanded that every Sunday they should be 'read . . . plainly and distinctly, in such order as they stand in the book – except any sermon be preached'. Another key text is the epistle to the queen, prefixed to the Geneva Bible of 1560, which contains an extended meditation on 'edification', the building of Solomon's temple. This is a figure for the rebuilding of the English church of which the monarch was now the head. (The word 'edification' derives from a Latin verb meaning 'to build'.)

The following comes from 'An Homily against Disobedience and Wilful Rebellion', which is found at the end of the expanded edition of the *Book of Homilies*:

As in reading of the holy scriptures, we shall find . . . that kings and princes, *as well the evil as the good*, do reign by God's ordinance, and that subjects are bounden to obey them: that God doth give princes [rulers] wisdom, great power, and authority: that God defendeth them against their enemies, and destroyeth their enemies horribly: that the anger and displeasure of the prince is as the roaring of a lion and the very messenger of death: and that the subject that provoketh him to displeasure sinneth against his own soul.

The double reconstitution of church and state meant, as the extract from the homily indicates, that seditious acts could be construed as rebellions against not just political but divine order. This was a useful argument to deploy against any who considered, in the words of King James's ambassador to Venice, that it was 'allowable for subjects to take up arms against or put their princes to death'.[3] Such arguments had been widely discussed at the time of the Wars of Religion in France (1562–98) and the revolt of The Netherlands against Spain's hegemony (1572–87).[4] The homily contains an implicit rebuke to what in the twentieth century came to be called 'liberation theology'.

Had he lived longer, Edward VI may well have introduced fundamentalist attempts at moral reformation, based on Mosaic injunctions, many of which would have been concerned with sexual reformation. A couple of years after the promulgation of the homilies this project was addressed in the *De Regno Christi* [*Concerning the Kingdom of Christ*] (1550) by Martin Bucer, Regius Professor of Divinity at Cambridge, and presented by him as a New Year's gift to the young king. Bucer, like Plato in the *Laws*, proposed the death penalty for adultery.[5] Fifty years later, certain reformed ministers allied themselves with magistrates in zealous attempts to root out this kind of sin:[6] Shakespeare's *Measure for Measure* is a sceptical meditation upon the practicalities of this kind of reform.

Sir Thomas More's *Utopia*

But poets had dreamt of new forms of state and empire since at least the time that Plato wrote his *Republic*. Well before the Act of Appeals and just a couple of years after Machiavelli's *Prince*, Sir Thomas More had written the best-known Renaissance description of a fictional realm, his *Utopia*. His storyteller, Raphael Hythloday, supposedly travelled in the company of Amerigo Vespucci (1454–1512). The name of that Genoese merchant and navigator had been given to 'America' and he is mentioned in More's text. In Greek *'utopia'* means 'no place'. The modern word 'utopian' means an imagined land where fantasies can become realities (as in fairy stories), but More's fantasies were *reforming* visions of the 'best state of a commonwealth'. The book, written in Latin and first published in 1516, was rapidly disseminated throughout Europe, although no translation into English appeared before that by Ralph Robinson printed during the reign of Edward VI in 1551. (Robinson translated the Latin word *'princeps'*, meaning a 'first official', as 'prince' and referred throughout to the ruler Utopus as 'King Utopus', thus turning More's republic into a kingdom.)[7]

More's narrative method adds to the irony of the title. On an embassy to Antwerp, More – the narrator is also a character in the text – tells how he was introduced to Hythloday, a mariner, who, after many travels, had determined that many of the lands he has visited beyond Europe were more fairly governed and had better laws than Christian commonwealths. The opinions of Hythloday (the name means 'expert in nonsense') need not be the opinions of the author, and Book 1 of the work (written it would seem after the description of Utopia in Book 2)[8] is a rhetorical dialogue where Hythloday's opinions are sceptically challenged – after the manner of Plato's dialogues. (This form is also used in the *Dialogue between Cardinal Pole and Thomas Lupset* by Thomas Starkey [1495?–1538], another work on social problems, and in Edmund Spenser's *View of the Present State of Ireland* of 1596.) However, underlying More's wit and play of ideas we are aware of a tough polemic against contemporary manners and injustices.

Utopia is scarcely an open society: in the interests of equality there is no private property, meals are taken communally, and all dress alike in simple plain attire. Euthanasia is the cure for the terminally ill, and convicted fornicators are forbidden ever to marry. Everyone must work for nine hours a day, each household has two bondmen or slaves; everyone must regularly labour for two years in the country. Both men and women must practise feats of arms, travelling is strictly controlled, and hunting and frivolous pastimes are forbidden. More had lived for four years in the Carthusian monastery or 'Charterhouse' next to Lincoln's Inn where he had studied law and always followed an ascetic life: many of the features of Utopia resemble medieval rules for monastic regimes – as well as recalling features of the communist regimes of the twentieth century.

But the rulers of this island republic listen to wise counsellors and take less 'delight in warlike matters and feats of chivalry . . . than in the good feats of peace'.[9] There, the enclosure of common land by the rich to provide grazing for sheep does not occur. In England, in Hythloday's famous words:

> your sheep . . . are become so great devourers and so wild that they eat up the men and swallow down the very men themselves . . . noblemen and gentlemen, yea and certain abbots . . . enclose all into pastures; they throw down houses; they pluck down towns, and leave nothing but only the church to be made into a sheep-house. And this is also the cause why victuals be now in many places dearer. Yet, besides this, the price of wool is risen, that poor folks, which were wont to work it and make cloth thereof, be now able to buy none at all:[10]

Poverty, according to both Hythloday and, obviously in this passage, to More, was the root of much criminality: in the words of *West Side Story*, delinquents were 'depraved on account of they were deprived'. Rather than being executed, thieves in Utopia were put to hard labour, while persistent adulterers were put to death. However, couples intending marriage saw each other naked before they committed themselves, and if it should happen later that

> the man and the woman cannot well agree between themselves, both of them finding other with whom they hope to live more quietly and merrily, that then by the full consent of both be divorced asunder and married again to other. But that not without the authority of the council, which agreeth to no divorces before they and their wives have diligently tried and examined the matter.[11]

Utopian laws were written so clearly that no lawyers were necessary – the joke is that More himself had been trained in the law. Women could be priests, priests need not be celibate, and varieties of religion were tolerated, many Utopians converting to Christianity when they heard from Hythloday of Christ's teaching.

The Literature of Folly

The Utopians 'have singular delight and pleasure in fools':[12] fools are recurrent figures in Renaissance texts. Sir Thomas More was a close friend of Erasmus of Rotterdam, whose *Praise of Folly* was conceived in the summer of 1509 when Erasmus was on his way to visit More in England. The *Moriae Encomium* ('Praise of Folly') was written in More's house: the punning title can be read as 'The Praise of More'. This book was printed in 1511 in Paris and then translated into English by Sir Thomas Chaloner in 1549.

The irony embedded in the *Praise of Folly*, which takes the form of a mock encomium (rhetorical commendation), matches that of the *Utopia*. Its satirical treatment of the virtues and follies of the age and its portraits of courtiers and worldly warrior popes, of scholars, poets, and other professionals, are sketched out by a fool (who is also a female). Are the opinions of the fool to be trusted any more than those of Hythloday? Does the title mean 'a praise of Folly' or 'a foolish praise'? The book is a rhetorical *tour de force*, copious of example and acute of wit, a mixture of tough reasonableness and agreeable sophistry. Characteristically, however, Folly denies both the art and the insight which generated the book: 'what thing these cunning rhetoricians, for all their long and forepenned orations can hardly bring about (I mean to drive care and pensiveness out of the hearers' minds), that have I with my only [sole] look and presence accomplished.'[13]

Near the beginning Folly delivers a long account of her genealogical descent, which parodies those of heroes in classical texts: Folly is daughter of Plutus (god of riches) and of Neotes (Youth); she was nursed by Drunkenness and Stupidity. Does this make her an unreliable narrator? If More had speculated about a commonwealth ruled by reason, Folly demolishes both the credentials and the arguments of the most wise:

> But now cometh Plato, [Socrates'] disciple, to defend his master at the bar, a gay [exuberant] advocate I promise you, who, being offended with the noise of the people thronging about him could scant make an end of the first clause of his tale . . . And yet . . . is that worthy saw of Plato much commended, how those commonweals most happily should flourish that were governed by philosophers, or whose governors applied themselves to philosophy. No, no, if ye look in histories ye shall find no

rulers were ever more pestilent to a commonweal that if the same at any time fall into the hands of such one as was given to any sect of philosophy.[14]

Is this folly, an inverted appeal for philosopher kings or wise scepticism?

Thomas Nashe followed Erasmus's method some eighty years later in *The Unfortunate Traveller* (1594). Nashe adopts the persona of a page at court, Jack Wilton, who presents himself as a wise fool; within descriptions of Wilton's adventures the author embeds satires on the defeat of the Anabaptists in Münster and the excesses of Rome under the popes. Nashe's vision of Italy is characteristically ambivalent: he implicitly endorses words of Roger Ascham that quickly became proverbial, 'An English Italianate is a devil incarnate',[15] but also reveals great admiration for the Venetian Pietro Aretino (1492–1556) whose notoriety in England was matched only by that of Machiavelli:

> one of the wittiest knaves that ever God made. If out of so base a thing
> as ink there may be extracted a spirit, he writ with nought but the spirit
> of ink, and his style was the spirituality of arts . . . His pen was sharp-
> pointed like poniard. No leaf he wrote on, but was like a burning glass
> to set on fire all his readers. With more than musket-shot did he charge
> his quill where he meant to inveigh . . . He was no timorous servile
> flatterer of the commonwealth wherein he lived . . . Princes he spared
> not that in the least point transgressed. His life he contemned in com-
> parison of the liberty of speech.[16]

'Aretine', because some sonnets were published with illustrations by Giulio Romano of positions for love-making, was associated in England with ribaldry or pornography. However, works like his *Ragionameni* (*Dialogues*) are a serious examination of the abuses of marriage and of the sexual double standard, and his political writings and satires gave him the title of the 'scourge of princes'.

Why are fools so prominent in late medieval and Renaissance culture, a period we might be inclined to think of as an age of wisdom? (Or why do modern readers make them central?) Erasmus was not the first to call fools into a circle: in 1494 the German poet Sebastian Brant wrote *Das Narrenshiff*, which was translated by Alexander Barclay in 1509 as *The Ship of Fools of the World*. Fools people many of the satirical comedies of the turn of the sixteenth century: notable are Ben Jonson's comedies of humours and George Chapman's *All Fools* (c.1601) – the latter play is also much indebted to classical New Comedy. In such plays, fools or foolish wits are 'gulled' or put down by 'heroes' of questionable virtue or by witty clowns. Similar figures appear in the cony-catching pamphlets that proliferated in the sixteenth century: these profiles of the period's underworld describe how rogues and cursitors (vagabonds) cozen and pillage their victims. A 'cony' was a rabbit: its period pronunciation 'cunny' generated a repertory of obscene jests. Some of these pamphlets delight in listing words from the secret cant or jargon of these thieves, gypsies and beggars.[17]

However, not all fools appear in a negative light. There is wisdom in folly: the topic derived from genealogies of folly upon which some of the greatest writers of the age – Erasmus, Shakespeare and Cervantes – drew. First was the assumption that there is wisdom in madness: Socrates had declared 'Our greatest blessings come to us by way of madness, provided the madness is given us by divine gift' (*Phaedrus*, 244a), and from this and other Platonic and neo-platonic texts came the notion of *divinus furor* which we examined in chapter 1. Thomas More and Shakespeare refer to fools as 'naturals', a word that also could be used for madmen and which, as we would expect, has both positive and negative connotations. The incurable fools locked away in the 'hospital' shown in Middleton and Rowley's *The Changeling* (1622) have paid with their wits for pursuing the follies of love and desire. Another image is of the simpleton, excluded from community and wandering the highways as a 'Bedlam' – like Edgar, disguised as Poor Tom, in *King Lear*. Images of truth may be perceived through their babble: as Edgar says, 'Thorough the sharp hawthorn blow the winds' (3.4.44–5). Such figures might have been expected to touch the consciences of those more 'normal' or more privileged.

The second tradition is embodied in the figure of the professional jester or court fool. These might resemble modern circus clowns, gambolling entertainers skilled in verbal games, droll repartee and improvisation. The flavour of one kind of performance is suggested in a compliment paid to Feste: 'Thou was in very gracious fooling last night when thou spokst of the Vapians passing the equinoctial of Queubus' (*Twelfth Night*, 2.3.22ff). However, Lear's fool (who, to many, seems not just witty but half-crazed) is given to delivering prophecies that contain mixtures of fantasies and satire. Such fools were 'licensed', given a space in which to perform their truth games, but could be whipped for overstepping the mark.

In Shakespeare's *1* and *2 Henry IV* Sir John Falstaff often plays the jester, and his discourse and presence are a touchstone for the vapourings of warriors and politicians. After his cowardice has been exposed at Gadshill (*1 Henry IV*), Falstaff and Hal take it in turns to play the king, to parody the role of Hal's father admonishing his son for the company he keeps in the taverns and stews of Eastcheap. When Falstaff is player king, Shakespeare invokes a pattern of inversion that has a long history: a lord of misrule presiding at a feast of fools. Erasmus's Folly describes the festive riots of which this is an example:

> of all such knacks I am the only devisor, like as this, that now is solemnly taken up at banquets, to chose a king by lots, to play at tables [board-games], to bring good luck, to quaff about the board, to sing carols [joyous songs] . . . was never ordained by the seven sages of Greece but through mine invention, for the conservation and avail [benefit] of mankind. Yet mark you the nature of all such devices and ye shall see that *the more folly they smell of, the more they do profit the life of moral men.*[18]

Falstaff is a corrupt knight, drunken, debauched, idle, but he stands for something positive: wit, ease, a capacity to take many roles, a nose for humbug, and, despite his years, a kind of sexiness or at least a talent for inspiring love among that most hard-bitten group, the harlots. Moreover, when Prince Hal threatens Falstaff with banishment, the fat knight responds: 'Banish plump Jack, and banish all the world' (*2 Henry IV*, 2.4.397–8). Revelry and riot cannot be abolished by the operation of the law: the reach of the Tudor state may have exceeded its grasp. Fools or jesters were 'real' men who, they claimed, were indistinguishable from 'artificial' men who had fashioned moral or social roles for themselves. Which is the puppet, the player, the actor, which the actual person?

This is a question raised in a tale inspired by Cervantes' *Don Quixote* (1605). The anecdote also looks forward to the tragic scenes played out by Charles I, who met his end on a scaffold that was all too like the scaffolds occupied by players:

> Such strange impressions makes strong fancies, and works not only upon women wonderful effects, but even the most masculine spirits have been (as well as our Don [Quixote]) shrewdly tainted with it. A gentleman [was] importuned, at a fire-night in the public hall, to accept

the high and mighty place of a mock-emperor, which was duly conferred upon him by seven mock-electors at the same time, with much
wit and ceremony. The emperor ascended his chair of state, which was
placed upon the highest table in the hall, and at his instalment all
pomp, reverence, and signs of homage were used by the whole company. Insomuch that our emperor (having a spice of self-conceit before,
was soundly peppered now) for he was instantly metamorphosed to the
stateliest, gravest, and commanding soul that ever eye beheld. Taylor
acting Arbaces [in Beaumont and Fletcher's *A King and No King*, 1611]
or Swanston [playing] D'Ambois [in Chapman's *Bussy D'Ambois*, 1604]
were shadows to him; his pace, his look, his voice, and all his garb was
altered. Alexander upon his elephant, nay upon the castle upon that
elephant, was not so high; and so close did this imaginary honour stick
to his fancy that for many years he could not shake off this one night's
assumed deportments until the times came that drove all monarchical
imaginations out, not only of his head but everyone's.[19]

'Monarchical imaginations': comedy is obviously not just a laughing
matter. Thinking about this sort of ritualized behaviour, Mikhail
Bakhtin was to argue that in carnival rituals we encounter elements
of the demotic, satirical, deflationary and extra-institutional, devoted
to the celebration of community and local solidarity at the expense of
national interest or hierarchical order or 'the specialized appreciation
of durable literary values'.[20]

Jonson's *Volpone* (1606) is another bravura exhibition of varieties of
folly, achieving gravity through complex entanglements of folly and
vice. It was written at a time when court grandees could become very
wealthy by being granted monopolies on the trading of particular
commodities or by venturing their capital in commercial projects. In
Renaissance terms, the hero is a 'monster' in that he is partly man and
partly beast: in his case a fox (the play owes allegiance to medieval
beast allegories). To the audience he also appears as a kind of jester
whose project is to gull the 'real' fools of Venice of their wealth. They
come to call upon Volpone who has put it abroad that he is terminally
ill. Anyone who brings tribute in the form of gifts will be remembered
in his will. His household is equally 'monstrous', being composed of
deformed beings, a dwarf, a hermaphrodite and a eunuch, who serve
as his fools and together sing a song beginning 'Fools, they are the only
nation [race], / Worth men's envy or admiration' (1.2.66–7). Another
conspicuous fool in the play, Sir Politic Would-be, a dim-witted English

traveller in Venice, imitates the get-rich-quick projects of native Venetian monsters, the birds of prey: the advocate Voltore (the vulture), the old gentleman Corbaccio (the raven) and the merchant Corvino (the crow). As Sir Politic, he is part Machiavel; as Sir Pol, he is part parrot who apes the doings of the vicious. This 'Englishman Italianate' is not a devil but an ass.

Jonson's mingling of the foolish and the vicious creates an acid satire upon the beginnings of venture capitalism that were apparent at the time. The pursuit of wealth denatures men, turning them from angels to beasts. In this comic world the 'good' characters, Bonario and Celia, appear ridiculous, although laughter may well cease when Celia proclaims:

> . . . punish that unhappy crime of nature,
> Which you miscall my beauty: flay my face,
> Or poison it with ointments, for seducing
> Your blood to this rebellion.   (3.7.250–3)

Her husband Corvino has prostituted Celia to Volpone. Volpone is about to rape her: in despair her tactic is to blame her beauty and, by implication, herself for triggering his ardour and raising an insurrection against the moral order. In this world of inverted values, virtue converts to guilt.

But the play preaches no simple moral. At its end, in an act of revenge rather than of justice, Volpone is 'mortified' ['consigned to death'] by being committed to the hospital of the *incurabili* by Venetian judges who had been outwitted by him. His counter-revenge is to make a kind of return from the dead in the Epilogue by adopting the role of the player who had taken his part:

> The seasoning of a play is the applause.
> Now, though the Fox be punished by the laws,
> He, yet, doth hope there is no suffering due
> For any fact, which he hath done 'gainst you;
> If there be, censure him: here he, doubtful, stands.
> If not, fare jovially, and clap your hands.

Laughter is subversive:[21] one man's wisdom is another man's folly – and vice versa. Jonson's actor begs applause, but is this for his performance or for the character he has been playing? If the latter, the audience has been gulled into applauding vice, or at least into delighting in the energy of the vicious.

A third tradition derives from the elevation of the simplicity of Christ's life and teaching to the degree that it becomes a kind of sublimated folly in the eyes of those who sought the meanings of life and existence through ratiocination. Erasmus parodied the speculative subtleties of the scholastic philosophers, often followers of St Thomas Aquinas (1224–74), which seemed to him to be irrelevant to moral experience:

> they expound the secrets of scripture at their pleasure, disputing how the world was first created and proportioned; by what channels sin was derived into Adam's posterity; what ways, by what measure, and in how short space Christ was complete in the womb of Mary the Virgin; and how in the sacrament of the altar, the accidents of bread and wine remain when the substance is gone . . . whether Christ might possibly have taken to him the likeness of a woman, of a fiend, of an ass, or of a gourd? Or how that gourd should have preached, done miracles, or been banged on the cross. Or what should Peter have consecrated if he had consecrated what time Christ's body hanged on the cross.[22]

It may be from this tradition of the holy fool or innocent that the use of the word 'fool' as a term of endearment derives. Sidney concludes *Astrophil and Stella* 73:

> O heav'nly fool, thy most kiss-worthy face
> Anger invests with such a lovely grace
> That Anger's self I needs must kiss again.

At the end of *Richard II*, the king who had been monarchizing upon the great stage of the world, alone in prison just before he dies, finds a kind of holy wisdom:

> Thus play I in one person many people,
> And none contented. Sometimes am I king,
> Then treasons make me wish myself a beggar,
> And so I am. Then crushing penury
> Persuades me I was better when a king,
> Then am I kinged again: and by and by
> Think that I am unkinged by Bullingbrook,
> And straight am nothing. But whate'er I be,

Nor I nor any man that but man is
With nothing shall be pleased, till he be eased
With being nothing.   (5.5.31–41)

The passage works on various levels: Richard engages with a foolish fantasy that a beggar may be happier than a king (a vaguely subversive notion), and he reaches his conclusion by complex, though childlike, wordplay: 'nothing' was pronounced at the time 'noting' and could mean 'knowing'. There is probably also an echo of St Paul: 'as having nothing, and yet possessing all things' (2 Cor. 6: 10).

The Writing of Travel and Exploration

Imaginary states were not constructed only in fictions but in what purported to be 'objective' accounts of other places. Discoveries in the New World provided huge amounts of gold and also showed that other kinds of social organization were possible. New World societies were almost always branded as 'barbarous', 'natural' or 'unnatural'. This last seeming contradiction is because words like 'natural' are seldom descriptive and generally evaluative. Particular social orders and political hierarchies had long been legitimated in terms of what is 'natural': most analogies between states and bodies, like Menenius' extended description of the Roman 'body politic' in Shakespeare's *Coriolanus* ([1608] 1.1.79–146), are revealed to be just endorsements of the customary. Richard Hooker derived human laws from divine and natural laws in his *Of the Laws of Ecclesiastical Polity* (1593–7); Michel de Montaigne was sceptical: 'oh man . . . thou seest but the order and policy of this little cell wherein thou art placed . . . This law thou allegest is but a municipal [national] law, and thou knowest not what the universal is.'[23] The natural is always a product of the cultural and not vice versa.

About 1580, Montaigne wrote an essay 'Of the Cannibals', a source for Shakespeare's *Tempest* (1611), in which he showed that virtue might reside among the barbarous or 'unnatural'. In a prefatory poem to the English translation of Montaigne by John Florio in 1603, Samuel Daniel showed how Montaigne's achievement had been to demonstrate the workings of what is now called ideology, or systems of ideas, conventions or beliefs that order the action or behaviour of a culture:

...this great potentate,
This prince Montaigne (if he be not more)
Hath more adventured of his own estate
Than ever man did of himself before:
And hath made such bold sallies out upon
Custom, the mighty tyrant of the earth,
In whose *seraglio of subjection*
We all seem bred-up, from our tender birth.

The 'natural', he too reminds us, is generally the customary – although modern readers may reject the casual slur against the seraglios of the Muslim world.

In 1596, Sir Walter Ralegh published his *Discovery of the Large, Rich, and Beautiful Empire of Guiana*. His description of the country is, as by now we might expect, deeply imprinted by ideology:

> The empire of Guiana is directly east from Peru towards the sea, and lieth under the equinoctial line, and it hath more abundance of gold than any part of Peru, and as many or more great cities than ever Peru had when it flourished most . . . Those commanders and chieftains that shoot at honour and abundance, shall find there more rich and beautiful cities, more temples adorned with golden images, more sepulchres filled with treasure, than either [Hernán] Cortés [1485–1547] found in Mexico or [Francisco] Pizarro [c.1476–1541] in Peru: and the shining glory of this conquest will eclipse all those so far extended beams of the Spanish nation . . . Guiana is a country that hath yet her maidenhead, never sacked, turned, nor wrought; the face of the earth hath not been torn, nor the virtue and salt of the soil spent by manurance, the graves have not been opened for gold, the mines not broken with sledges [hammers], nor their images pulled down out of their temples. It hath never yet been entered by any army of strength, and never conquered or possessed by any Christian prince.[24]

The book is a rhetorical manifesto, a prospectus for the colonization or invasion of these magnificent cities, from which Ralegh himself doubtless hoped to profit. It is a nice critical question to determine whether the sexualized imagery of a virgin country never 'possessed' tells us something about the politics of sexual behaviour in the period or was used by Ralegh as a means to sell his anti-Spanish prospectus.

However, the Americas had been surveyed from a very different perspective in a work that probably introduced the phrase 'New World':

the *De Novo Orbe* by Pietro Martire d'Anghiera (1457–1526), partially translated by Richard Eden in 1555 as *The Decades of the New World*. There, in the translator's Preface to the Reader, the 'Indians' (it was still believed that the Americas were part of 'India' approached from the West) are branded as barbarian cannibals and the Spaniards hailed as liberating crusaders:

> [The] bondage [of the Indians] is such as is much rather to be desired than their former liberty, which was to the cruel cannibals rather a horrible licentiousness than a liberty, and to the innocent so terrible a bondage that, in the midst of their fearful idleness, they were ever in danger to be a prey to those man-hunting wolves. But now, thanks be to God, by the manhood and policy of the Spaniards, this devilish generation [race] is so consumed, partly by the slaughter of those that could by no means be brought to civility, and partly by reserving such as were overcome in the wars and converting them to a better mind . . . Moses, as the minister of the law of wrath and bondage given in fire and tempests, was commanded in his wars to save neither man, woman, nor child . . . But the Spaniards, as the ministers of grace and liberty, brought into these new gentiles the victory of Christ's death, whereby they, being subdued with the worldly sword, are now made free from the bondage of Satan's tyranny.[25]

The pro-Spanish spin on this is easily explained: in the year of publication the Roman Catholic Mary Tudor, wife of King Philip of Spain, ruled over England. Once again, we see another culture viewed in terms of an informing myth, this time from the Old Testament.

Houses and Gardens

So far we have looked at designs for living and for government in prose discourses and theatrical representations. In verse, a good focus for these topics is the sub-genre of the 'country house poem'. These generally work by offering set-piece descriptions of the architecture of mansions and their surrounding gardens and parks. They define and focus on borders, or what are often called 'thresholds', spaces where art or culture (the building) and nature (the park or garden) meet. Poets writing in this genre usually propose a union between the cultural and an idealized nature: the description of a *'natural'* order within the park or estate serves to legitimate the house and the *social* order it represents. Country estates, therefore, which seem to be private places, often become emblems of politics. They tell us something about the quality of life of their owners – indeed, the great houses of the time were generally designed to be 'read' as well as to be seen.

Henry VIII, his descendants and their ministers often built magnificent palaces for themselves that replaced the fortified castles that feudal nobility had previously inhabited. In emulation of these, men of wealth who, under James I, were often knighted in return for giving to the royal exchequer, erected what have been called 'prodigy houses' designed to proclaim both wealth and status. These are signs of cultural competition, analogous to the theatrical contests that, as we shall see, are enacted on the stage in city comedies. When estates are described in topographical poems the descriptions are written not just to bring realities to mind, but to inculcate ideas and often, somewhat surreptitiously, define ideals.

We can track back to earlier allegorical descriptions of buildings: here is Spenser's House of Pride to which Duessa guides the Knight of the Red Cross:

> at last they see
> A goodly building, brauely garnished,
> The house of mightie Prince it seemd to bee:
> And towards it a broad high way that led,
> All bare through peoples feet, which thither traueiled.
>
> Great troupes of people traueild thitherward
> Both day and night, of each degree and place,
> But few returned, hauing scaped hard,
> With balefull beggerie, or foule disgrace,
> Which euer after in most wretched case,
> Like loathsome lazars, by the hedges lay.
> Thither Duessa bad him bend his pace:
> For she is wearie of the toilesome way,
> And also nigh consumed is the lingring day.
>
> A stately Pallace built of squared bricke,
> Which cunningly was without morter laid,
> Whose wals were high, but nothing strong, nor thick,
> And golden foile all ouer them displaid,
> That purest skye with brightnesse they dismaid:

High lifted vp were many loftie towres,
And goodly galleries farre ouer laid,
Full of faire windowes, and delightfull bowres;
And on the top a Diall told the timely howres.

It was a goodly heape for to behould,
  And spake the praises of the workmans wit;
But full great pittie, that so faire a mould
  Did on so weake foundation euer sit:
For on a sandie hill, that still did flit,
  And fall away, it mounted was full hie,
That euery breath of heauen shaked it:
  And all the hinder parts, that few could spie,
Were ruinous and old, but painted cunningly.

(The Faerie Queene, 1.4.2–5)

This generic example of what Thorstein Veblen was to term 'conspicuous display' is also a house built on an unsure foundation (see Matthew 7: 26–7); nor does it offer hospitality, a virtue regularly praised in the period.

The first country house poem that celebrated an actual estate was probably the 'Description of Cookham' (1609–10) by Aemilia Lanyer (see chapter 1); this was followed by Ben Jonson's 'To Penshurst' (1611?), Thomas Carew's 'Saxham' (published 1640), Denham's 'Co-oper's Hill' (1642), and Marvell's 'Upon Appleton House' (1652). The tradition surfaced in Alexander Pope's description of Timon's Villa in his 'Epistle to Bathurst' (1730–2) and was used in novels – Jane Austen's Mansfield Park and Evelyn Waugh's Brideshead establish political ideals.

Such poems use history as well as geography: they evoke traditions, often associated with images of national identity, just as the National Trust's country houses now serve as sites of pilgrimage to shrines of Englishness. As in the case of other cultures, images of lost worlds, Eden, or the Golden Age were often imposed on descriptions of actual estates. Jonson's country house poem 'To Penshurst' (which might be read alongside his praise of country living in 'To Sir Robert Roth') creates an emblem of Jonsonian virtues and values. It was written at a time when gentlemen were migrating to the city, which was the new centre of wealth and diversion: in 1590 Sir Henry Unton complained from the country that 'my clownish life doth deprive me of all intelligence and comfort.'[26] Penshurst is the anti-type of households in the plays, Volpone's and Lovewit's in *The Alchemist*, to which people unwittingly bring tribute, and of the New Inn, a place of vacuous and indecorous behaviour in the play of the same name (1629).

Historically, Penshurst was the home of the Sidney family, and the poem contains reminiscences of Kalander's house in Book 1, chapter 2 of Sidney's *Countess of Pembroke's Arcadia* (1593 edn). Sir Philip Sidney, who was for many the epitome of chivalry, had died in 1586, and the poem belongs among a number of Stuart texts that are nostalgic for the age of Elizabeth.[27] Jonson compares a fairly modest Elizabethan manor with Jacobean prodigy houses like Audley End in Essex, seat of Thomas Howard, Duke of Suffolk, which was being built when the poem was written. The poem offers a variety of pastoral in that rusticity here is imbued with courtliness; Jonson uses the technique of instructing plutocratic citizens and depraved courtiers by praising the inhabitants of his earthly paradise, a little Eden in Kent.

The poem's opening praises the propriety of the mansion's design, its decorum – the way its form of architecture suits its function as a dwelling. The conceit that informs the description of the estate is of natural creatures voluntarily sacrificing themselves to those that live there:

> And if the high-swoll'n Medway fail thy dish,
>> Thou hast thy ponds that pay thee tribute fish:
> Fat, agèd carps that run into thy net;
>> And pikes, now weary their own kind to eat,
> As loath the second draught [netting] or cast to stay [await],
>> Officiously [obligingly], at first, themselves betray.   (31–6)

These witty images derive from commonplaces that can be traced back to Martial, Juvenal, and Virgil's *Georgics*. We soon realize that what Jonson has done, however, is to suppress the labour that sustains the estate. There is no mud in pastorals, nor is there any depiction of everyday work: representing the pains of lowly paid labour, as began to happen in the nineteenth century, might have been deemed subversive. The poem is a celebration not only of hospitality but also of consumption, and the means of production are suppressed. Nor is there any sign of the burgeoning agrarian capitalism, the enclosing and engrossing of land.[28]

Andrew Marvell in 'Upon Appleton House' offers a more ironic view. He imagines becoming like Gulliver in Brobdingnag:

> And now to the abyss I pass
> Of that unfathomable grass,
> Where men like grasshoppers appear,
> But grasshoppers are giants there;
> They, in their squeaking laugh, contemn
> Us as we walk more low than them:
> And, from the precipices tall
> Of the green spurs, to us do call.

Lost in the depths of a meadow, he finds all that is human belittled and disdained by the 'natural' denizens of the estate.

City Comedy and the Court

As we have seen, country estates appear in texts as versions of pastoral, indicative of values opposed to those of cities as portrayed in the plays of Ben Jonson. Other dramatists, notably Thomas Dekker and Thomas Middleton, contributed to another sub-genre, city comedy. In Jonson's texts allegorical traditions generated both households and characters. Similarly, cities, in the theatrical fictions of the early seventeenth century, are constructions: it is misleading to speak of them as 'portrayals' or perhaps even as 'representations'. Rather they are 'anti-pastorals', conceptual centres, ideological spaces and not really places, fashioned by authors, their actors, or their readers, and poised in opposition to other centres of values, the country and the court. In many literatures, the country suggests images of the past, cities evoke those of the future; the country stands for integration and hospitality, the city for individualism and alienation.

Actual cities in early modern Britain were new, or at least made news. London grew at a phenomenal rate: in 1500 its population was about 35,000, in 1550 about 120,000, in 1600 about 200,000, in 1700 about 500,000. The magnetism of the court 'now-a-days much greater and more gallant than in former times', and now for the most part resident in London, swelled its population, drawing gentlemen of the shires to the city, 'the younger sort of them to see and show vanity, and the elder to save the cost and charge of country hospitality and housekeeping'.[29] Wealth created confidence: Frederick, Duke of Wirtemberg, describing London in 1592, wrote:

> The inhabitants are magnificently apparelled, and are extremely proud and overbearing; and because the greater part, especially the trades-people, seldom go into other countries, but always remain in their houses in the city attending to their business, they care little for foreigners, but scoff and laugh at them; and moreover one dare not oppose them, else the street-boys and apprentices collect together in immense crowds and strike to the right and left unmercifully without regard to person; and because they are the strongest, one is obliged to put up with the insult as well as the injury.[30]

This xenophobia is registered throughout Thomas Dekker's *The Shoemaker's Holiday* (1599, see below).[31] Another factor in the growth of London was the ever-increasing importance of the court as an administrative centre: in *1 Henry IV* Falstaff and Bardolph at Gadshill feel licensed to steal gold on its way to the king's exchequer (2.2.43).

Nowadays, 'the City' is a synecdoche (a part for the whole) that designates one part of London, the financial node of British capitalist enterprise. Although in the age of Jonson and Middleton there was much more artisanal manufacture in London than there is now, it was non-manufacturing entrepreneurialism and adventurism rather than industry that featured in literature. Although there were no fewer than 160 craft guilds, 'the City was dominated by the twelve great Livery Companies which were effectively associations of merchants and wholesalers rather than occupational groupings.'[32] Stow observed that 'retailers and artificers, at the least of such things as pertain to the back or belly, do leave the country towns, where there is no vent [sale], and do fly to London where they be sure to find ready and quick market.'[33]

Population growth was punctuated by outbreaks of the plague or Black Death which killed tens of thousand of citizens. Inflation and dearth caused by plague added to the problems caused by immigration, generating not only 'masterless men' but poverty; penury amidst the splendours of the city made both more visible. Vagrancy arrests rose twelvefold between 1560 and 1625.[34] The city became an ambivalent and contradictory image, of magnificence and destitution: failure to understand the economic changes that generated these phenomena made many aspects of city life seem 'unnatural'.

This striking contrast between the beginnings of civic splendour and social deprivation provided material for *morality plays*, but we must also consider why London is among the few cities to have generated a distinctive tradition of *city drama*. The answer, according to a contemporary, may lie in England's caste system: in 1617 Fynes Moryson wrote: 'The gentlemen disdain traffic, thinking it to debase gentry; but in Italy, with graver counsel, the very princes disdain not to be merchants by the great [in gross], and hardly leave the retailing commodity to men of inferior sort.'[35] We cannot speak with assurance of 'classes' in a pre-industrial society, but there was certainly competition between nobility and gentry, on the one hand, and merchants, on the other – as inscribed in Shakespeare's romantic comedy *The Merchant of Venice* (1596).

The competing interests of court and city are at the centre of many plays. Dekker's *The Shoemaker's Holiday* was performed at court on New Year's Day 1600, presumably after successful performances at the Rose.[36] Simon Eyre, a master shoemaker and a 'merry madcap' and 'frolic fellow', presides over the play. His catchphrase, 'Prince am I none though I am princely born' (vii. 49–50) is, significantly, adapted from Greene's dramatic romance *Orlando Furioso*. He rises to become Lord Mayor of London, but it is worth noting that he makes his fortune not from honest labour but from an investment in merchandise that nets him £3,000. Ironically, however, the play celebrates industriousness, although work is not actually represented. Instead, we are treated to a feast of work-related talk: 'a good rubbing-pin, a good stopper, a good dresser, your four sorts of awls, and your two balls of wax, your paring-knife, your hand- and thumb-leathers, and good Saint Hugh's bones [those of the patron saint of shoemakers] to smooth up your work' (iv. 83–7). Dekker constructs a moral economy, in which work is associated with festivity, eating and quaffing, and with 'tickling it' (xi. 74). Songs are dotted through the text and there is a morris dance (xi. 55). The celebratory presentational skills of the players win us over to the ethos of the characters they are playing.

Two romantic tales make up a double plot, that of the love of an unthrift gentleman, Rowland Lacy, for Rose, a citizen's daughter, and that of the wooing by Master Hammon, a city gentleman, first of Rose and then of Jane, wife to Ralph, a journeyman shoemaker. Ralph has been pressed into the army fighting against France, and towards the end of the play he comes back wounded. His appearance is presumably intended to prick the conscience of warmongers, and the play invokes citizen values to question those of the aristocracy. Is it right for Lacy, who is the nephew of the Earl of Lincoln and who manages to buy himself out of the army, to marry Rose, daughter of Sir Roger Oatley, Lord Mayor of London? The text suggests that social and economic factors are creating adjustments in the relationships between caste or rank and status. (This was registered when, at the beginning of his reign, James, in order to raise revenue, put knighthoods up for sale. Jonson and Chapman girded at this debasement of that rank in *Eastward Ho* [1605] and were imprisoned for their pains.) Love, of course, overcomes adversity, and the 'King of England', historically Henry VI but here invested with the attributes of Henry V, arrives on Shrove Tuesday (xxi. 182), the day of carnival, as *deus ex machina* to resolve the plots and heal social divisions. But is he just papering over cracks?

Even more threatening to contemporaries than the rapid accumulations of gold was usury, a topic that informs many complaints in citizen comedies popular in the first decades of the seventeenth century.[37] Usury had been forbidden by canon law: Bacon says that this was because, after Eden, Adam had been commanded to eat bread made by the sweat of his brow and not that of another. Calvin, however, had condoned the taking of interest, and parliamentary acts in the reigns of Henry VIII and Elizabeth allowed it, provided that the charges levied did not exceed 10 per cent. The raising of capital by borrowing with interest was necessary to finance ventures and projects – as well as to maintain display. Bacon again: 'To speak of the abolishing of usury is idle: all states have ever had it in one kind or rate or other, so as that opinion must be sent to Utopia.' The consequence was that money-lenders became very rich and their status, acquired through wealth, seemed to threaten political order. Usury caused 'the decay of customs of kings or states, which ebb or flow with merchandizing'.[38] Donne wrote self-deprecatingly, arguing that Dame Usury was coming to have the same power as Dame Nature:

> I, when I value gold, may think upon
> The ductileness, the application,
> The wholesomeness, the ingenuity,
> From rust, from soil, from fire ever free,
> But if I love it, 'tis because 'tis made
> By our new Nature, Use [usury], the soul of trade.
> (Elegy XVIII, 'Love's Progress', 11–16)

In *The Merchant of Venice*, Shylock is demonized both as a Jew and as a money-lender, and the usurer Dampit ('damned pit') figures as a 'trampler of the times', a destroyer of all social values, in Middleton's *A Trick to Catch the Old One*.

Jonson's Volpone (the fox), whose remorseless pursuit of wealth endows him with the nature of a beast, sophisticates justifies his gulling tricks by arguing that he is guilty of neither the evils attendant upon industrialism nor those of the usurer:

> I glory
> More in the cunning purchase of my wealth
> Than in the glad possession, since I gain
> No common way: I use no trade, no venture;
> I wound no earth with ploughshares; fat no beasts
> To feel the shambles; have no mills for iron,
> Oil, corn, or men, to grind them into powder;
> I blow no subtle glass; expose no ships
> To threatenings of the furrow-faced sea;
> I turn no monies in the public bank,
> Nor *usure private*. (1.1.30–49)

Like the city, the court was a mythic construction that could be viewed from opposite perspectives. In *Old Fortunatus* (1599) Dekker offered an idealized vision of Elizabeth's court in a prologue written for a court performance after the play had appeared in a public playhouse:

> Our eyes are dazzled by Eliza's beams;
> See (if at least thou dare see) where she sits:
> This is the great pantheon of our goddess,
> And all those faces, which thine eyes thought stars,
> Are nymphs attending on her deity . . .
> I weep for joy to see so many heads
> Of prudent ladies, clothed in the livery
> Of silver-handed age, for serving you,
> Whilst in your eyes youth's glory doth renew.

In other plays, however, courtiers are presented from a city point of view as idle and corrupt, obsessed with conspicuous display and consumption. When, in *Eastward Ho*, Quicksilver asks Touchstone 'What would you ha' me do?', he replies, 'Why, do nothing, be like a gentle-man, be idle; the curse of man is labour. Wipe thy bum with testons [small coins] and make ducks and drakes with shillings' (1.1.115–16).

Citizens equally abhorred the roaring boys, rioters, wastethrifts, and brothel-masters[39] that brought disorder to their domain. Margot Heinemann was right to insist that Middleton was not writing a series of anti-city theatrical diatribes from the point of view of the court, but rather celebrating those industrious virtues that have been associated with 'Puritanism'.[40]

These plays, however, accommodate both satire and celebration. Many are based on the pattern of classical 'New Comedy', which pits age against youth, and, as in the cony-catching pamphlets, greedy moneylenders are gleefully cozened of their wealth by the witty rap-acity of their would-be heirs or apprentices, who are the 'heroes' of this sort of dramatic action.

When we consider the examples and passages in this chapter, it is apparent that, as Bertolt Brecht considered, literature tends to consist not of reflections *of* but of reflections *on* reality. We must concen-trate upon the interpretative metaphors that authors use as much as upon what they describe. To close, here are some lines from yet another text by Dekker, *The Wonderful Year* (1603), which describes a twelvemonth in which James succeeded Elizabeth and the country was racked by the plague. Dekker describes the last illness of Elizabeth as 'a hideous tempest, that shook cedars, terrified the tallest pines, and cleft in sunder even the hardest hearts of oak'. He then reflects: 'Oh what an earthquake is the alteration of a state! Look from the cham-ber of presence to the farmer's cottage, and you shall find nothing but distraction: the whole kingdom seems a wilderness, and the people in it are transformed to wild men.' Reverting to the plague, he invokes one of the most famous Elizabethan playhouse figures, reminding his readers of the terror of overwhelming military force:

> Imagine then that all this while Death, like a Spanish Leaguer [enemy of the French Protestant Huguenots], or rather like stalking *Tamburlaine*, hath pitched his tents (being nothing but a heap of winding-sheets stitched together), in the sinfully polluted suburbs [where playhouses and brothels were to be found]: the Plague is muster-master, and mar-shal of the field.[41]

It is hard to establish one perspective on this as Dekker makes Death, Plague, and Tamburlaine representations of one another, while seemingly endorsing and repudiating the sinfulness of his own calling as a dramatist. We have examined designs for various kinds of brave new worlds: these metaphors of storm, earthquake and plague, applied to social and historical events, remind us that even though London was spared serious social unrest at the end of the sixteenth century, the structures that sustained the order of early modern England were perceived to be all too fragile.[42]

CHAPTER 6

Fictive Persons and Places

Characterization in the Playhouse

Revenge, Rape and Murder: these are the disguises worn in 5.2 of Shakespeare's *Titus Andronicus* (1591) by the Queen of the Goths, Tamora, and two of her sons, when they come to visits Titus. A couple of years earlier, Thomas Kyd had opened *The Spanish Tragedy* with the entrance of Revenge accompanied by the Ghost of Don Andrea. These sequences remind us of two things: that allegorical methods of characterization, found, for example, in fifteenth-century morality plays, survived well into the English high Renaissance, and that it was not indecorous to mingle, within particular sequences, 'real' characters with figures that were obviously personifications or figurative types. Morality plays continued to be revived, written and performed until the beginning of the seventeenth century, and plays with strong allegorical structures flourished in the universities and Inns of Court until the 1640s.

Many Romantic and post-Romantic readers, however, have had problems with allegory. Coleridge found cause to disparage Ben Jonson because he often used allegorical schemes of virtues and vices to fashion his characters: 'The observation I have prefixed to . . . *Volpone* is the key to the faint interest which these noble efforts of intellectual power excite, with the exception of *The Sad Shepherd*; because in that piece only is there any character with whom you can morally sympathize.'[1] At worst, allegorical figures in the playhouse can be used for dreary declamation, but, as medieval vice figures demonstrate, they often display as much energy as do more particularized figures. An audience's experience of 'character' in performance derives not just from the texts we read, but also from the presence and skill of the player who might bring in touches of felt life. However, given that such personifications serve as instruments for their play's exploration of moral or theological issues, attempts by readers to feel for or sympathize with such figures, even with the 'real' non-allegorical figures in the plays in which they occur, may be inappropriate. They were conceived for purposes of demonstration rather than identification. Both allegorical and typical figures take their being from their place in the moral rather than the emotional structures of the fictions they inhabit.

Many characters in seasonal plays and moralities were given an opening speech of self-presentation – and the convention survived into the Renaissance. Nature, in the anonymous *The Marriage of Wit and Science*, probably performed at court around 1568, opens the play by defining her own attributes as she addresses her son Wit:

> Grand lady, mother of every mortal thing,
> Nurse of the world, conservative of kind,
> Cause of increase, of life and soul the spring.
> At whose instinct the noble Heaven doth wind,
> To whose award all creatures are assigned.
> I come in place to treat with this my son
> For his avail how he the path may find,
> Whereby his race in honour he may run:

The first scene in which Shakespeare's Edmond appears, 1.2 of *King Lear*, also begins with self-presentation, a proclamation of his allegiance to a very different kind of Nature based on self-interest and action without conscience. Later, in the morality play *Marriage of Wit and Science*, a speech of Science shows how allegory informs not only character but also the narrative:

> I have a mortal foe
> That lurketh in the wood hereby as you come and go;
> This monstrous giant bears a grudge to me and mine,
> And will attempt to keep thee back from this desire of thine.
> The bane of youth, the root of ruin and desires,
> Devouring those that sue to me, his name is Tediousness.
> No sooner he espies the noble Wit begin

To stir and pain itself the love of me to win,
But forth he steps and with strong hands by might and main
He beats and buffets down the force and liveliness of brain.
That done in deep despair, he drowns him villainously:
Ten thousand suitors in a year are cast away thereby.   (4.1.141–52)

After falling into the lap of Idleness, who has intoxicated him with her singing, Wit, with the help of Will, duly defeats Tediousness. The play ends with him betrothed to Science.

Furthermore, when we look at the earliest editions of Renaissance plays we often find Shakespeare and his fellow dramatists using generic speech headings, even for major named personages. In the second Quarto of *Hamlet*, which derives from a manuscript Shakespeare wrote himself, we find 'King', 'Queen' and 'Clown' used to prefix speeches by Claudius, Gertrude and the Gravedigger. This indicates that even if such characters derive ultimately from historical chronicles rather than being allegorical personifications, authors were often as much concerned with universal attributes as with singular character traits. In Middleton's citizen comedy *A Trick to Catch the Old One*, the hero sports the name Theodorus Witgood, while his girl is merely 'Courtesan' – in fact 'Witgood' means both quick of mind and producer of fine semen.[2]

The ubiquity of type characters might help us overcome the prejudice against what are unthinkingly branded as 'stereotypes'. In a famous letter of 1888, Friedrich Engels wrote to Margaret Harkness about her novel, *A City Girl*: 'If I have any criticism to make, it is perhaps that your novel is not quite realistic enough. Realism to my mind, implies, besides truth of detail, the truthful rendering of typical characters under typical circumstances.' It is through typifying personalities that authors can critique their societies.

Character could also be created by styles, verbal as we saw in chapter 1, and physical. Many personages in drama have to be played by actors possessed of superior performance techniques. Some of these, drama students study today: singing, dancing and fencing, for example. Other roles must have enabled them to present the mime techniques, funny walks, pratfalls, distortions of the body, feats of juggling and the *lazzi* or stock routines, physical and verbal, that we associate with *commedia dell'arte* ('skilled comedy'), which was developed in the Italian Renaissance.

Sometimes 'character' is embedded in dialogue in the form of extended images. In Shakespeare's Henry IV plays, Falstaff and Justice Shallow are described as personifications of Carnival and Lent.[3] The prince invents for his father a speech that he delivers to Falstaff, the subject of the oration:

> There is a devil haunts thee in the likeness of an old fat man; a tun of man is thy companion. Why dost thou converse with that trunk of humours, that bolting-hutch of beastliness, that swollen parcel of dropsies, that huge bombard of sack, that stuffed cloak-bag of guts, that roasted Manningtree ox with the pudding in his belly, that reverend Vice, that grey Iniquity, that father Ruffian [i.e. the Devil], that Vanity in years? (*1 Henry IV*, 2.4.370–6)

Hal conjures images of Shrovetide feasting along with characters from the old moralities. Conversely, Falstaff recreates Justice Shallow as though he were a figure in a Brueghel engraving:

> I do remember him at Clement's Inn, like a man made after supper of a cheese paring. When a [he] was naked, he was for all the world like a forked radish, with a head fantastically carved upon it with a knife. A was so forlorn that his dimensions, to any thick sight, were invisible. A was the very genius of famine, yet lecherous as a monkey and the whores called him mandrake . . . And now is this Vice's dagger become a squire . . . you might have thrust him and all his apparel into an eel-skin: the case of a treble hautboy was a mansion for him, a court. And now has he land and beef. (*2 Henry IV*, 3.2.250–65)

There is, of course, no evidence that these lines were cues for players or costumiers: they are rather fantastic exercises in writing the body in a grotesque mode. Similar sketches are to be found in prose and, visually, in Inigo Jones's designs for the masques of Ben Jonson.[4]

Character could also be established by costumes. The inventory made in 1598 by the Elizabethan theatrical impresario Philip Henslowe contains a list of what he called 'antic suits' which, besides a 'red velvet horseman's coat', itemized 'Daniel's gown' and 'Will Summers' suit':[5] a play of *Daniel in the Lion's Den* was performed in Nördlingen by English players in 1604, and before the Queen in 1600 there may have been a revival of Nashe's *Summer's Last Will and Testament* (1592), a play in which Will Summers, who had become court fool in 1525, appeared along with personifications of the four seasons. 'Antic suits' probably included costumes for such allegorical personages. The costume 'painted full of tongues' for Rumour, who is Prologue to *2 Henry IV*, is of this type.

In a seventeenth-century drawing that seems to represent aspects of *Titus Andronicus* in performance,[6] we see some attempt at Roman costume for Titus, who is in a toga, but surrounding soldiers are clearly wearing Elizabethan costumes. Similarly, there are references in *Woodstock* (1590,[7] about the virtuous uncle of King Richard II) to characters wearing medieval shoes with long pointed toes. The inference we might draw is that occasionally a sort of 'costume property' might have been added to a standard Elizabethan costume.

Money was certainly spent on elaborate dress for those who played leading roles, but these garments were used to define the natures of those who wore them rather than mark the period of the play. The scarlet costume for Tamburlaine and the frieze (coarse woollen cloth) for Woodstock, an emblem of probity, are obviously emblematic of their natures. Minor characters were costumed out of the company's stocks – within the Elizabethan repertory system there can have been no question of finding a uniform style for each production. Many parts required conventional or vocational costumes: characters of high degree wore robes with heraldic or ecclesiastical emblems, the ceremonial dress of the present rather than fancy dress from the past. Kings wore crowns, devils wore horns, doctors' gowns were of scarlet, lawyers' gowns of black, rustics and clowns wore 'startups' (boots that reached to mid-calf), licensed fools wore long coats of motley, woven of coarse wool and parti-coloured green and yellow, prologues wore black with a crown of bays, ghosts wore leather 'pilches' (garments made of skins dressed with hair), shepherds wore white coats and carried staff and bottle, sailors wore canvas suits, servants blue coats or slops. Henslowe's inventory lists 'a robe for to go invisible', presumably something like the 'shape [costume] invisible' worn by Ariel in *The Tempest* (4.1.185). Faustus went invisible with a simple girdle (3.2.17–18). Obviously, such costumes served a useful function in identifying characters quickly as they entered. In general, the players' use of regular contemporary clothing rather than the fancy dress of the past doubtless enhanced the political resonance of performances.

Another source of costumes was described by Thomas Platter in 1599:

The comedians [players] are most expensively and elegantly apparelled, since it is customary in England, when distinguished gentlemen or knights die, for nearly the finest of their clothes to be made over and given to their servants, and as it is not proper for them to wear such clothes but only to imitate them, they give them to the comedians to purchase for a small sum.[8]

Platter's citation of propriety refers to the Elizabethan sumptuary laws, which were an attempt to maintain what Shakespeare called 'degree' and we would call a 'status-system': expensive fabrics could be worn only by those of higher rank.[9] Some of the most obvious transgressors, of course, were the players who might bring back to court rich costumes lately seen on the backs of deceased nobility.

The word 'character' originally meant something engraved: in Renaissance drama, 'character' is often a kind of badge, and many persons were simply 'badged', verbally or visually. The first use of the word to designate something about a person comes from Shakespeare:

> I will believe thou hast a mind that suits
> With this thy fair and outward character.
> (*Twelfth Night*, 1.2.51)

The implication is that the moral make-up of the sea-captain whom Viola addresses matches the costume that establishes him as a type of the lowly born but totally worthy. That is all we need to know about him.

If there was what we might now call a psychological interest, it was likely to be schematic, deriving from the theory of humours that was set up by the ancient Greek philosopher Hippocrates.[10] He believed that a healthy temperament derived from a balanced mixture of four bodily fluids or 'humours': blood, phlegm, yellow bile and black bile. Each of these was associated with particular organs and particular seasons, and their respective qualities, warm and moist, cold and moist, warm and dry, and cold and dry, were held to generate particular characteristics: those who were sanguine were courageous, the phlegmatic were calm, the choleric easily angered, and the melancholic despondent. Humours could also combine to create more complex types. The scheme is set out in the Induction to Jonson's *Every Man Out of his Humour* (1599):

Why, humour (as 'tis *ens*) we thus define it
To be a quality of air, or water,
And in itself holds these two properties,
Moisture, and fluxure; as, for demonstration,
Pour water on this floor, 'twill wet and run;
Likewise the air (forced through a horn, or trumpet)
Flows instantly away and leaves behind
A kind of dew; and hence we do conclude,
That whatsoe'er hath fluxure and humidity,
As wanting power to contain itself,
Is humour. So in every human body
The choler, melancholy, phlegm, and blood,
By reason that they flow continually
In some one part, and are not continent,
Receive the name of 'humours'. Now thus far
It may, *by metaphor*, apply itself
Unto the general disposition:
As when some one peculiar quality
Doth so possess a man that it doth draw
All his affects, his spirits, and his powers,
In their confluctions, all to run one way,
This may be truly said to be a 'humour'.

Jonson does not consider that bodily processes *determine* a person's disposition, but that they constitute a *metaphoric system* that can be used to describe personality or 'inwardness'.

Affecting a humour became fashionable:

COB   Nay, I have my rheum, and I can be angry as well as another, sir.
CASH Thy rheum, Cob? Thy humour, thy humour! Thou mistak'st.
COB   Humour? Mack, I think it be so indeed: what is that humour?
   Some rare thing, I warrant.
CASH Marry, I'll tell thee, Cob: it is a gentleman-like monster, bred, in
   the special gallantry of our time, by affectation; and fed by folly.
                              (Jonson, *Every Man in his Humour*, 1616 version, 3.4)

The sequence indicates that a distinction between 'comedy of humours' (psychological), which we associate with Renaissance drama, and 'comedy of manners' (social), which was prevalent after the Restoration, does not really hold.

A convention that modern readers or spectators might find strange is that of sudden mood swings – or changes of 'humour'. Like the sudden onset of a disease, hatred can turn to love, grief to joy, or equanimity to rage. The sudden jealousy of Shakespeare's Othello and Leontes has been the topic of countless student essays that misguidedly seek for psychological realism. In Heywood's *A Woman Killed with Kindness* (1603), two close friends suddenly fall out when out hawking, and the noble-minded Sir Charles Mountford kills two of Sir Francis Acton's men:

> SIR CHARLES My God, what have I done! What have I done!
>   My rage hath plunged into a sea of blood
>   In which my soul lies drowned . . .
>   'Twas in the heat of blood,
>   And anger quite removes me from *my self.* (1.3.43–51)

His anger has changed his character completely; choleric humour has possessed him. (In a context like this we must read 'my self' and not the reflexive pronoun 'myself'.) As a consequence of his actions, he falls into poverty and is imprisoned. Later, the villainous Wendoll woos and wins the angelic Anne Frankford, his friend's wife, all in a sequence of only eighty lines (2.3). (Anne is not punished but 'kindly' banished by her husband and dies of grief.) Later Susan, sister of Sir Charles, agrees to marry Sir Francis, erstwhile enemy of the family who, having sought to seduce her, redeems her brother from gaol.

> SUSAN I will yield to fate,
>   And learn to love where I till now did hate. (5.1.147–8)

It is difficult to tell whether such moments reveal character being sacrificed to plot or whether, in the case of sudden rage, tempers in the period, as some historians have argued, were short and outbursts of violence or vituperation were in life all too common. (One offered explanation is that the inefficacy of medicine meant that many minor ailments, pains or itches, could never be cured and that people were almost always uncomfortable or irritable.)

Inwardness could also be revealed through soliloquy. However, it is important to remember that, until about the time of *Hamlet*, soliloquies would seem to have been directed to spectators rather than into some kind of mental space. The player at such a moment is, strangely enough, distanced from the role he is taking, sometimes establishing a perspective upon the morality of his actions: Richard III's opening soliloquy in Shakespeare's play is an attempt to rationalize his villainy, a challenge to the audience to see through the false logic of the character's game-plan.

Whether there was distance or perspective between the female characters and the boy players who took their parts is difficult to tell. Experience of modern productions where players of the same gender take all the parts reveals that the convention of cross-gendered acting can rapidly become invisible. Paradoxically, it may have become more visible in the large number of texts that contain 'breeches parts' (when female characters were called upon to disguise themselves as males) when spectators are regularly reminded of the convention through wordplay or asides. In plays for the coterie companies there are, however, moments that suggest that boys were invited to flaunt their sexuality and enjoy their travesty roles to the delight of some and the outrage of moralistic members of the audience.[11] (Boys joined playing companies between the ages of ten and thirteen and played female roles until they were about twenty – many women were therefore played by youths whose voices had broken.)

An individual 'personality' could also be portrayed by several players. The fourth-century Latin poet Prudentius' allegorical poem *Psychomachia* ('Battle of the Soul') had created a structure for morality plays, many of which depict a struggle between spirit and flesh, virtues and vices, for the allegiance of a central figure named, for example, 'Everyman', 'Mankind' or 'Anima' (Soul). The Good Angel in *Dr Faustus* who warns the hero against his demonic pact, and the Bad Angel who urges him to persevere in evil, dramatize a mental struggle 'within the mind' of the hero: in modern productions they have been played by glove puppets held by the actor playing the central role.

Certain parts, those for singers, dancers and, particularly interestingly, fools, were not really 'characters' in that they did not take part in the stage action, but played on the threshold between representation and presentation, as much 'themselves' as the figures they personated. In the Epistle to his translation of Erasmus' *Praise of Folly* (see chapter 5), Sir Thomas Chaloner in 1549 described how fools in some ways were like modern stand-up comedians within the dramatic action: 'And seeing the vices of our days are such as cannot enough be spoken against, what know we, if Erasmus in this book thought good between *game and earnest* to rebuke the same?'

In later plays, particularly those written for coterie audiences after 1600, many characters are stylizations of earlier characterizations. The discontented and satirical Hamlet spawned many progeny, among them Malevole in Marston's *Malcontent* (1603) and Philaster in Beaumont and Fletcher's play of the same name (1609). Hamlet speaks of putting on an 'antic disposition' (2.1.173) – the word 'antic' had connotations of both madness and monstrosity. The moment kindles a comparison with the way in which actors visibly adopted a role or disposition: characters so created often spoke both for themselves and for the play or company. As 'antics' they had a licence for scabrous lampooning: here is Malevole, in fact the disguised Duke Altofront, slagging off a court parasite with accusations of sodomitical behaviour:

> MALEVOLE Yaugh, God o'man, what dost thou there? Duke's Ganymede, Juno's jealous of thy long stockings. Shadow of a woman, what wouldst, weasel? Thou lamb o'court, what dost thou bleat for? Ah, you smooth-chinned catamite!
>
> PIETRO Come down, thou ragged cur, and snarl here. I give thy dogged sullenness free liberty: trot about and bespurtle whom thou pleasest.
>
> MALEVOLE I'll come among you, you goatish-blooded toderers [libertines], as gum into taffeta, to fret [fray], to fret. I'll fall like a sponge into water to suck up, to suck up. Howl again. I'll go to church and come to you. (1.2.5–16)

'Ganymede', the name provocatively adopted by Rosalind in *As You Like It*, was slang for a catamite or male whore.

The bawdy asides often sprinkled through dialogue like this signal camaraderie between player and audience. But even in the public playhouses wordplay and meta-theatrical references ('If this were played upon a stage, now, I could condemn it as an improbable fiction' [*Twelfth Night*, 3.4.108–9]) must have established a circuit of wit running between player and spectator that did not always encompass the character whose deeds were being enacted.

The donning of a self-created self was also a technique for a politician. At the end of *Richard III* the tyrant asks himself in soliloquy:

> What do I fear? My self? There's none else by.
> Richard loves Richard; that is, I am I. (5.5.136–7)

The mask of villainy will not come off: the proud vaunt of the martial hero, 'I am I' (*soy quién soy* in the plays of the seventeenth-century Spanish dramatist Calderón), here acknowledges a spiritual wound. Bacon wrote of another politic counterfeiter, Perkin Warbeck: 'Nay, himself, with long and continued counterfeiting, and with oft telling a lie, was turned by habit almost into the thing he seemed to be; and from a liar to a believer.'[12]

It can be argued that, in contrast to these theatrical personages, audiences did not 'believe in' the characters exhibited in the theatrical plays – so much like games (see chapter 2) – that they attended. We might also remember that the notion of play can encompass the imaginative feats of children at play who offer highly stylized versions of the characters they enact. In this kind of context, 'character' is not equivalent to 'personality'.

When grown-ups take part in sports or watch sporting fixtures they too are engaging in highly codified or stylized feats of activity. Modern spectator sports take place upon playing fields; early modern stages are usefully considered as 'fields of play'. A familiar version of games of supposes in Shakespearean comedy is that of the instability of gender. Rosalind in *As You Like It* disguises herself as a man and then in masculine attire plays the part of a woman. On the stage, through disguise or techniques of personation, players could read and change the gender inscriptions or attributes that were written upon their bodies.[13]

Perhaps the conclusion is that our prime effort should not be to uncover the inward life of characters we encounter when reading texts like the ones mentioned above. Inwardness, however, as the twentieth-century philosopher Ludwig Wittgenstein considered, may be perceived in theatrical performance. One of his examples is Shakespeare's Macbeth:

> Here is the point of Behaviourism: it isn't that they deny there are feelings. But they say our description of behaviour *is* our description of feelings.
>
> 'What did he feel when he said: "Duncan is in his grave"?' Can I describe his feelings better than by describing how he said it? All other descriptions are crude compared with a description of the gesture he made, the tone of voice with which he made it.
>
> What is a description of feeling at all? What is a description of pain?
>
> Discussion of a comedian doing imitations, sketches. Suppose you want to describe the experience of the audience – why not describe first

of all what they saw? Then perhaps that they shook with laughter, then what they said.

'This can't be a description of their feelings.' One says this because one is thinking of their organic feelings – tension of the muscles in their chest, etc. This would obviously be an experience. But it doesn't seem half as important as the fact that they said so and so. *One thinks of a description of experience not as a description of an action, but as a description of pain or organic feelings.*[14]

We might attend primarily not to attributing feelings to the personages we construct in our minds as we read, but to deciphering the performances of players representing these personages. The success of such a performance will derive not necessarily from congruence to a postulated inner life of the person represented but from the way it coheres with all other aspects of the particular production.

People as Objects in Verse and Prose

Rhetorical handbooks included sets of exercises (*progymnasmata*) intended to prepare students for the writing of exercise orations and the like (*gymnasmata*). The set put together by Aphthonius of Antioch (AD c.400) was still used in the Renaissance. These are his notes on *ekphrasis* (which then meant simply 'description'):

Description is an expository discourse that brings the object exhibited vividly into view.

One may describe persons and things, times and places, irrational creatures and in addition plants. Persons: e.g., Homer's 'He was round-shouldered, dark-skinned, with curly hair'; things: e.g., sea-battles and land-battles, like the historian; times: e.g., spring and summer, explaining what flowers grow during them; places: e.g., Thucydides spoke of the shape of the Thesprotian harbour Chimerium. In describing persons one should proceed from beginning to end, i.e. *from head to feet*; in describing things, from what precedes them, what is in them, and what tends to result from them; in describing times and places, from what surrounds them and what is contained in them.[15]

That rhetorical method for writing the body, for proceeding from 'head to feet' – known as a 'blazon' – is evident in countless Renaissance love poems:

Her goodly eyes like Sapphires shining bright,
Her forehead ivory white,
Her cheeks like apples which the sun hath rudded,
Her lips like cherries charming men to bite,
Her breast like to a bowl of cream uncrudded,
Her paps like lilies budded,
Her snowy neck like to a marble tower,
And all her body like a palace fair,
Ascending up with many a stately stair,
To Honour's seat and Chastity's sweet bower.
                    (Spenser, *Epithalamion*, 171–80)

However, it is patently not the case that this passage brings the woman to the mind's eye or, in Aphthonius' phrase, 'vividly into view'. Nor does the following, a description of Shakespeare's Tarquin as he with his eyes devours the sleeping Lucrece:

As the grim lion fawneth o'er his prey,
Sharp hunger by the conquest satisfied,
So o'er this sleeping soul doth Tarquin stay,
His rage of lust by gazing qualified;
Slaked not suppressed for standing by her side,
    His eye, which late this mutiny restrains,
    Unto a greater uproar tempts his veins;

And they like straggling slaves for pillage fighting,
Obdurate vassals fell exploits effecting,
In bloody death and ravishment delighting,
Nor children's tears nor mothers' groans respecting,
Swell in their pride, the onset still expecting.
    Anon his *beating heart*, alarum striking,
    Gives the hot charge, and bids them do their liking.

His drumming heart cheers up his burning eye,
His eye commends the leading to his hand;
His hand, as proud of such a dignity,
Smoking with pride marched on to make his stand
On her bare breast, the heart of all her land;
    Whose ranks of blue veins as his hand did scale
    Left their round turrets destitute and pale.

They, must'ring to the quiet cabinet
Where their dear governess and lady lies,
Do tell her she is dreadfully beset,
And fright her with confusion of their cries.
She, much amazed, breaks ope her locked-up eyes,
    Who, peeping forth this tumult to behold,
    Are by his flaming torch dimmed and controlled.
                (Shakespeare, *The Rape of Lucrece*, 421–48)

The modulation of imagery, from Tarquin as beast of prey through the description of the battle of his faculties until he becomes a warlord commanding pillage, says a lot about this kind of masculinity.[16] The unusual use of feminine rhymes in the second stanza quoted may evoke his 'beating heart'. Description in the Renaissance, as well as being a technique, was built around rhetorical topics which were used as means to a general end, that of working upon the reader or auditor's (moral) sensibility. The language in these two passages is suited not to truth to reality, but truth to type: the purpose in the first is to eulogize and say something about the way that beauty is an index of the good; in the second to say something about the relationship between Tarquin's rampaging desire and the culture he inhabits.

From a rhetorical point of view (see chapter 1) we also find poets 'inventing' and arranging stock images. In 1582, twenty-five-year-old Thomas Watson published *The Hekatompathia or Passionate Century of Love*. As well as supplying marginal notes to the passages in classical texts from which he had borrowed details, he prefixed each of his (eighteen-line) sonnets with a headnote that describes its quality. This is the seventh sonnet:

This passion of love is lively expressed by the author in that he lavishly praiseth the person and beautiful ornaments of his love, one after another as they lie in order. He partly imitateth herein Aeneas Silvius [Enea Silvio Piccolomini (1405–64), later Pope Pius II] *who setteth down the like in describing Lucretia, the love of Euryalus* [in his erotic narrative *Euryalus and Lucretia*]; *and partly he followeth Ariosto* [*Orlando Furioso*], *Canto 7, where he describeth Alcina; and partly borroweth from some others where they describe the famous Helen of Greece . . .*

Hark you that list to hear what saint I serve:
Her yellow locks exceed the beaten gold,

Her sparkling eyes in heaven a place deserve,
Her forehead high and fair of comely mould,
   Her words are music all of silver sound,
   Her wit so sharp as like can scarce be found,
Each eyebrow hangs like Iris in the skies,
On either cheek a rose and lily lies,
Her breath is sweet perfume, or holy flame,
   Her lips more red than any coral stone,
   Her neck more white than agèd swans that moan,
Her breast transparent is, like crystal rock,
Her fingers long, fit for Apollo's lute,
Her slipper such as Momus [the personification of criticism] dare
   not mock,
Her virtues all so great as make me mute:
   What other parts she hath I need not say,
   Whose face alone is cause of my decay. (sig. A4^r)

Shakespeare parodied such catalogue poems in 'My mistress' eyes are nothing like the sun' (Sonnet 130), as did Donne in his second elegy, 'The Anagram', which remarks of Flavia:

Though all her parts be not in th'usual place,
She hath yet an anagram of a good face. (15–16)

The jest was reduced to absurdity in Charles Sorel's, *The Extravagant Shepherd: An Anti-Romance* (1627), translated into English in 1654, in which the hero, having requested a picture of his beloved Charite, finds that:

Anselm had in this business acted a piece of ingenious knavery. Observing what the shepherd had told him of the beauty of his mistress, and imitating the extravagant descriptions of the poets, he had painted a face which, instead of being of a flesh-colour, was of a complexion white as snow. There were . . . upon each cheek a lily and a rose, crossing one the other. Where there should have been eyes, there was neither white nor apple, but two suns sending forth beams, among which were observed certain flames and darts. The eye-brows were black as ebony, and were made like two bows . . . Above that . . . was Love, like a little child, seated in his throne . . . The hair floated about all this in diverse manners: some of it . . . was twisted and made like networks, and in many places there hanged lines, with hooks ready baited. There were a many hearts taken with the bait.[17]

FIGURE 4 'The metaphorical picture', illustration to Charles Sorel, *The Extravagant Shepherd, or the History of Lysis: An Anti-Romance* [1627], trans. John Davies (London, 1660 edn), pp. 22–3, London, British Library.

As well as being an amusing parody of narrative and descriptive techniques in the manner of *Don Quixote*, this passage reminds us that 'images' very seldom resemble pictures, but rather offer a way of examining the way in which the poet's mind is making sense of the world.

This 'metaphorical picture' is a version of the topic of the tyrant woman. Poems that contain any kind of narrative and which involve women are likely to follow in the tradition of Petrarch and ascribe absolute power to the mistress. Petrarch had allegorized this topic in his *Trionfo d'Amore* (c.1358), illustrated by Botticelli and others with a triumphant chariot bearing armed Cupids. Poets adorned such fables with conceits depicting, for example, wounds inflicted by Cupids hiding in the lady's eyebrows:

> Fly, fly, my friends, I have my death wound; fly.
> See there that boy, that murth'ring boy I say,
> Who like a thief hid in dark bush doth lie
> Till bloody bullet get him wrongful prey.
> So, tyrant he, no fitter place could spy,
> Nor so fair level in so secret stay,
> As that sweet black which veils the heav'nly eye;
> There himself with his shot he close doth lay.
> (Sidney, Astrophil and Stella, 20.1–8)

Eros is usually apprehended only through metaphor: here the metaphoric structure is of sweet warfare. In other poems, courtesy or courtly love draws upon the discourses of hunting or of political transactions and on the rhetoric of power.

However, women could and did respond. Lady Mary Wroth wrote a sequence of sonnets, probably in the second decade of the seventeenth century, *Pamphilia to Amphilanthus* ('The All-loving to the Equivocator in Love'). In this sonnet she reduces Cupid, the dauntless god of love, to a lost child:

> Late in the forest I did Cupid see
>   Cold, wet, and crying, he had lost his way
>   And, being blind, was farther like to stray;
> Which sight a kind compassion bred in me.
>
> I kindly took and dried him, while that he
>   (Poor child) complained he starvèd was with stay

And pined for want of his accustomed prey,
For none in that wild place his host would be.

I glad was of his finding, thinking sure,
  This service should my freedom still procure,
    And in my arms I took him then unharmed,
Carrying him safe unto a myrtle bower;
  But in the way he made me feel his power,
    Burning my heart, who had him kindly warmed. (No. 139)

It would be easy to deduce from the content alone of this poem that
it was written by a woman, and tempting to conjecture that it is a
description not just of Cupid but of the helplessness and perfidious-
ness of men in general.

Person and Persona

Just as characters in the playhouse are much involved with self-
presentation, certain kinds of poem demand that the reader apprehend the temperament or disposition of its speaker or 'persona'. (The
Latin word *persona* means 'mask'.) In 1753 Georges-Louis Leclerc,
Conte de Buffon was to coin the famous aphorism *'le style est l'homme
même'* (style is the man himself). In Renaissance poems, particular
styles are adopted to create both speaker and an implied reader or
listener for the poem. This obviously occurs in the sonnets quoted
above; more extended examples are to be found in poems from the
complaint tradition, some of which derive from *The Mirror for Magistrates* (1559), and which look forward to nineteenth-century dramatic
monologues. Samuel Daniel's 'The Complaint of Rosamond' (1592)
tells the story of the seduction and death of Rosamond Clifford, mistress to Henry II. It opens with a confession, which suggests that the
text will unfold moralistically:

Out from the horror of infernal deeps
My poor afflicted ghost comes here to plain it,
Attended with my shame that never sleeps,
The spot wherewith my kind [character] and youth did stain it.
My body found a grave where to contain it:
  A sheet could hide my face, but not my sin,
  For Fame finds never tomb t'enclose it in.

And which is worse, my soul is now denied
Her transport to the sweet Elysian rest,
The joyful bliss for ghosts repurified,
The ever-springing Gardens of the Blest:
Charon [the ferryman over the river Styx in Hades] denies me
     waftage with the rest.
  And says my soul can never pass the river
  Till lovers' sighs on earth shall it deliver. (1–14)

However, Rosamond's inner thoughts are interestingly explored by having her inspect and decipher the ornamentation upon a casket presented to her by the king:

The day before the night of my defeature
He greets me with a casket richly wrought;
So rare that Art did seem to strive with Nature
T'express the cunning workman's curious [ingenious] thought;
The mystery whereof I prying sought
  And found engraven on the lid above,
  Amymone, how she with Neptune strove.

Amymone, old Danaus' fairest daughter,
As she was fetching water all alone
At Lerna, whereas Neptune came and caught her;
From whom she strived and struggled to be gone,
Beating the air with cries and piteous moan;
  But all in vain, with him she's forced to go;
  'Tis shame that men should use poor maidens so.

There might I see describèd how she lay
At those proud feet, not satisfied with prayer:
Wailing her heavy hap, cursing the day,
In act so piteous to express despair;
And by how much more grieved, so much more fair.
  Her tears upon her cheeks (poor careful [grief-ridden] girl)
  Did seem against the sun crystal and pearl:

Whose pure clear streams (which lo so fair appears)
Wrought hotter flames (O miracle of love
That kindles fire in water, heat in tears,
And makes neglected beauty mightier prove,
Teaching afflicted eyes affects to move);

> To show that nothing ill becomes the fair,
> But cruelty, which yields unto no prayer.   (379–406)

Her reading of this *ekphrasis* (here designating not simply description but a representation of a representation) of a classical rape reveals that she was fully aware not only of the vigour of masculine sadism but also of the consequences that were likely to ensue if she continued her dalliance:

> I saw the sin wherein my foot was ent'ring,
> I saw how that dishonour did attend it,
> I saw the shame whereon my flesh was vent'ring,
> Yet had I not the power for to defend it:
> So weak is sense, when error hath condemned it.
>   We see what's good, and thereto we consent,
>   But yet we choose the worst, and soon repent.   (428–34)

Daniel alludes to one of the most quoted utterances in classical literature: *video meliora proboque deteriora sequor* (translated by Arthur Golding as 'The best I see and like: the worst I follow headlong still'), spoken by Ovid's Medea as she strives to quench her love for Jason (*Metamorphoses*, 7, 20–1). But dally Rosamond did.

Lyrics, too, can be dramatic and not merely melodic. Often we feel that the author's style has created a speaker or persona who may, as in a theatrical soliloquy, be addressing himself or be heard as one side of a dialogue, addressing an imagined presence. Generally, this is a loved one, but Donne's 'Go and Catch a Falling Star', for instance, may be taken to be addressing a friend who shares the scorn for feminine constancy proclaimed by the persona. Deducing possible responses to the declarations or persuasions is a way of detecting irony in such texts.

In both verse and drama, lyrical registers in soliloquies or dialogue may allow us to impute subjectivity or inwardness. Their characteristic richness of imagery can give the impression of a mind in action. Modern readers often judge verse by its seeming degree of sincerity. Such a criterion, as we have seen, may be inappropriate for a lot of Renaissance verse, but if we assume that some of the period's love poems were written to persuade the loved one of the lover's passion rather than to conjure admiration from members of a coterie for the poet's technique, it was obviously necessary to convey some kind of 'truth'. This might come not only from idiosyncratic variations upon familiar topics, but also from the sound or tone of the poem. One method is to play the *rhythm* of the persona's speaking voice against the *metre* of the poem (the normative pattern of stressed and unstressed syllables), and to avoid fitting sentences and syntactic breaks to line endings (the trick of enjambment). John Donne prided himself on his 'strong lines', his 'masculine persuasive force' (Elegy 16, 'On his Mistress'). The fervency of some of the poems comes from this striving between rhythm and metre, as in 'The Good Morrow' where the speaker urges his lover to ignore conformist worldly heroisms and to force their two private spheres into one, distinctive and secure:

> Let sea-discoverers to new worlds have gone;
> Let maps, to others, worlds on worlds have shown;
> Let us possess one world: each hath one and is one.

Thomas Carew described the effect in his 'Elegy upon the Death of Dr John Donne': 'to the awe of thy imperious wit / Our stubborn language bends'. But we also note a paradox: that Donne has provided a technical code or convention for sincerity.

Persons in Prose

Set descriptions of people in prose narratives are less common than in verse. In order to create character, authors as different as Sir Philip Sidney and Thomas Deloney (1543–1600) rely upon dialogue. In Sidney's *Arcadia*, however, one of the main characters, Musidorus, is described after being found shipwrecked. He appears as an icon of virtue:

> upon the mast they saw a young man . . . bearing show of about eighteen years of age, who sat as on horse-back having nothing upon him but his shirt which, being wrought with blue silk and gold, had a kind of resemblance to the sea: on which the sun (then near his western home) did shoot some of his beams. His hair (which the young men of Greece used to wear very long) was stirred up and down with the wind, which seemed to have a sport to play with it, as the sea

had to kiss his feet; himself full of admirable beauty, set forth by the strangeness both of his seat and gesture: for, holding his head up full of unmoved majesty, he held a sword aloft with his fair arm, which often he waved about his crown as though he would threaten the world in that extremity.[18]

In contrast, in Nashe's *The Unfortunate Traveller* (1594), we find this description of a Roman master craftsman, in fact an executioner:

At the first chop with his wood-knife would he fish for a man's heart and fetch it out as easily as a plum from the bottom of a porridge pot. He would crack necks as fast as a cook cracks eggs; a fiddler cannot turn his pin so soon as he would turn a man off the ladder. Bravely did he drum on this Cutwolf's bones, not breaking them outright but, like a saddler knocking in of tacks, jarring on them quaveringly with his hammer a great while together. No joint about him but, with a hatchet he had for the nonce, he disjointed half, and then with boiling lead soldered up the wounds from bleeding. His tongue he pulled out, least he should blaspheme in his torment. Venomous stinging worms he thrust into his ears to keep his head ravingly occupied; with cankers scruzed [caterpillars squeezed] to pieces he rubbed his mouth and his gums. No limb of his but was lingeringly splintered in shivers. In this horror left they him on the wheel as in hell – where yet living he might behold his flesh legacied amongst the fowls of the air.[19]

The description may seem crammed with gruesome detail, but its energy comes from its bravura figures of speech: like the passages from the Henry IV plays quoted above, it is a feat of language rather than documentary, and stands at the end of this picaresque fiction as a epiphany of the outlandish horrors of papist Rome.

More descriptive writing about people occurs in 'character books', which became popular about 1608 when Joseph Hall published his *Characters of Virtues and Vices*. Such texts draw from the *Characters* of the Greek philosopher Theophrastus (c.372–287 BC) and resemble brief essays in conversational style on moral types or satirical sketches. The following defence of the profession of playing and definition of quality in acting is cast in this mould. It was published anonymously with Sir Thomas Overbury's poem 'A Wife' in 1615, and is now attributed to the dramatist John Webster:

An Excellent Actor

Whatsoever is commendable in the grave orator is most exquisitely perfect in him, for, by a full and significant action of body, he charms our attention. Sit in a full theatre and you will think you see so many lines drawn from the circumference of so many ears whiles the actor is the centre. He doth not strive to make Nature monstrous: she is often seen in the same scene with him, but neither on stilts nor crutches; and for his voice, 'tis not lower than the prompter nor louder than the foil and target [small shield]. By his action he fortifies moral precepts with examples; for what we see him personate, we think truly done before us. A man of deep thought might apprehend the ghosts of our ancient heroes walked again, and take him (at several times) for many of them. He is much affected to painting [making of images], and 'tis a question whether that make him an excellent player or his playing an exquisite painter. He adds grace to the poet's labours: for what in the poet is but ditty, in him is both ditty and music. He entertains us in the best leisure of our life, that is between meals, the most unfit time either for study or bodily exercise. The flight of hawks and chase of wild beasts, either of them are delights noble: but some think this sport of men worthier despite all calumny. All men have been of his occupation: and indeed what he doth feignedly that do others essentially: this day one plays a monarch, the next a private person. Here one acts a tyrant, on the morrow an exile; a parasite this man tonight, tomorrow a precisian [puritan], and so of divers others. I observe of all men living a worthy actor in one kind is the strongest motive of affection that can be: for when he dies, we cannot be persuaded any man can do his parts like him. Therefore the imitating characterist was extreme idle in calling them rogues. His muse, it seems, with all his loud invocation, could not be waked to light him a snuff [candle-end] to read the statute [against 'rogues, vagabonds, and sturdy beggars' of 1598]: for I would let his malicious ignorance understand that rogues are not to be employed as main ornaments to His Majesty's Revels; but the itch of bestriding the press, or getting up on this wooden Pacolet [magical horse] hath defiled more innocent paper then ever did laxative physic [medicine]. Yet is their invention such tired stuff that, like Kentish post-horse, they cannot go beyond their ordinary stage, should you flay them. But to conclude, I value a worthy actor by the corruption of some few of the quality as I would do gold in the ore; I should not mind the dross but the purity of the metal.

Places

Just as, to modern eyes, many of the persons we have looked at seem 'artificial' rather than derived from experience, few fictive places originate from reportage. Landscapes (the word entered the language in 1598) tended not to be descriptions but based on rhetorical topics that were inserted into texts in order to persuade readers to accept moral doctrines (see also the examples of pastoral discussed in chapter 3).

In playhouses, as we have seen, there were no sets to represent places – there were certainly, for example, no painted flats to replicate Simon Eyre's workshop in Dekker's *The Shoemaker's Holiday*. However, *settings* were, when appropriate, established by three-dimensional mansions or devices. A Swiss traveller, Thomas Platter, observed tents ('*Zelten*') on the stage during a performance at the Curtain playhouse in 1599.[20] The various trees and 'mossy banks' listed among Henslowe's properties[21] must have signified to contemporary audiences not 'woodlands' but 'pastoral', not place but mode.

Just as Dekker offered a banquet of technical language in *The Shoemaker's Holiday*, Jonson parades London place-names in the opening chorus to *The Devil is an Ass* (1616):

> I will fetch thee a leap
> From the top of Paul's steeple to the Standard in Cheap . . .
> We will survey the suburbs and make forth our sallies
> Down Petticoat Lane and up the Smock Alleys,
> To Shoreditch, Whitechapel, and so to Saint Kather'n's,
> To drink with the Dutch there, and take forth their patterns.

Such profusion of local names is rare, but many play texts contain references to real places. Jonson's use of old-fashioned metre reminds us that details are codified: not there to create a likeness of urban *reality* but to offer what Roland Barthes' termed a 'reality effect' (*effet de réel*),[22] an indication that the fantastic action has to do with political and social *actuality*.

When Sidney turns to describe the landscape of Arcadia, the effect of idealization is as apparent as in his description of Musidorus. The aesthetic serves a moral conviction rather than a desire to portray sensuousness or reality:

There were hills which garnished their proud heights with stately trees; humble valleys whose base estate seemed comforted with refreshing of silver rivers; meadows enamelled with all sorts of eye-pleasing flowers; thickets, which, being lined with most pleasant shade, were witnessed so too by the cheerful deposition [testimony] of many well-tuned birds; each pasture stored with sheep feeding with sober security, while the pretty lambs with bleating oratory craved the dams' comfort; here a shepherd's boy piping, as though he should never be old; there a young shepherdess knitting, and withal singing, and it seemed that her voice comforted her hands to work, and her hands kept time to her voice's music. As for the houses of the country – for many houses came under their eye – they were all scattered, no two being one by the other, and yet not so far off as that it barred mutual succour: a show, as it were, of *an accompanable* [sociable] *solitariness, and of a civil wildness.*[23]

Inscribed upon this *paysage moralisé* is a *public* ideal: the hills and valleys reproduce social hierarchy, the fields have not been enclosed, the pastoral society of shepherds implicitly critiques court and city, and the houses are set in a very English way to combine community with privacy. The passage is locked up with two conspicuous oxymorons. We realize that the landscape described is itself a *representation* of an ideal order, so Sidney's description is another kind of *ekphrasis*, a representation in words of what was represented in the idealized landscape.[24] There is practically no description of landscape or cityscape in another important prose romance, Lyly's *Euphues and his England* (1580): descriptive passages there concentrate on the manners of those Euphues meets on his travels.

In verse, as we might now expect, we find no more 'realism' than in prose. At the opening of *The Faerie Queene*, the Knight of the Red Cross accompanied by Una is forced to take shelter from a storm of rain:

> Enforst to seeke some couert nigh at hand,
>   A shadie groue not far away they spide,
>   That promist ayde the tempest to withstand:
>   Whose loftie trees yclad with sommers pride,
>   Did spred so broad, that heauens light did hide,
>   Not perceable with power of any starre:
>   And all within were pathes and alleies wide,
>   With footing worne, and leading inward farre:
> Faire harbour that them seemes; so in they entred arre.

And foorth they passe, with pleasure forward led,
   Ioying to heare the birdes sweet harmony,
   Which therein shrouded from the tempest dred,
   Seemd in their song to scorne the cruell sky.
   Much can they prayse the trees so straight and hy,
   The sayling Pine, the Cedar proud and tall,
   The vine-prop Elme, the Poplar neuer dry,
   The builder Oake, sole king of forrests all,
The Aspine good for staues, the Cypresse funerall.

   The Laurell, meed of mightie Conquerours
   And Poets sage, the Firre that weepeth still,
   The Willow worne of forlorne Paramours,
   The Eugh [yew] obedient to the benders will,
   The Birch for shaftes, the Sallow for the mill,
   The Mirrhe sweet bleeding in the bitter wound,
   The warlike Beech, the Ash for nothing ill,
   The fruitfull Oliue, and the Platane round,
The caruer Holme [holm-oak suitable for carving], the Maple seeldom
   inward sound.

Led with delight, they thus beguile the way,
   Vntill the blustring storme is ouerblowne;
   When weening to returne, whence they did stray,
   They cannot finde that path, which first was showne,
   But wander too and fro in wayes vnknowne,
   Furthest from end then, when they neerest weene,
   That makes them doubt, their wits be not their owne:
   So many pathes, so many turnings seene,
That which of them to take, in diuerse doubt they been.

(The Faerie Queene, 1.1.7–10)

This grove combines features of the idealized 'mixed forest' with an epic catalogue of trees, which can be traced back to Virgil and Ovid as well as Chaucer's *Parliament of Fowls*, and the rhetorical topic of the *locus amoenus* (see chapter 1).[25] It melds into a place of confusion and error, characteristically glossed only later in the episode as the 'Wandering Wood' (i.e. a forest where one is likely to wander) or 'Error's Den' (stanza 13). This is an emblem of man's life that recalls Dante's *selva oscura* ('dark wood') at the beginning of his *Inferno*. It is a mental space, a very literary place.

When we turn to non-fictional prose, pictorializing descriptions are also spare. Even those who wrote accounts of the first colonizing ventures in the New World, for example Thomas Harriot's *A . . . Report of the New Found Land of Virginia* (1588), tend to catalogue what Harriot calls 'merchantable commodities'. Their descriptions are refracted through myths like that of Atlantis, the Golden Age, the isles of the blessed, or the lost tribes of Israel.[26] They turn out not to be simple documentaries or romances, reflections *of* other cultures, but, yet again, reflections *upon* the culture inhabited by their audiences.

We realize how seldom we encounter literary landscapes when we turn to Michael Drayton's immense poem in hexameter couplets, *Poly-Olbion*, published in two parts in 1612 and 1622. The title, from the Greek, means 'many blessings' and the title page of the 1613 edition calls it 'A chorographical description of tracts, rivers, mountains, forests and other parts of this renowned isle of Great Britain'. 'Chorographia' was a rhetorical figure for a description of a particular country or perhaps 'nation'. Like Harriot, Drayton feels that his task is to enumerate geographical features, particularly the rivers, which feature on the maps which divide the parts of the book one from another, and to intersperse his 'songs' with digests of the lives of the historical worthies associated with each place. This union of geography and history is part of a project of nation-building: 'Great Britain' at this time was, of course, a fiction as the legislative union of England and Scotland was not to take place until 1707. Here, for example, is part of his account of Glastonbury in Somerset, the reported place of the tomb of both King Arthur and, it was believed, Joseph of Arimathea:

> O three times famous isle, where is that place that might
> Be with thyself compared for glory and delight
> Whilst Glastonbury stood, exalted to that pride,
> Whose monastery seemed all other to deride?
> Oh, who thy ruin sees, whom wonder doth not fill
> With our great fathers' pomp, devotion, and their skill?
> Thou more than moral power (this judgement rightly weighed)
> Then present to assist at that foundation laid;
> On whom for this sad waste should Justice lay the crime?
> Is there a power in Fate, or doth it yield to Time?
> Or was their error such that thou couldst not protect
> Those buildings, which with their zeal erect?

To whom didst thou commit that monument to keep,
That suffreth with the dead their memory to sleep?[27]

Even when describing a site as distinctive as Glastonbury, Drayton makes it a topic for an historical meditation, interesting for its veiled condemnation of Henry VIII's dissolution of the monasteries some eighty years earlier, but creating no feeling or spirit of place.

This is no charge against a minor poet: Milton uses the topic of the *locus amoenus*, the cataloguing conventions of epic poetry, combined with reflection upon the arts of poetry and horticulture, to create in 1667 his famous description of the Garden of Eden. Once more we are reminded that Renaissance *ekphrasis* involves a representation of a representation: the natural objects listed in the passage are not to be seen in the mind's eye but to be understood as ways of demonstrating that nature shares in the divine:

> in this pleasant soil
> His far more pleasant garden God ordained;
> Out of the fertile ground he caused to grow
> All trees of noblest kind for sight, smell, taste;
> And all amid them stood the tree of life,
> High eminent, blooming ambrosial fruit
> Of vegetable gold; and next to life
> Our death the tree of knowledge grew fast by,
> Knowledge of good bought dear by knowing ill.
> Southward through Eden went a river large,
> Nor changed his course, but through the shaggy hill
> Passed underneath ingulfed, for God had thrown
> That mountain as his garden mould [soil] high raised
> Upon the rapid current, which through veins
> Of porous earth with kindly thirst up drawn,
> Rose a fresh fountain, and with many a rill
> Watered the garden; thence united fell
> Down the steep glade, and met the nether flood,
> Which from his darksome passage now appears,
> And now divided into four main streams,
> Runs diverse, wandering many a famous realm
> And country whereof here needs no account,
> But rather to tell how, if art could tell,
> How from that sapphire fount the crispèd brooks,

Rowling on orient pearl and sands of gold,
With mazy error under pendant shades
Ran nectar, visiting each plant, and fed
Flowers worthy of Paradise which not nice art
In beds and curious knots, but nature boon
Poured forth profuse on hill and dale and plain,
Both where the morning sun first warmly smote
The open field, and where the unpierced shade
Embrowned the noontide bowers: thus was this place,
A happy rural seat of various view . . .

(*Paradise Lost*, 4.214–47)

The essential features of this topic are all there: 'a beautiful, shaded natural site . . . trees . . . a meadow, and a spring or brook'.[28] Milton's narrative voice moves without strain from description of this earthly paradise into meditation upon the great paradox of the 'fortunate fall', 'knowledge of good bought dear by knowing ill'. What is intriguing in this depiction is the prolepsis, the anticipation of the fall of mankind, the indistinct omens of the river emerging from its 'darksome passage' and of the stream rolling 'with mazy error', as well as the witty appropriation of what so many gentlemen of England aspire to, 'a happy rural seat of various view'.

As so often, Shakespeare may be the great innovator: is the earliest true 'landscape' in English literature Edgar's description of the view from Dover Cliff in *King Lear* (4.6.11–24)?

CHAPTER 7

Godliness

Sectarianism and 'Atheism'

Then the soldiers, when they had crucified Jesus, took his garments
and made them into four parts, to every soldier a part, and his coat; and
the coat was without seam, woven from the top throughout. Therefore
they said one to another, 'Let us not divide it, but cast lots for it, whose
it shall be.' (John 19: 23–4, Geneva Version)

From the time of the church fathers, the seamless robe of Christ had
been the sign for a unified Christian church. This ideal was ripped
asunder by the waves of Reformation and Counter-Reformation that
made the English Renaissance an age of schism and sectarianism. In
1628, the satirist and parliamentary poet George Wither forcefully
deployed the gospel figure:

> We that have but one father and one mother,
> Do persecute and torture one another
> So hotly, we oppose not Antichrist
> As we our fellow brethren do resist.
> The Protestant, the Protestant defies;
> And, we ourselves, ourselves do scandalize.
> Our church we have exposèd to more scorn
> And *her fair seamless vestment rent and torn*
> By our own fury more than by their spite
> Who are to us directly opposite:
> To save an apple, we the tree destroy,
> And quarrels make for every needless toy.[1]

It is imperative to remember the religious factionalism of the period. We certainly cannot airily refer to what 'Christians' believed: through most of the period Christians, because of doctrinal differences, were slaughtering each other. (This also makes any invocation of '*the* Elizabethan world picture' at the least tendentious.) Catholic priests were tortured by being hung by the hands for up to twelve hours to extract the names of their co-religionists, then hanged by the neck before being cut down and disembowelled alive. Such theatrical executions inspired terror and were meant to inspire terror. They were far more to do with social control than with justice: priests were impeached as traitors because they were presumed to be fomenting rebellion. Catholic sectaries were not permitted freedom of conscience and were often deprived of their lands and wealth. It was to question this that the Catholic priest and poet Robert Southwell wrote *An Humble Supplication to Her Majesty,* secretly printed after his execution in 1595. 'Why should it be more treasonable to be made priests', he wrote, 'in the midsummer day of your first year than the next day before, or the last of Queen Mary's reign?'[2] He went on to envision the torments of English Catholics:

> They water their fountains with the showers of our tenderest veins and build their houses with the ruins of ours, tempering the mortar of their foundations with our innocent blood. Our livings are but snares for the owners' lives, commonly made the fee of every mercenary mouth that can, by sounding our disgraces into credulous ears, procure themselves warrants to seize upon our substance. They make our wills before we be sick, bequeathing to their own uses what share they like and, by displacing our offspring, adopt themselves to be heirs of our lands, begging and broking for them as if we were either condemned for fools or in perpetual minority; and not contented with our wealth, they persecute our lives, never thinking their possessions sure till the assurance be seasoned with our death.[3]

It was, however, not just a question of rooting out the papists: reformation stimulated a cultural revolution. The first part of a ditty by Richard Corbett (1582–1635) indicates the way in which so many aspects of the nation's life and beliefs were infused by religious change:

A Proper New Ballad, Entitled 'The Fairies' Farewell' . . . To be Sung or Whistled to the Tune of 'The Meadow Brow' by the Learned, by the Unlearned to the Tune of 'Fortune [My Foe]'

'Farewell rewards and fairies',
  Good housewives now may say,
For now foul sluts in dairies
  Do fare as well as they;
And though they sweep their hearths no less
  Than maids were wont to do,
Yet who of late for cleanliness,
  Finds sixpence in her shoe?

Lament, lament, old abbeys,
  The fairies lost command;
They did but change priests' babies –
  But some have changed your land;
And all your children stolen from thence
  Are now grown Puritans
Who live as changelings ever since
  For love of your domains.

At morning and at evening both
  You merry were and glad,
So little care of sleep and sloth,
  These pretty ladies had:
When Tom came home from labour
  Or Cis to milking rose,
Then merrily went their tabor
  And nimbly went their toes.

Witness those rings and roundelays
  Of theirs which yet remain,
Were footed in Queen Mary's days
  On many a grassy plane;
But since of late Elizabeth
  And later James came in,
They never danced on any heath
  As when the time had been.

By which we note the fairies
  Were of the old profession,

> Their songs were Ave Maries,
>   Their dances were procession [Romish litanies sung in procession];
> But now alas they all are dead
>   Or gone beyond the seas,
> Or further from religion fled –
>   Or else they take their ease.[4]

Given such effects of religious change upon common life, it is often more apt to refer to 'Reformation England' than 'Renaissance England' (as the title of this book implies).

Obviously, therefore, unlike the eighteenth-century Enlightenment, secularizing movements in England did not lead to widespread religious disbelief. A small piece of evidence for secularization comes from John Florio: in 1598, part of his translation of the Italian word '*sapiéntia*' was 'knowledge of things divine and human'. This is the summary Stoic definition of wisdom, *rerum humanarum divinarumque scientia*, reported by St Augustine and repeated countless times throughout the Middle Ages and the Renaissance. Yet, by 1611, Florio apparently considered that this translation of *sapiéntia*, used in the first edition of his Italian–English dictionary only thirteen years before, was out of date and replaced it with a doubtless more modern and provocatively secular concept, 'knowledge of many things'.[5] Yet when, in 'An Anatomy of the Word: The First Anniversary', Donne famously proclaimed that 'new philosophy calls all in doubt', his 'all' did not encompass godhead. So when Fulke Greville inveighed against 'atheism' towards the end of the sixteenth century, the word, as for most of his contemporaries, had connotations of 'godless' behaviour:

> Thy powerful laws, Thy wonders of creation,
> Thy word incarnate, glorious heaven, dark hell,
> Lie shadowed under man's degeneration;
> Thy Christ still crucified for doing well;
>   Impiety, O Lord, sits on thy throne,
>   Which makes Thee, living light, a God unknown.
>
> Mans' superstition hath thy truth entombed,
> His *atheism* again her pomps defaceth;
> That sensual unsatiable vast womb
> Of Thy seen church Thy unseen Church disgraceth.
>   There lives no truth with them that seem Thine own,
>   Which makes thee, living Lord, a God unknown.
>   (*Caelica*, Sonnet 109: 13–24)

Martin Luther, commenting on Exodus 33 where Moses is allowed to see only the back parts of God and not his face, had put into circulation the concept of '*deus absconditus*' (a hidden God), but God was almost always deemed to exist.

In some instances, the word 'atheism' had a more technical meaning: the insistence that God had to be known through reason rather than through faith. This is the meaning it has in a passage from an elegy by William Habington:

> Who will with silent piety confute
> *Atheistic sophistry,* and by the fruit
> Approve [attest] religion's tree? Who'll teach his blood
> A virgin law, and dare be great and good?[6]

When, in Marlowe's play, Dr Faustus attempts to disprove the possibility of life after death, he picks up Jerome's Bible and, with seeming skill, proves syllogistically from scriptural texts (Rom. 6: 23 and 1 John 1: 8) that all men are condemned to everlasting death (B text, 1.1.36–48). Many in the audience would have been familiar with this argument, for it is found in the *Book of Homilies*. In 'The First Part of the Sermon of the Misery of Man', the same texts are clearly expounded and the same conclusion reached. But the deduction, the homily asserts, is false:

> It hath been manifestly declared unto you that no man can fulfil the law of God, and therefore by the law all men are condemned; whereupon it followed necessarily that some other thing should be required for our salvation than the law, and that is a true and lively faith in Christ, bringing forth good works and a life according to God's commandments.[7]

Fulke Greville, like his intellectual hero, Sir Philip Sidney, whose biography he wrote, was deeply imbued with the teachings of John Calvin. Calvin's theology stressed what *Caelica* 109 called 'man's degeneration'. Near the end of the *Arcadia*, Sidney had written 'In . . . a shadow or rather pit of darkness the wormish mankind lives, that neither they know how to foresee nor what to fear, and are but like tennis balls, tossed by the racket of the higher powers.'[8] Men's fortunes and fates were predestined, and Calvinists believed that only the 'elect' or chosen would achieve salvation. About 1634, the doctrine was parodied in a poem probably by a priest whose pseudonym was 'John Brereley':

But Protestants serve such a tyrant God
As doth (say they) inflict the dreadful rod
Of his eternal wrath, no care once had
Of any of their actions good or bad:
Yea, though they be the chief in Virtue's school,
They must be damned. Which is the greatest fool?[9]

Scepticism

One of the period's greatest religious poems, John Donne's third satire, 'Of Religion', squarely confronts the scepticism that must have tempted any thinking person during this time of religious war: civil wars, fired by religious difference, raged in France through the second half of the sixteenth century. The poem was written around 1592, about the same time as Marlowe's *Dr Faustus*, and it shares many of its themes. The poem enjoins its readers to regard the struggle for faith as more strenuous than that with the traditional temptations of the World, the Flesh, and the Devil (see Luke 4: 13) – although these, of course, must be eschewed:

So the World's self, thy other loved foe, is
In her decrepit wane; and thou, loving this,
Dost love a withered and worn strumpet. Last,
Flesh (itself death), and joys which flesh can taste,
Thou lovest; and thy fair goodly soul, which doth
Give this flesh power to taste joy, thou dost loathe.   (37–42)

The theatricality of these lines is not born from the cynicism of a young man who has not yet reconciled his sexual urges with his need to love and be loved, but from grave seriousness. The poem's persona is established at the poem's opening as a courtier who demands the attention of auditors inclined to frivolity or insouciance:

Kind pity chokes my spleen [seat of both mirth and melancholy];
   brave scorn forbids
Those tears to issue which swell my eyelids.
I must not laugh (nor weep) sins and be wise.   (1–3)

He then asks why religion is not as venerated as virtue was by the ancients before the incarnation of Christ. What follows is a review of

contemporary religious sectaries, Catholics, Calvinists, members of the
Church of England, as well as those who commit themselves to no
sect or are happy with any. They are figured as mistresses for Donne's
fellow wits, among whom the poem circulated in manuscript:

> Seek true religion. O where? Mirreus,
> Thinking her unhousèd here and fled from us,
> Seeks her at Rome: there because he doth know
> That she was there a thousand years ago;
> He loves the rags so, as we here obey
> The statecloth where the Prince sat yesterday.
> Crants to such brave loves will not be enthralled,
> But loves her only who at Geneva is called
> Religion: plain, simple, sullen, young,
> Contemptuous, yet unhandsome – as among
> Lecherous humours, there is one that judges
> No wenches wholesome but coarse country drudges.   (43–54)

The procedures of classical scepticism (set out in the writings of
Sextus Empiricus who flourished around AD 190) involved this disposition of contradictory positions. Such a procedure must induce
doubt but, like Michel de Montaigne (died 1592), whose motto was
'*Que scais-je?*' (What do I know?), Donne insists upon *wise doubt*:

> To adore, or scorn an image, or protest,
> May all be bad; *doubt wisely*: in strange way
> To stand inquiring [investigating] right is not to stray:
> To sleep, or run wrong, is: (76–9)

His exhortation turns to a magnificent image of the intellectual life:

> On a huge hill,
> Cragged and steep, Truth stands, and he that will
> Reach her, about must, and about must go;
> And what the hill's suddenness [steepness] resists, win so;
> Yet strive so, that before age, death's twilight,
> Thy soul rest, for none can work in that night;
> To will implies delay: therefore, now do.   (79–85)

He ends with an insistence that religious faith must be based upon
strength rather than self-abasement, but a strength that, paradoxically,
shuns mortal power and commits itself to trust in God:

As streams are, power is; those blest flowers that dwell
At the rough stream's calm head, thrive and do well,
But having left their roots and themselves given
To the stream's tyrannous rage, alas are driven
Through mills, and rocks, and woods, and at last, almost
Consumed in going, in the sea are lost:
So perish souls, which more choose men's unjust
Power from God claimed, than God himself to trust.   (103–10)

What T. S. Eliot wrote about Tennyson might be applied to this poem: 'In Memoriam can, I think, justly be called a religious poem, but for another reason than that which made it seem religious to his contemporaries. It is not religious because of the quality of its faith, but because of the quality of its doubt.'[10]

Donne, probably like Shakespeare, had been brought up in the Roman faith: about the time he wrote his elegies he apostatized by committing himself to the Church of England. In the third elegy, 'Change', he accosts his inconstant mistress with ribald images, wrenched from their places in religious controversy:

Although thy hand and *faith*, and *good works* too
Have sealed thy love, which nothing should undo,
Yea, though thou fall back, that *apostasy*
Confirm thy love, yet much, much I fear thee.   (1–4)

Perhaps this represents a kind of projection, perhaps the obscenities were intended to exorcize in some way a degree of religious agony. Whatever our conclusions, the poem reveals that it may be that both love and God can be known only through metaphor. In one of his holy sonnets, 'Show me, dear Christ, thy spouse so bright and clear', Donne reverses the metaphoric polarities of the secular poem and, in the fervency of his quest for a secure religious home, actually sexualizes the *topos* of the church as bride of Christ:

Dwells she with us, or, like adventuring knights,
First travel we to seek and then make love?
Betray, kind husband, thy spouse to our sights,
And let mine amorous soul court thy mild dove
Who is most true, and pleasing to Thee, then
When she's embraced and open to most men.   (9–14)

The religious poems of Andrew Marvell (1621–78), like those of Donne and George Herbert, use language from the domains of love, sexuality and politics to explore religious experience. In 'A Dialogue between the Resolved Soul and Created Pleasure' the two voices seem gendered: the part of Soul, we might imagine, being spoken by a chaste woman, Pleasure by a seducer. They might equally seem politicized, Soul having the sensibility of a principled parliamentarian, Pleasure that of a cavalier Royalist. Dramatizing these two points of view creates ironical detachment: in 1657 Marvell had succeeded Milton as Latin secretary to the Council of State under Cromwell, but his 'Horatian Ode upon Cromwell's Return from Ireland' (1650) is as critical of Cromwell as it is admiring.

The 'Dialogue' begins with the persona's romanticized visualization of (Royalist?) soldiers preparing to attack those supporting the cause of virtue:

> Courage, my soul, now learn to wield
> The weight of thine immortal shield;
> Close on thy head thy helmet bright,
> Balance thy sword against the fight.
> See where an army, strong as fair,
> With silken banners spreads the air.
> Now, if thou be'st that thing divine,
> In this day's combat let it shine:
> And show that Nature wants an art
> To conquer one resolvèd heart.
>   PLEASURE
> Welcome the creation's guest,
> Lord of earth and heaven's heir.
> Lay aside that warlike crest
> And of Nature's banquet share:
> Where the souls of fruits and flow'rs
> Stand prepared to heighten yours.
>   SOUL
> I sup above, and cannot stay
> To bait [stop at an inn] so long upon the way.
>   PLEASURE
> On these downy pillows lie,
> Whose soft plumes will thither fly;
> On these roses strewed so plain [smoothly]
> Lest one leaf thy side should strain.

SOUL
My gentler rest is on a thought,
Conscious of doing what I ought.   (1–24)

After tempting Soul with further courses of 'alluring sense' (47), Pleasure tempts his interlocutor with the gift of that knowledge for which Faustus sold his soul:

PLEASURE
Thou shalt know each hidden cause
And see the future time;
Try what depth the centre draws,
And then to heaven climb.
SOUL
None thither mounts by the degree [stair]
Of knowledge, but Humility.   (69–74)

Soul's response generates a final 'Chorus':

Triumph, triumph, victorious soul;
The world has not one pleasure more:
The rest does lie beyond the pole [pole-star],
And is thine everlasting store.   (75–8)

This would seem a fit conclusion were it not for the religious banality, pounding operatic rhythms and unfocused images of that final stanza. These suggest Marvell's rejection of his own moralization, a degree of sceptical detachment from orthodoxy.

The Diffusion of Catholic Spirituality

Like many of his contemporaries, Donne had been influenced by the methods of meditation that had been developed by St Ignatius of Loyola (1491–1556), founder of the Jesuits and one of the most influential figures of the Counter- (or Catholic) Reformation of the sixteenth century. Loyola had written a set of spiritual exercises that encouraged the practitioner first to bring to memory an episode of scriptural narrative, then to compose a place, rendered with the sight of the imagination, and then to place himself within the scene. Donne's

'Good Friday, 1613, Riding Westward' is an example of this genre. In 'The Burning Babe' the recusant priest Robert Southwell likewise conjures a vision methodically:

> As I in hoary winter's night stood shivering in the snow,
> Surprised I was with sudden heat, which made my heart to glow;
> And lifting up a fearful eye to view what fire was near,
> A pretty babe all burning bright did in the air appear;
> Who, scorchèd with excessive heat, such floods of tears did shed
> As though his floods should quench his flames, which with his tears
>   were fed.
> 'Alas,' quoth he, 'but newly born in fiery heats I fry,
> Yet none approach to warm their hearts or feel my fire but I!
> My faultless breast the furnace is, the fuel wounding thorns,
> Love is the fire, and sighs the smoke, the ashes shame and scorns;
> The fuel justice layeth on, and mercy blows the coals,
> The metal in this furnace wrought are men's defilèd souls,
> For which, as now on fire I am to work them to their good,
> So will I melt into a bath to wash them in my blood.'
> With this he vanished out of sight and swiftly shrunk away,
> And straight I called unto mind that it was Christmas day.

Protestant as well as Catholic poets took up Ignatian methods. (Many works by Catholics were openly published even though their authors were persecuted.) In Southwell's long poem *Saint Peter's Complaint*, three editions of which appeared in 1595, the year of his execution, we find a short meditation that dramatizes St Peter entering into dialogue with those within a house of sorrows:

> At Sorrows' door I knocked; they craved my name:
> I answered, 'One unworthy to be known.'
> 'What one?' say they. 'One worthiest of blame.'
> 'But who?' 'A wretch, not God's, nor yet his own.'
> 'A man?' 'O no, a beast, much worse.' 'What creature?'
> 'A rock.' 'How called?' 'The rock of scandal, Peter.'
>
> 'From whence?' 'From Caiphas' house.' 'Ah, dwell thou there?'
> 'Sin's farm [lease] I rented there, but now would leave it.'
> 'What rent?' 'My soul.' 'What gain?' 'Unrest and fear.'
> 'Dear purchase.' 'Ah, too dear. Will you receive it?'
> 'What shall we give?' 'Fit tears and times to plain [lament] me.'
> 'Come in', say they. Thus Griefs did entertain me.   (703–14)

George Herbert wrote a similar dialogue-lyric, 'Love (III)', placed at the end of the 'Church' section of his collection, *The Temple* (1633):

> Love bade me welcome; yet my soul drew back,
>   Guilty of dust and sin.
> But quick-eyed Love, observing me grow slack
>   From my first entrance in
> Drew nearer to me, sweetly questioning
>   If I lacked anything.
>
> 'A guest', I answered, 'worthy to be here';
>   Love said, 'You shall be he.'
> 'I, the unkind, ungrateful? Ah, my dear,
>   I cannot look on thee.'
> Love took my hand and smiling did reply,
>   'Who made the eyes, but I?'
>
> 'Truth, Lord, but I have marred them: let my shame
>   Go where it doth deserve.'
> 'And know you not', says Love, 'who bore the blame?'
>   'My dear, then I will serve.'
> 'You must sit down', says Love, 'and taste my meat'.
>   So I did sit and eat.

This dialogue-lyric is a meditation upon partaking of communion in heaven when the Lord 'will gird himself about, and make them to sit down at table, and will come forth and serve them' (Luke 12: 37). Herbert's follower Henry Vaughan (1621–95) often meditated upon creatures from the natural world: 'Cock-Crowing', 'The Star', 'The Palm-Tree'.

Another tradition that served both Protestants and Catholics is that laid out in emblem books. Emblems amalgamated an engraving, generally of a symbolic object or scene, a brief motto that the image illustrated, and a moralizing poem. They had emerged with Andrea Alciati's *Emblematum Liber* (1531). Alciati had been influenced by a set of religious and secular allegorical emblems supposed to have been written by an Egyptian magus, Horapollo Niliacus, *The Hieroglyphics*, which was translated into Greek in 1505 and had a major influence on Renaissance iconology. The elaboration of sacred emblems is associated with the Jesuits, but Georgette de Montenay's *Emblèmes, ou Devises*

Chrestiennes (1571) was produced by a Protestant woman, and a work of a Dutch Protestant, John van der Noot, *A Theatre for Worldlings*, appeared in England in 1569 with translations by the seventeen-year-old Edmund Spenser. (This work does not contain the usual Latin mottoes.) The twelfth poem describes the Beast of Revelation, chapter 12; in the engraving the Pope kneels before it in prayer:

> I saw an ugly beast come from the sea,
> That seven heads, ten crowns, ten horns did bear,
> Having thereon the vile blaspheming name.
> The cruel leopard she resembled much,
> Feet of a bear, a lion's throat she had.
> The mighty dragon [the devil] gave to her his power.
> One of her heads yet there I did espy,
> Still freshly bleeding of a grievous wound [the gospel].
> One cried aloud, 'What one is like' (quod he)
> 'This honoured dragon, or may him withstand?'
> And then came from the sea a savage beast,
> With dragon's speech, and showed his force by fire,
> With wondrous signs to make all wights adore
> The beast, in setting of her image up.

Richard Crashaw (1612/13–49), son of a Protestant divine, having converted to the Church of Rome, wrote an ecstatic poem about St Theresa, 'The Flaming Heart'. The poem is about an emblematic picture that shows Theresa swooning as she is struck by a seraph's dart of love. The argument is that the power of St Theresa exceeds that of the seraph, a power enshrined in her flaming heart:

> Leave her that, and thou shalt leave her
> Not one loose shaft but love's whole quiver.
> For in love's field was never found
> A nobler weapon than a wound.
> Love's passives are his activ'st part,
> The wounded is the wounding heart.
> O heart, the equal poise of love's both parts,
> Big alike with wound and darts.
> Live in these conquering leaves; live all the same,
> And walk through all tongues one triumphant flame.
> Live here, great heart, and love and die and kill,
> And bleed and wound, and yield and conquer still.

D.iij.

FIGURE 5 'An emblem from Van der Noot's *Theatre [for] Worldlings*', page from Jan Baptista van der Noot, *A Theatre, wherein be represented as well the miseries and calamities that follow the voluptuous Worldlings, as also the great joys and pleasures which the faithful do enjoy*, translated out of French by T. Roest, with Epigrams and Sonnets prefixed, the former translated from the *Sonnets* of Petrarch, and the latter from the *Visions* of Du Bellay, by Edmund Spenser (London, 1569), sig. Diij[r], London, British Library.

Let this immortal life, where're it comes,
Walk in a crowd of loves and martyrdoms.
Let mystic deaths wait on't, and wise souls be
The love-slain witnesses of this life of thee.
O sweet incendiary, show here thy art
Upon this carcase of a hard, cold, heart!
Let all thy scattered shafts of light that play
Among the leaves of thy large books of day,
Combined against this breast, at once break in
And take away from me my self and sin:
This gracious robbery shall thy bounty be,
And my best fortunes such fair spoils of me.
O thou undaunted daughter of desires,
By all thy dower of lights and fires,
By all the eagle in thee, all the dove,
By all thy lives and deaths of love,
By thy large draughts of intellectual day,
And by thy thirsts of love more large than they,
By all thy brim-filled bowls of fierce desire,
By thy last morning's draught of liquid fire,
By the full kingdom of that final kiss
That seized thy parting soul and sealed thee His,
By all the heav'ns thou hast in Him.
Fair sister of the Seraphim,
By all of Him we have in thee,
Leave nothing of my self in me.
Let me so read thy life that I
Unto all life of mine may die.   (69–108)

This flamboyantly conceited and paradoxical style, culminating in the breathless ecstatic invocation, derives from the Neapolitan poet Giambattista Marino (1569–1625): its high ornamentation and unification of forms, here painting and poetry, led later critics to consider it a manifestation of the Baroque.

Protestant Poetics

Protestantism was above all a religion of the Word: even though Thomas Traherne (1637–74) left in manuscript a prose work, *The Meditations on the Six Days of Creation*, which followed the precepts set out in the translation by John Heigham of *Meditations upon the Mysteries of our Holy Faith* by the Jesuit Luis de la Puente (1619), he 'Protestantized' his texts by including extensive passages from the Bible.[11] Crucial to the development of Protestant verse was fresh attention to the Psalms, the devotional poems in the Bible. The headnote to the Geneva Version (1560) of the Book of Psalms called them 'present remedies against all temptations and troubles of mind and conscience'. Eleven years earlier, Thomas Sternhold and John Hopkins had published a clumsy metrical version of the texts, designed to present God's word directly as well as to counter the polyphonic settings used in the masses of the Catholic Church. Plain 'church tunes' were printed in Geneva a few years later, and this version of the psalms went through around 300 versions before 1640.

Sir Philip Sidney undertook the production of a new metrical version that had reached Psalm 42 at the time of his death; his sister, Mary Herbert, Countess of Pembroke (1561–1621) continued the project. Here is the seventh verse of Psalm 142 in the Geneva Version: 'Bring my soul out of prison that I may praise Thy name: then shall the righteous come about me, when Thou art beneficial unto me.' Sternhold and Hopkins's version depends upon awkward inversion and clumsy rhyme:

> That I may praise Thy name, my soul
>   From prison, Lord, bring out:
> When Thou art good to me, the just
>   Shall compass me about.

Mary Sidney's version is far more interesting: her metaphors read as though they grow out of experience as well as out of doctrinal commonplace, and her words stand in a more normal order:

> Oh, change my state, unthrall my soul enthralled;
>   Of my escape then will I tell the story;
> And, with a crown enwalled
>   Of godly men, will glory in thy glory.

The Reformation, in fact, might well be categorized as a flight from dogma to experience. Fulke Greville put it aphoristically:

Yet when each of us in his own heart looks,
He finds the God there, far unlike his books.
('Chorus Sacerdotum', from *Mustapha* [1609])

Aemilia Lanyer incorporated into her *Salve Deus, Rex Judaeorum* (1611), a long poem that begins with a meditation upon the Passion of Christ, an exercise in moral theology entitled 'Eve's Apology in Defence of Women'. Pontius Pilate's wife speaks the lines strongly and passionately:

... Our mother Eve, who tasted of the tree,
Giving to Adam what she held most dear,
Was simply good, and had no power to see;
The after-coming harm did not appear:
    The subtle serpent that our sex betrayed,
    Before our fall so sure a plot had laid

That undiscerning Ignorance perceived
No guile or craft that was by him intended;
For, had she known of what we were bereaved,
To his request she had not condescended;
But she (poor soul) by cunning was deceived,
No hurt therein her harmless heart intended:
    For she alleged God's word, [in] which He denies
    That they should die, but even as gods, be wise.

But surely Adam cannot be excused,
Her fault, though great, yet he was most to blame;
What Weakness offered, Strength might have refused,
Being lord of all, the greater was his shame:
Although the serpent's craft had her abused,
God's holy word ought all his actions frame:
    For he was lord and king of all the earth,
    Before poor Eve had either life or breath.

Who being framed by God's eternal hand
The perfect'st man than ever breathed on earth,
And from God's mouth received that strait command,
The breach where of he knew was present death:
Yea, having power to rule both sea and land,
Yet with one apple won to loose that breath,

Which God hath breathèd in his beauteous face,
Bringing us all in danger and disgrace.

And then to lay the fault on Patience' back,
That we (poor women) must endure it all;
We know right well he did discretion lack,
Being not persuaded thereunto at all;
If Eve did err, it was for knowledge sake,
The fruit being fair persuaded him to fall:
   No subtle serpent's falsehood did betray him:
   If he would eat it, who had power to stay him? . . .

Then let us have our liberty again,
And challenge to yourselves no sov'reignty;
You came not in the world without our pain –
Make that a bar against your cruelty;
Your fault being greater, why should you disdain
Our being your equals, free from tyranny?
   If one weak woman simply did offend,
   This sin of yours hath no excuse nor end.   (763–832)

Here the experience of a woman speaking for women confronts the misogyny that informed so much of the Christian doctrine of the time.

Devotion and the Problems of Language and Style

When it came to devotional verse, Protestants aimed to celebrate clarity and simplicity. George Herbert, whose father was descended from the Earls of Pembroke, took orders in the Anglican Church. In his poem called simply 'Divinity', he contrasted what seemed to be the super-subtle ratiocination of scholastic Catholic theology with the attempts to apprehend godhead directly that were at the basis of Protestant thought. He begins with an analogy between theological ingeniousness and astronomical sophistication, the invention of invisible material objects, the planetary spheres that were deemed to impel the sun, moon and stars:

As men, for fear the stars should sleep and nod
   And trip at night, have spheres supplied,
As if a star were duller than a clod,
   Which knows his way without a guide;

Just so the other heav'n they also serve,
  Divinity's transcendent sky,
Which with the edge of wit they cut and carve:
  Reason triumphs and faith lies by.

Could not that wisdom, which first broached the wine,
  Have thickened it with definitions?
And jagged [slashed] his seamless coat, had that been fine,
  With curious questions and divisions?

But all the doctrine, which he taught and gave,
  Was clear as heav'n, from whence it came.
At least those beams of truth, which only save,
  Surpass in brightness any flame.   (1–16)

Herbert here dons the role of a humorous uncle, exploring matters of
high seriousness in an engagingly witty manner. Yet, in a way, the
poem is a noble failure: having fought off the devils of reason, the
poet takes refuge in a thicket of metaphor. We cannot 'look through'
the poem to the experience that engendered it: the poem is the experience. It is not a poem of rustic beatitude (Herbert was Rector of
Bemerton in Wiltshire). In its way, this, like Donne's 'Of Religion', is
a remarkable poem of doubt: the poet implicitly admits to a distinction between what he would like to feel and 'the expression of what
he really feels'.[12] The metaphors portend sincerity and security, but
the mind of the poet knows them for what they are.

The resonance of St John's Gospel – 'In the beginning was the
Word, and the Word was with God, and that Word was God . . . And
the word was made flesh' (John 1: 1–14, Geneva Version) – has
always been heard clearly by poets, and particularly by those writing
after the Reformation. Yet although the mystery of the incarnation
here seems to be plainly set out, poets attempting to apprehend the
divine word found they could not leap from the everyday to the
ineffable. In many passages in his writing, St Augustine spoke about
how, having begun to perceive God, one could not express him. He
often quoted St Paul: 'For now we see through a glass, darkly' (1 Cor.
13: 12). The problem implicitly lies with language: when Milton in
Paradise Lost spoke of hoping to obtain an 'answerable [corresponding]
style' (9.20) from Urania, his heavenly muse, he implicitly admitted
that she might not bestow it upon him. This sense of inhabiting what

Nietzsche was to conceive of as a kind of prison-house of language has, of course, been central to modern epistemology. As Nietzsche wrote:

> The drive toward the formation of metaphors is the fundamental human drive, which one cannot for a single instant dispense with in thought, for one would thereby dispense with man himself. This drive is not truly vanquished and scarcely subdued by the fact that a regular and rigid new world is constructed as its prison from its own ephemeral products, the concepts.[13]

One way forward seemed to pursue simplicity, which, according to the demands of decorum, required clarity, a plain style and freedom from verbal artifice. Donne famously opined in 'The Cross':

> So when thy brain works, ere thou utter it,
> Cross and correct concupiscence of wit.   (57–8)

Characteristically, however, he challenges his own injunction with a pun upon the poem's title and the act of revising a text. Herbert, too, wanted a new decorum for religious verse, a union of pious certainty and prosodic truth. In 'A True Hymn' he wrote:

> The fineness which a hymn or psalm affords,
> Is when the soul unto the lines accords.   (9–10)

This desire to make the form of the poem fit for its purpose is further exemplified in his 'pattern poems': the shape on the printed page of 'The Altar' and 'Easter Wings' shadows the topics they explore.

Herbert described the end of the journey for writers of devotional verse in another sacral parody, 'Jordan (I)':

> Who says that fictions only and false hair
> Become a verse? Is there in truth no beauty?
> Is all good structure in a winding stair?
> May no lines pass, except they do their duty
>   Not to a true, but painted chair?
>
> Is it no verse, except enchanted groves
> And sudden arbours shadow coarse-spun lines?
> Must purling streams refresh a lover's loves?

> Must all be veiled, while he that reads, divines,
> Catching the sense at two removes?
>
> Shepherds are honest people; let them sing:
> Riddle who list, for me, and pull for prime [draw for a winning hand
>   in a card game];
> I envy no man's nightingale or spring;
> Nor let them punish me with loss of rhyme,
>   Who plainly say, 'My God, my King.'

Again, there is a clash between intention and practice: the metonymic conceit of verse lines doing obeisance to the throne of God, rather than an earthly throne, is as ingenious as the romantic metaphors of trees shading and validating the plain but true utterances of pastoral lovers. The re-dedication of secular poetry to divine ends is unsuccessful – it serves to reveal that God can be seen only through concepts, as an analogue of the fictions Herbert deems to be inappropriate, and not in his own domain. Moreover, the conclusion of the poem defeats itself; it creates a kind of hermeneutic circle: the poem's speaker says that God is the sole king he will serve, but admits, albeit tacitly, that God can be known only through metaphor, as a 'king'.

The visionary poet Thomas Traherne also addressed the problem of 'truth', beginning with the commonplace of Truth as a naked female:

> The naked truth in many faces shown,
> Whose inward beauties very few have known,
> A simple light, transparent words, a strain
> That lowly creeps, yet maketh mountains plain,
> Brings down the highest mysteries to sense
> And keeps them there; that is our excellence:
> At that we aim; to th'end thy soul might see
> With open eyes thy great felicity,
> Its objects view, and trace the glorious way
> Whereby thou may'st thy highest bliss enjoy.
>
> No curling metaphors that gild the sense,
> Nor pictures here, nor painted eloquence;
> No florid streams of superficial gems,
> But real crowns and thrones and diadems!
> That gold on gold should hiding shining lie
> May well be reckoned baser heraldry.

An easy style drawn from a native vein,
A clearer stream than that which poets feign,
Whose bottom may, how deep soe'er, be seen,
Is that which I think fit to win esteem:
Else we could speak Zamzummim [Old Testament giants] words,
    and tell
A tale in tongues that sound like Babel-Hell;
In meteors speak, in blazing prodigies,
Things that amaze, but will not make us wise.

('The Author to the Critical Peruser')

His advocacy of a plain style is familiar; his rapturous desire for 'real crowns and thrones and diadems' impossible.

Sermons

Preaching was one of the dominant religious forms of the day and a far greater proportion of the population than in modern times enjoyed listening to sermons. Sermons were occasions when preachers could both deploy their theological rhetorical training, their reading in theology, their knowledge of Latin, Greek and Hebrew, and study of Biblical translations, and also engage with the religious cultures of the times. (In reality, there were many complaints about almost illiterate clergy.) They might re-construe Biblical narratives or, in Catholic times, engage with the liturgical experiences of the congregation: interpret hymns and images, explore typology (see chapter 4), reflect upon the worship of saints, on mystery and miracle plays, and the festivals of the Christian year. When and where Protestantism had become established, preachers tended to anatomize and interpret biblical texts before attempting to create a devotion to the moral life in the congregation as well as condemning enormities such as witchcraft and carnality. Great preachers became celebrities, and individual and collected sermons were widely published – as well as manuals on the office of preaching. Sermons could be instruments of cultural change. With the Reformation, important feminine influences upon religion disappeared with the condemnation of saints and idolatory: Eire describes a Protestant 'masculinization of piety'.[14]

On Ash Wednesday 1599 the popular preacher Lancelot Andrewes (1555–1626), who rose to be Bishop of Winchester, preached a sermon at court, 'At what time the Earl of Essex was going forth upon the Expedition for Ireland', which engages with the intoxication of chivalric notions of war as a kind of game:

> I know not what we reckon of war: peace is [God's] blessing . . . and a special favour it is from Him . . . for a land to spend more iron in scythes and ploughshares than in swordblades or spearheads. And, if peace be a blessing, and a chief of His blessings, we may deduce from thence what war is. To make no otherwise of it, then, it is the rod of God's wrath (as Esay termeth it), his iron flail (as Amos), the hammer of the earth (as Jeremy) whereby he dasheth two nations together. One of them must in pieces; both, the worse for it. *War is no matter of sport.* Indeed, I see Abner esteem of it as of a sport: 'Let the young men now arise' (sayth he to Joab) 'and show us some sport' [2. Sam. 2: 14]). But I see the same Abner, before the end of the same chapter, weary of his sport and treating with Joab for an end of it: 'How long shall the sword devour?' sayth he, 'shall it not be bitterness in the end' [2 Sam. 2: 26], if it hold long? War then being God's rod, His fearful rod, and that so fearful that King David (though a warrior too), when both were in his choice preferred the plague before it and desired it of the twain.[15]

This assembles a characteristically 'puritan' mass of scriptural citations with direct plain speech, asking whether the realities attendant upon the military expedition to quell rebellion in Ireland ought not be weighed against romantic and debonair visions of military glory. The same kind of ideological questioning emerges in Shakespeare's *Henry V*, which was being written at almost exactly this time.

The sermons of John Donne, who was equally popular as a preacher, and who, in 1621, procured the deanery of St Paul's through the offices of King James's favourite, the Duke of Buckingham, engagingly combine wit and intellectual ingenuity with reflections upon mortal behaviour and images of homely life, all obviously delivered with the rhetorical aplomb of an actor (see also chapter 2). Here, in a sermon preached to Charles I at Whitehall in 1628, he considers the same text that Dr Faustus struggled with:

> There is the punishment for sin: 'The reward of sin is death' [Rom. 6: 23]. If there remain no death, there remains no punishment, for 'the reward of sin is death'. And death complicated [folded together] in itself, death wrapped in death? And what is so intricate [interwinding], so entangling as death? Whoever got out of a winding-sheet? It is death

aggravated [burdened] by itself, death weighted down by death. And what is so heavy as death? Whoever threw off his gravestone? It is death multiplied by itself. And what is so infinite as death? Whoever told over the days of death?

The Latinate meanings indicate his perennial concern with language. He then modulates into a passage upon 'dying' – the word was used jocularly for sexual orgasm – which reveals a complex and somewhat disconcerting meditation upon themes he had investigated in his love poetry:

And then for the other calamities in this life, which we call *morticulas*, little deaths, the children, the issue, the off-spring, the propagation of death. If we would speak properly, no affliction, no judgment of God in this life hath in it exactly the nature of a punishment: not only not the nature of satisfaction, but not the nature of a punishment. We call not coin base coin till the alloy be more than the pure metal: God's judgments are not punishments except there be more anger than love, more justice than mercy in them, and that is never.[16]

That is revealing of the period's deep fear of the weakening of the male body by the spending of 'seed'.[17]

On 12 December 1626 Donne had preached upon prayer at the funeral of Sir William Cokayne. His text was John 11: 21: 'Then said Martha unto Jesus, Lord, if thou hadst been here, my brother had not died':

But when we consider with a religious seriousness the manifold weaknesses of the strongest devotions in time of prayer, it is a sad consideration. I throw myself down in my chamber, and I call in and invite God and His angels thither and, when they are there, I neglect God and His angels for the noise of a fly, for the rattling of a coach, for the whining of a door. I talk on, in the same posture of praying: eyes lifted up, knees bowed down, as though I prayed to God, and if God or His angels should ask me when I thought last of God in that prayer, I cannot tell. Sometimes I find that I had forgot what I was about, but when I began to forget it I cannot tell. A memory of yesterday's pleasures, a fear of tomorrow's dangers, a straw under my knee, a noise in mine ear, a light in mine eye, an anything, a nothing, a fancy, a chimera in my brain, troubles me in my prayer. So certainly there is nothing, nothing in spiritual things, perfect in this world.[18]

Recognizing the difficulty of prayer and the constant possibility of poetic failure, several poets of the period labelled their poems 'ejaculations', as in the sub-title to Herbert's *The Temple*: 'Sacred Poems and Private Ejaculations' (1633). The *Oxford English Dictionary* defines this sense of the word as 'A short prayer "darted up to God" (Fuller) in an emergency'. In 1636, Thomas Cranley, in a work entitled *Amanda or The Reformed Whore*, rebuked his mistress (?) for neither attending to sermons nor praying properly:

> Thou dost not keep one Sunday in a year
> Nor hear'st a sermon once in two years' space;
> Thou carest neither for to read nor hear,
> Devotion dwells not in thee, nor yet grace.
> No divine thought hath in thy heart a place.
>   Thou hast no resolution or intent
>   Once to take comfort of the sacrament.
>
> Thou know'st not what to prayer doth belong,
> Private, or public, nor to meditation;
> Thou dost not use to exercise thy tongue
> In vocal sound, or silent adoration,
> Nor send'st thy thoughts up by *ejaculation*,
>   Nor worship'st any deity above
>   But Venus and her son, the god of love.[19]

'Metaphysical' Verse and Platonism

Mutual dependency between the languages of love and religion is at the key of what is somewhat misleadingly termed 'metaphysical verse', written by a school of poets who took their cue from Donne – the term as we use it now was not so used in Donne's lifetime. The word 'metaphysics' probably derives from the book by Aristotle that was found in medieval codices 'after' his *Physics*. That work dealt with the first principles of things: time and space, causation and identity. In the eighteenth century the word came generally to designate the study of what lies beyond the empirical – a warning that the metaphysical verse of the English Renaissance is not necessarily 'about' godhead or religion.

Drummond of Hawthornden (1585–1649) used the term in a letter of about 1628: 'In vain have some men of late (transformers of everything) consulted upon [Poetry's] reformation, and endeavoured to abstract her to metaphysical ideas and scholastical quiddities, denuding her of her own habits and those ornaments with which she hath amused the whole world some thousand years.'[20] These 'ornaments' were doubtless part of the repertory of stock images and epithets found, for example, in the poems of the Elizabethan sonneteers. Some decades later, Dryden also made a pejorative use of the word in *A Discourse of the Original and Progress of Satire* (1692) with reference to Donne: 'He affects the metaphysics not only in his satires, but in his amorous verses, where nature only should reign, and perplexes the minds of the fair sex with nice speculations of philosophy.' Dryden here is not only sexist – assuming that the women in Donne's circle were ignorant (which is far from being the case) – but also unperceptive of irony.

In a poem such as 'The Ecstasy', Donne does imply an auditor who is familiar with the Platonic concept that the soul can withdraw from the body. Castiglione's *The Book of the Courtier* ends with Cardinal Bembo's description of the way in which the soul is enflamed by emanations of heavenly beauty, which is itself a manifestation of the good. The soul ascends what Bembo, using a figure that derives ultimately from Plato's *Symposium* (211), calls 'the stair of love':

Therefore waxed blind about earthly matters, [she] is made most quick of sight about heavenly. And otherwhile when the stirring virtues [motive forces] of the body are withdrawn [absorbed] . . . she feeleth a certain privy smell [perfume] of the right angelic beauty, and . . . coveting to couple herself with it, having found . . . the footsteps of God, in the beholding of whom (as in her happy [beatific] end) she seeketh to settle herself . . .

Thus the soul, kindled in the most holy fire of true heavenly love, fleeth to couple herself with the nature of angels, and not only clean forsaketh sense but hath no more need of the discourse of reason, for, being changed into an angel, she understandeth all things that may be understood, and, without any veil or cloud, she seeth the main [immense] sea of the pure heavenly beauty and receiveth it unto her, and enjoyeth the sovereign happiness that cannot be apprehended of the senses . . .

Therefore vouchsafe, Lord, to hearken to our prayers, pour thyself into our hearts, and with the brightness of thy most holy fire lighten our darkness . . . Make us to smell those spiritual savours that relieve [quicken] the virtues of the understanding, and to hear the heavenly harmony so tunable, that no discord of passion take place any more in us.[21]

In 'The Ecstasy', Donne narrates how, when lying on a bank, the souls of the two lovers, after 'negotiation', had so united in ecstasy that they were in danger of forgetting their bodies:

> So must pure lovers' souls descend
>   T'affections and to faculties,
> Which sense may reach and apprehend,
>   Else a great prince in prison lies.
>
> To our bodies turn we then, that so
>   Weak men on love revealed may look:
> Love's mysteries in souls do grow,
>   But yet the body is his book.
>
> And if some lover, such as we,
>   Have heard this dialogue of one,
> Let him still mark us; he shall see
>   Small change when we're to bodies gone.   (65–76)

Donne's wit enables the poem to be read both as a mannerly celebration of the mysteries of 'pure' or 'Platonic' love and as a cavalier poem of seduction in which ascent and descent allegorize the crescendo and relief of passion. The speaker may be inviting the mistress to accept the invitation to carnal pleasure gracefully or hinting that he would not be surprised if she firmly rejected the moral sophistry of the latter part of his persuasion.

Again, reversing the polarities of the kinds of metaphor Donne had used, Herbert, in 'Denial', uses the language of an unsuccessful lover to address God:

> When my devotions could not pierce
>   Thy silent ears,
> Then was my heart broken, as was my verse:
>   My breast was full of fears
>   And disorder . . .

Therefore my soul lay out of sight,
    Untuned, unstrung;
My feeble spirit, unapt to look right,
    Like a nipped blossom, hung
        Discontented.

O cheer and tune my heartless breast,
    Defer no time,
That so thy favours granting my request,
    They and my mind may chime,
        And mend my rhyme.   (1–4, 21–30)

Some decades earlier in *Fowre Hymnes* (1596) Edmund Spenser had created two Platonic discourses, 'An Hymn in Honour of Love' and 'An Hymn in Honour of Beauty'. Then, as he claims in a prefatory epistle, because his patrons, Margaret, Countess of Cumberland, and Mary, Countess of Warwick, had deemed them likely to increase 'strong passion' in the young, he added 'by way of retractation',[22] 'An Hymn of Heavenly Love' and 'An Hymn of Heavenly Beauty'. In all the poems he includes a narrative of cosmological creation that depicts the imposition of order upon the chaotic elements. In 'An Hymn in Honour of Love' he narrates how Clotho, the Fate who span the thread of life, raised Cupid from Venus' lap (symbolizing the union of Love and Beauty) to create a cosmos ruled by love:

For ere this world's still moving mighty mass
Out of great Chaos' ugly prison crept,
In which his goodly face long hidden was
From heaven's view, and in deep darkness kept,
Love, that had now long time securely slept
In Venus' lap, unarmèd then and naked,
Gan rear his head, by Clotho being waked,

And, taking to him wings of his own heat,
Kindled at first from heaven's life-giving fire,
He gan to move out of his idle seat,
Weakly at first, but after, with desire
Lifted aloft, he gan to mount up higher,
And, like fresh eagle, make his hardy flight
Through all that great wide waste, yet wanting [lacking] light.

Yet wanting light to guide his wand'ring way,
His own fair mother, for all creatures' sake,
Did lend him light from her own goodly ray.
Then through the world his way he gan to take,
The world that was not till he did it make;
Whose sundry parts he from themselves did sever,
The which before had lyen confusèd ever.

The earth, the air, the water, and the fire
Then gan to range them selves in huge array
And with contrary forces to conspire
Each against other, by all means they may,
Threat'ning their own confusion and decay:
Air hated earth, and water hated fire,
Till Love relented [abated] their rebellious ire.

He then them took and, tempering goodly well
Their contrary dislikes with lovèd means,
Did place them all in order, and compel
To keep themselves within their sundry reigns,
Together linked with adamantine chains;
Yet so, as that in every living wight
They mix themselves, and show their kindly might. (57–91)

The Cupid figure here derives ultimately from the pre-Socratic philosopher Empedocles (c.490–430 BC), who saw the elements ruled by competing powers of Love and Strife – the mischievous 'blind Cupid', god of carnal desire wearing a blindfold, emerged much later.[23]

The equivalent passage in 'An Hymn of Heavenly Love' replaces Cupid with Christ as the true 'God of Love' but, although the two countesses were supposedly puritanical in attitude,[24] this new creation myth and the description of the Trinity are not much more attached to scripture than the first:

Before this world's great frame, in which all things
Are now contained, found any being place,
Ere flitting Time could wag his eyas' [young hawk's] wings
About that mighty bound, which doth embrace
The rolling spheres, and parts their hours by space,
That high eternal power which now doth move
In all these things, moved in itself by love.

It loved itself because itself was fair –
For fair is loved – and of itself begot
Like to itself his eldest son and heir,
Eternal, pure, and void of sinful blot,
The firstling of his joy, in whom no jot
Of love's dislike or pride was to be found,
Whom he therefore with equal honour crowned.

With him He reigned, before all time prescribed,
In endless glory and immortal might,
Together with that third from them derived,
Most wise, most holy, most almighty Sprite,
Whose kingdom's throne no thought of earthly wight
Can comprehend, much less my trembling verse
With equal words can hope it to rehearse [recount].   (22–42)

Even the 'retractation' may derive from the precedent set by Petrarch in his sonnets of repentance.[25] We can only conclude that Spenser was in sympathy with the great project of the Florentine scholar Marsilio Ficino (1433–99), through whose *Commentary upon Plato's Symposium* (1469, also known as the *De Amore*) Platonic ideas had filtered across the whole of Europe. Provided that this kind of platonizing was doctrinally vague and placed God as the goal for intellectual and spiritual ardour, it was likely to find favour with many godly persons – indeed, such emphasis on purification and unmediated communion with deity was central to much Protestant discourse.

Platonic and Ovidian Banquets

As we have seen, the notion of the soul ascending towards divinity though the senses was central to Platonic thought: because the figure was associated with the *Symposium* ('banquet') it became known as a 'Platonic banquet'. In 1595, George Chapman published a poem on love and learning, *Ovid's Banquet of Sense*. Ovid, straying into a garden where Julia (or Corynna) sits bathing and playing her lute, is moved by four of his five senses, hearing, smell, sight, and taste. He celebrates their virtues in songs that he sings to the lady and, when she grants him a kiss, for satisfaction of his taste, he would proceed 'to entreaty

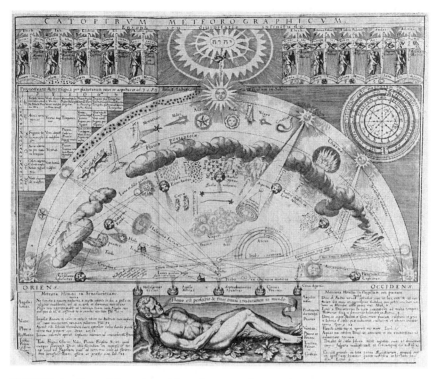

FIGURE 6 'Seraphim, cherubim, thrones, dominations, powers, planets, meteorology, and man', engraving from Robert Fludd, *Philosophia Sacra et Vere Christiana* (Frankfurt, 1626), pp. 140–41, London, British Library.

for the fifth sense' (the poem's 'Argument') – touch, but coitus is interrupted and the poem ends.

Ficino, from whom Chapman adapted the poem's scheme, had distinguished between two loves: Venus Ourania, celestial or divine love, which 'possesses itself of the highest faculty in man, i.e. the Mind or intellect, and impels it to contemplate the intelligible splendour of divine beauty'; and Venus Pandemos, 'natural' love, which 'takes hold of the intermediary faculties in man, i.e. imagination and sensual perception, and impels him to procreate a likeness of divine beauty in the physical world'.[26] Divine love belongs to the contemplative man, natural love to the active. Yet this second Venus is not necessarily inferior: natural love can ascend through the senses and the mind to the contemplation of divine beauty. If, however, the progression is not from the basest sense to the highest, but is instead a descent to touch, Ficino called the love 'bestial' (*amor ferinus*) and associated it with a third type, the voluptuous man. The Platonic banquet led to divine wisdom, the banquet of sense to carnal knowledge. Ovid, of course, was held to be the archetype of the voluptuous man, the opposite of Plato, the supreme contemplative,[27] and in the poem Ovid, like the speaker in Donne's 'The Ecstasy', uses a sophistical Platonic argument to gain his desires.

Three years later, Chapman published a continuation of Marlowe's *Hero and Leander*, which lay unfinished at Marlowe's death. When she read the contributions of the two men, Katherine Mansfield wrote: 'I read *Hero and Leander* last night. That's incredibly lovely. But how extremely amusing Chapman's *finish* is! Taking that magical poem and putting it into a body [bodice] and skirt!'[28] In fact, Marlowe's opening sestiads are ironically moral, by no means merely erotic, and it is too simple to say that Chapman imposed a pattern of retributive tragedy onto Marlowe's sexy narrative. Leander, in the first of two episodes added by Chapman, is visited by Ceremony whose worship he had neglected while he is boasting of his union with Hero to his sister:

> The goddess Ceremony, with a crown
> Of all the stars and heaven with her, descended;
> Her flaming hair to her bright feet extended,
> By which hung all the bench of deities;
> And in a chain, compact of ears and eyes,
> She led Religion; all her body was
> Clear and transparent as the purest glass:
> For she was all presented to the sense.
> Devotion, Order, State, and Reverence,
> Her shadows were; Society, Memory –
> All which her sight made live, her absence die.
> A rich disparent [diversely coloured] pentacle she wears,
> Drawn full of circles and strange characters:
> Her face was changeable to every eye:
> One way looked ill, another graciously,
> Which while men viewed, they cheerful were and holy,
> But looking off, vicious and melancholy.
> The snaky paths to each observèd law,
> Did Policy in her broad bosom draw;

One hand a mathematic crystal sways,
Which gathering in one line a thousand rays
From her bright eyes, Confusion burns to death,
And all estates of men distinguisheth.
By it Morality and Comeliness,
Themselves in all their sightly figures dress;
Her other hand a laurel rod applies,
To beat back Barbarism and Avarice,
That followed eating earth and excrement
And humane limbs, and would make proud ascent
To seats of gods, were Ceremony slain.
The Hours and Graces bore her glorious train,
And all the sweets of our society
Were sphered and treasured in her bounteous eye.
Thus she appeared, and sharply did reprove
Leander's bluntness in his violent love;
Told him how poor was substance without rites,
Like bills unsigned, desires without delights,
Like meats unseasoned, like rank corn that grows
On [thatched] cottages, that none or reaps or sows:
Not being with civil [proper] forms confirmed and bounded,
For human dignities and comforts founded,
But loose and secret all their glories hide:
Fear fills the chamber, darkness decks the bride.   (3.112–154)

Although Ceremony leads Religion by a chain, Chapman proposes her as the only liberator for men whose lives are bounded by their senses. The chain, 'compact of ears and eyes', not only signifies the constraint that fallen, sensual man has placed upon the intellectual truths of religion, but is also a form of Homer's golden chain (*Iliad*, 8.18–27). Chapman rather clumsily transfers its attributes to Ceremony's hair by which mankind might progress to the highest orders of existence. Ceremony is thus an ambivalent symbol of humility and hope. She wears a magic pentangle signifying the marriage of heaven and earth effected by the ceremonies of the white magician, displays the 'snaky paths to each observèd law' (the difficult but prudent ways of right action), and beats back her enemies with a laurel rod, Apollo's laurel, the laurel of arts and science.[29]

Chapman attempted in this passage a fusion of Christianity and Platonism, of politics and morality, of spiritual magic and optical science, of public civility and private comeliness, of practice and ritual, of the sublime and the homely, and, in so far as it represents a triumphant procession in the manner of Petrarch's *Trionfi*, of image and word. I know of no other brief text that integrates so ambitiously both Renaissance learning and Reformation principle, a focalization of the cultural forces of the age.

Notes

Introduction: New Worlds of Words

1   Patrick Collinson, *The Religion of Protestants: The Church in English Society 1559–1625* (Oxford: Oxford University Press, 1982), pp. 141–88.

Chapter 1   Speaking and Writing

1   John Florio, *A World of Words* (London, 1598), p. 202.
2   Raymond Williams, *Keywords* (London: Fontana, 1976), pp. 183–8.
3   Michael Drayton's epistle to Henry Reynolds, 'Of Poets and poesie', gives a graceful account both of the progression of his education and of the formation of a canon of English literature; see David Norbrook and H. R. Woudhuysen (eds), *The Penguin Book of Renaissance Verse 1509–1659* (Harmondsworth: Penguin, 1993 edn), pp. 728–34.
4   Sir Philip Sidney, *An Apology for Poetry*, ed. G. Shepherd (Manchester: Manchester University Press, 1965), p. 134.
5   *Poetics*, ch. ix.
6   George Puttenham, *The Arte of English Poesie* (London, 1589), p. 89.
7   John Florio, *His First Fruits* [1578], ed. Arundell del Re (Formosa: Taihoku Imperial University Memoirs, 1936), fo. 50^{r-v}.
8   Cicero, *De Officiis*, I. xvi. 50.
9   'A Defence of an Essay of Dramatic Poesie', in John Dryden, *Poetry, Prose and Plays*, ed. Douglas Grant (London: Rupert Hart-Davis, 1952), p. 447.
10   William Empson, *Argufying: Essays on Literature and Culture*, ed. John Haffenden (London: Chatto and Windus, 1987), p. 167.

11 A form of reasoning in which a conclusion is derived from two premises which contain a common term, exemplified by 'Every man is mortal; Socrates is a man: Therefore Socrates is mortal.'

12 *Eighty Sermons preached by that learned and reverend divine John Donne* (London, 1640), p. 549.

13 For commonplace books, see R. R. Bolgar, *The Classical Heritage and its Beneficiaries* (Cambridge: Cambridge University Press, 1954), pp. 265–75.

14 Puttenham, *Arte of English Poesie*, p. 67.

15 Norbrook and Woudhuysen (eds), *Renaissance Verse 1509–1659*, pp. 414–15.

16 Ernst Robert Curtius, *European Literature and the Latin Middle Ages*, trans. Willard R. Trask (London: Routledge and Kegan Paul, 1953), p. 195.

17 Alberti, *Della Pittura* (1438), cited in François Quiviger, 'Renaissance art theories', in *A Companion to Art Theory*, ed. Paul Smith and Carolyn Wilde (Oxford: Blackwell, 2002), pp. 49–60, at p. 57.

18 M. P. Tilley, *A Dictionary of the Proverbs in England in the Sixteenth and Seventeenth Centuries* (Ann Arbor: University of Michigan Press, 1950).

19 Thomas Blount, *The Academy of Eloquence* (London, 1654). pp. 121–2; see also Abraham Fraunce, *The Arcadian Rhetoric* (London, 1588).

20 Jean Klene (ed.), *The Southwell–Sibthorpe Commonplace Book, Folger MS V.b.198*, Medieval and Renaissance Texts and Studies, vol. 147 (Tempe, AZ, 1997), pp. 105–7.

21 Cited from *The Advancement of Learning*, by Blount, sig. A4^r.

22 William Wordsworth and Samuel Taylor Coleridge, *Lyrical Ballads 1805*, ed. Derek Roper (London: MacDonald and Evans, 1976 edn), p. 22.

23 Ben Jonson, *Timber, or Discoveries Made upon Men and Matter* [1641], ed. Felix E. Schelling (Boston, MA: Ginn and Company, 1892), p. 74.

24 Sidney, *Apology for Poetry*, p. 100.

25 Jonson, *Timber, or Discoveries*, p. 77.

26 T. S. Eliot, *Selected Essays* (London: Faber and Faber, 1951 edn), p. 293.

27 Sidney, *Apology for Poetry*, p. 138.

28 The tag '*ars est celare artem*' is often quoted, but its exact origin is unknown.

29 Baldassare Castiglione, *The Book of the Courtier*, trans. Sir Thomas Hoby [1561] (London: Everyman, 1928), p. 46.

30 Sidney, *Apology for Poetry*, p. 101.

31 For *enargeia*, see Lucy Gent, *Picture and Poetry 1560–1620* (Leamington Spa: James Hall, 1981).

32 Robin Robbins, 'Poets, friends and patrons: Donne and his circle; Ben and his tribe', in *A Companion to English Renaissance Literature and Culture*, ed. Michael Hattaway (Oxford: Blackwell, 2000), pp. 419–41.

33 See Joseph Anthony Mazzeo, 'A critique of some modern theories of metaphysical poetry', *Modern Philology*, 50 (1952), 88–96.

34 *The Reason of Church Government* [1641], *The Prose Works of John Milton*, 3 vols (London: Henry G. Bohn, 1848), vol. 2, p. 479.

35 Stanley Wells and Gary Taylor, *William Shakespeare: A Textual Companion* (Oxford: Clarendon Press, 1987), pp. 72ff.

36 Puttenham, *Arte of English Poesie*, pp. 1–2.

37 Tilley, *Dictionary of Proverbs*, p. 451.

38 Thomas Wilson, *The Art of Rhetoric* (London, 1553), fo. 1^r.

39 Puttenham, *Arte of English Poesie*, p. 5.

40 John Northbrooke, *A Treatise against Dicing, Dancing, Plays and Interludes* . . . (London: Shakespeare Society, 1843), p. 54.

41 Alexander Pope, *An Essay on Criticism*, ll. 317–18.

42 Peter Dixon, *Rhetoric* (London: Methuen, 1971), pp. 22–3.

43 Madeleine Doran, *Endeavors of Art: A Study of Form in Elizabethan Drama* (Madison: University of Wisconsin Press, 1954), p. 47.

44 Wilson, *Art of Rhetoric*, fo. 7^v.

45 Ibid., fo. 4^r.

46 Brian Vickers, *Classical Rhetoric in English Poetry* (London: Macmillan, 1970), p. 85.

47 Joel B. Altman, *The Tudor Play of Mind: Rhetorical Inquiry and the Development of Elizabethan Drama* (Berkeley, CA: University of California Press, 1978).

48 Pierre de La Primaudaye, *The French Academy*, trans. T. B. (London, 1586), p. 72.

49 'A brief apology of poetry', in Ludovico Ariosto, *Orlando Furioso in English Heroical Verse*, trans. John Harington (London, 1591).

50 Puttenham, *Arte of English Poesie*, p. 115.

51 Paul Valéry, *Degas, Manet, Morisot*, trans. David Paul (Princeton, NJ: Princeton University Press, 1989), p. 62.

52 Michael Pincombe, *The Plays of John Lyly: Eros and Eliza* (Manchester: Manchester University Press, 1996).

53 Richard Hooker, *Of the Laws of Ecclesiastical Polity*, 2 vols (London: Everyman, 1907), vol. I, p. 157.

54 Francis Bacon, *The Advancement of Learning*, I. iv. 2. For the contention that the utilitarian drive of this argument is continued by those seventeenth-century scientists who contributed to the founding of the Royal Society in 1660, see Robert Adolph, *The Rise of Modern Prose Style* (Cambridge, MA: MIT Press, 1968).

55 Bacon, *Advancement of Learning*, II. xvii. 7; compare Jonson, *Timber, or Discoveries*, p. 62.

Chapter 2 Reading, Publication, Performance

1 See N. F. Blake, *Caxton: England's First Publisher* (London: Osprey, 1976).
2 John Donne, *Sermons on the Psalms and Gospels*, ed. Evelyn M. Simpson (Berkeley, CA: University of California Press, 1963), p. 140.
3 'Statistical tables', in *The Cambridge History of the Book in Britain, 1557–1695*, vol. 4, ed. John Barnard and D. F. McKenzie (Cambridge: Cambridge University Press, 2002), pp. 779–84.
4 Nigel Wheale, *Writing and Society: Literacy, Print and Politics in Britain, 1590–1660* (London: Routledge, 1999), pp. 55 and 79–84.
5 See Debora Shuger, 'Dead men talking', in *Renaissance Refractions: Essays in Honour of Alexander Shurbanov*, ed. Boika Sokolova and Evgenia Pancheva (Sofia: St Kliment Ohridski University Press, 2001), pp. 28–37; E. S. Needham-Green, *Books in Cambridge Inventories*, 2 vols (Cambridge: Cambridge University Press, 1986).
6 Roger Ascham, *The Schoolmaster* [1570], in *English Works*, ed. W. A. Wright (Cambridge: Cambridge University Press, 1904), p. 201.
7 Adam Fox, *Oral and Literate Culture in England, 1500–1700* (Oxford: Clarendon Press, 2000), p. 318; music for this and some of the other ballads listed in this section can be found in Claude M. Simpson, *The British Broadside Ballad and its Music* (New Brunswick: Rutgers University Press, 1966).
8 Thomas Robinson, *The Anatomy of the English Nunnery at Lisbon in Portugal* (London, 1622), pp. 13, 17; an edition of a work entitled *The Merry Conceited Jests of George Peele, Sometime a Student in Oxford* appeared in 1627.
9 Peter Blayney, 'The publication of playbooks', in *A New History of Early English Drama*, ed. J. D. Cox and D. S. Kastan (New York: Columbia University Press, 1997), pp. 383–422, at pp. 411–12.
10 Quoted in Gerald Eades Bentley, *The Professions of Dramatist and Player in Shakespeare's Time, 1590–1642* (Princeton, NJ: Princeton University Press, 1971), p. 52.
11 For the phrase, see Margaret Spufford, *Small Books and Pleasant Histories: Popular Fiction and its Readership in Seventeenth-century England* (Cambridge: Cambridge University Press, 1981), p. xvii.
12 F. J. Furnivall, *Captain Cox, his Ballads and his Books; or, Robert Laneham's Letter* (London: Ballad Society, 1871), pp. xii–xiii.
13 Natascha Würzbach, *The Rise of the English Street Ballad, 1550–1650*, trans. Gayna Walls (Cambridge: Cambridge University Press, 1990), pp. 326–9.

14 Tessa Watt, *Cheap Print and Popular Piety, 1550–1640* (Cambridge: Cambridge University Press, 1991), pp. 333–7.

15 Sir Philip Sidney, *An Apology for Poetry*, ed. G. Shepherd (Manchester: Manchester University Press, 1965), p. 118.

16 R. C. Simmons, 'ABCs, almanacs, ballads, chapbooks, popular piety, and textbooks', in *The Cambridge History of the Book in Britain*, vol. 4, ed. Barnard and McKenzie, pp. 504–13.

17 Patrick Collinson, Arnold Hunt and Alexandra Walsham, 'Religious publishing in England 1557–1640', in *The Cambridge History of the Book in Britain*, vol. 4, ed. Barnard and McKenzie, pp. 26–99.

18 Patrick Collinson, *The Religion of Protestants: The Church in English Society 1559–1625* (Oxford: Oxford University Press, 1982), p. 267.

19 Patrick Collinson, *The Reformation* (London: Weidenfeld and Nicolson, 2003).

20 Ibid., p. 36.

21 *The Whole Works of William Tindale etc.* (London, 1572–3), sigs Aii^r–Aiii^r, cited in Margaret Aston, 'Lollardy and the Reformation: survival or revival', *History*, 49 (1964), pp. 149–70, at p. 169. For an earlier praise of the benefits of printing, see Sir Thomas More, *Utopia* [1516], ed. Richard Marius, trans. Ralph Robinson (London: Everyman, 1994), pp. 96–7.

22 The phrase derives from a retort by William Tyndale to a priest who condemned his beliefs: 'If God spare my life, ere many years I will cause a boy that driveth a plough shall know more of the Scripture than you do.'

23 Fox, *Oral and Literate Culture*, pp. 22–3.

24 *Eighty Sermons preached by that learned and reverend divine John Donne* (London, 1640), pp. 267–74.

25 Roger Chartier, *The Order of Books: Readers, Authors, and Libraries in Europe between the Fourteenth and Eighteenth Centuries*, trans. Lydia Cochrane (Cambridge: Cambridge University Press, 1994), p. 19.

26 David Cressy, *Literacy and the Social Order: Reading and Writing in Early Modern England* (Cambridge: Cambridge University Press, 1980), pp. 55–9.

27 This is surveyed in John Pitcher, 'Literature, the playhouse and the public', in *The Cambridge History of the Book in Britain*, vol. 4, ed. Barnard and McKenzie, pp. 351–75, at pp. 368–70.

28 Cressy, *Literacy and the Social Order*, pp. 55–9.

29 F. J. Furnivall (ed.), *The Babees Book* (London: Early English Text Society, 1868), p. xiii.

30 See, for example, Philbert de Vienne, *The Philosopher of the Court*, trans. George North (London, 1575), pp. 13, 37–9.

31 Francis Bacon, *The Advancement of Learning*, I. v. 11.

32 Robert Burton, *The Anatomy of Melancholy*, ed. Floyd Bell and Paul Jordan-Smith (New York: Tudor, 1948), 1. 2. iii. 15.

33 Dante, *A Translation of the Latin Works*, trans. Philip H. Wicksteed (London: J. M. Dent and Sons, 1904), pp. 347–8.

34 William Tyndale and John Frith, *The Works of the English Reformers: William Tyndale and John Frith*, 3 vols (London: E. Palmer, 1831), vol. I, p. 303.

35 John Donne, *Sermons on the Psalms and Gospels*, ed. Evelyn M. Simpson (Berkeley, CA: University of California Press, 1963), p. 7.

36 'A brief apology of poetry', in Ludovico Ariosto, *Orlando Furioso in English Heroical Verse*, trans. John Harington (London, 1591), sig. ¶iiij^{r-v}.

37 Sidney, *Apology for Poetry*, p. 109.

38 Richard Dutton, *Mastering the Revels: The Regulation and Censorship of English Renaissance Drama* (London: Macmillan, 1991), p. xi.

39 John Taylor, *A Common Whore with all the Graces Graced* (London, 1622), cited in David Norbrook and H. R. Woudhuysen (eds), *The Penguin Book of Renaissance Verse 1509–1659* (Harmondsworth: Penguin, 1993), p. 740. This volume also offers a text of Michael Drayton's verse epistle to Henry Reynolds that includes a defence of publishing poetry in print (pp. 733–4).

40 Natalie Zemon Davis, 'Printing and the people: early modern France', in *Literacy and Social Development in the West*, ed. Harvey J. Graff (Cambridge: Cambridge University Press, 1981), pp. 69–95; see also Arthur F. Marotti, '"Love is not love": Elizabethan sonnet sequences and the social order', *English Literary History*, 49 (1982), pp. 396–428.

41 See Malcolm Jones, '"Such pretty things would soon be gone": the neglected genres of popular verse', in *A Companion to English Renaissance Literature and Culture*, ed. Michael Hattaway (Oxford: Blackwell, 2000), pp. 442–63.

42 Margaret Cavendish, *Philosophical Fancies* (London, 1653), p. 86.

43 Würzbach, *Rise of the English Street Ballad*, p. 2.

44 Possibly Thomas Bond, secretary to the Lord Chancellor.

45 Baird W. Whitlock, *John Hoskyns, Serjeant-at-Law* (Washington, DC: University Press of America, 1982), pp. 292, 326.

46 William Carew Hazlitt and Henry Huth (eds), *Fugitive Tracts Written in Verse . . . 1600–1700*, 2 vols (London: Chiswick Press, 1875).

47 Arthur F. Marotti, *Manuscript, Print, and the English Renaissance Lyric* (Ithaca NY: Cornell University Press, 1995), p. 81.

48 For nearly all the topics in this section, see ibid.

49 David Scott Kastan, *Shakespeare and the Book* (Cambridge: Cambridge University Press, 2001), p. 16.

50 See Joseph Loewenstein, 'The script in the market place', *Representations*, 12 (1985), pp. 101–14.

51 Peter Corbin and Douglas Sedge (eds), *Three Jacobean Witchcraft Plays* (Manchester: Manchester University Press, 1986), p. 84.
52 Richard A. McCabe, '"Right puisante and terrible priests": the role of the Anglican church in Elizabethan state censorship', in *Literature and Censorship in Renaissance England*, ed. Andrew Hadfield (Basingstoke: Palgrave, 2001), pp. 75–94.
53 Glynne Wickham, Herbert Berry and William Ingram (eds), *English Professional Theatre, 1530–1660: Theatre in Europe, A Documentary History* (Cambridge: Cambridge University Press, 2000), p. 51.
54 Ibid., p. 94.
55 For a discussion of all relevant issues, see Richard Dutton, *Licensing, Censorship, and Authorship in Early Modern England* (Basingstoke: Palgrave, 2000), pp. 132–61.
56 Wheale, *Writing and Society*, p. 72.
57 N. W. Bawcutt (ed.), *The Control and Censorship of Caroline Drama: The Records of Sir Henry Herbert, Master of the Revels, 1623–73* (Oxford: Clarendon Press, 1996), p. 177.
58 See David Mann, *The Elizabethan Stage Player: Contemporary Stage Representation* (London: Routledge, 1991).
59 See Michael Shapiro, *Gender in Play on the Shakespearean Stage: Boy Heroines and Female Pages* (Ann Arbor: University of Michigan Press, 1994).
60 Simpson, *The British Broadside Ballad*, p. 246.

Chapter 3   Forms Ancient and Modern

1 Thomas Campion, *Works*, ed. Walter R. Davis (London: Faber and Faber, 1969), p. 293.
2 Edmund D. Jones (ed.), *English Critical Essays (Sixteenth, Seventeenth and Eighteenth Centuries)* (Oxford: Oxford University Press, 1947 edn), p. 72.
3 George Puttenham, *The Art of English Poesie* (London, 1589), p. 20.
4 See John N. King, *English Reformation Literature: The Tudor Origins of the Protestant Tradition* (Princeton, NJ: Princeton University Press, 1982).
5 See James Simpson, *The Oxford English Literary History, 1350–1547: Reform and Cultural Revolution*, vol. 2, ed. Jonathan Bate (Oxford: Oxford University Press, 2002).
6 An exception is Dante's justification of his *Paradiso* in his letter to Can Grande (1319).
7 Edmund Spenser, *The Shorter Poems*, ed. William A. Oram et al. (New Haven, CT: Yale University Press, 1989), p. 17.
8 'A brief apology of poetry', in Ludovico Ariosto, *Orlando Furioso in English Heroical Verse*, trans. John Harington (London, 1591).

9   Ben Jonson, *Timber, or Discoveries Made upon Men and Matter* [1641], ed. Felix E. Schelling (Boston, MA: Ginn and Company, 1892), p. 66; cf. Sir Walter Ralegh, *Works*, ed. William Oldys and Thomas Birch, 8 vols (Oxford: Oxford University Press, 1829), vol. 2, p. xlv.

10 See Barbara Kiefer Lewalski (ed.), *Renaissance Genres: Essays on Theory, History, and Interpretation* (Cambridge, MA: Harvard University Press, 1986).

11 Samuel Taylor Coleridge, *Shakespearian Criticism*, ed. Thomas Middleton Raysor, 2 vols (London: Constable, 1930), vol. 1, p. 199.

12 Graham Bradshaw, *Shakespeare's Scepticism* (Brighton: Harvester, 1987), p. 93.

13 For this kind of self-conscious dramaturgy, see A. R. Braunmuller, 'The arts of the dramatist', in *The Cambridge Companion to English Renaissance Drama*, 2nd edn, ed. A. R. Braunmuller and Michael Hattaway (Cambridge: Cambridge University Press, 2003), pp. 53–92.

14 Mikhail Bakhtin, *Rabelais and his World*, trans. Hélène Iswolsky (Bloomington, IN: Indiana University Press, 1984).

15 Puttenham, *Art of English Poesie*, p. 20.

16 Spenser, *Shorter Poems*, pp. 13–14.

17 Sir Philip Sidney, *An Apology for Poetry*, ed. G. Shepherd (Manchester: Manchester University Press, 1965), p. 164.

18 Joshua Fisher, '"He is turned a ballad-maker": broadside appropriations in early modern England', *Early Modern Literary Studies*, 9.2 (2003), pp. 1–21 (available at http://www.shu.ac.uk/emls/09-2/fishball.html).

19 Henry Wotton, *The Elements of Architecture* (London, 1624), pp. 86–7.

20 Harington, 'Brief apology', sigs ¶iii^v, ¶vi^v.

21 Lucius Annaeus Seneca, *Seneca his Ten Tragedies, Translated into English*, trans. Jasper Heywood, John Studley, et al. (London, 1581), p. 195.

22 *Seneca in English*, ed. Don Share (London: Penguin, 1998), p. 75. Procne, wife to Tereus, was sister to Philomela who was raped by her brother-in-law. To revenge her sister, Procne killed her own son Itys and served up his flesh to her husband.

23 See Martin Wiggins (ed.), *Four Jacobean Sex Tragedies* (Oxford: Oxford University Press, 1998).

24 Title page to Thomas Preston's *Cambises*, c.1561.

25 See Mikhail Bakhtin, *The Dialogic Imagination*, ed. Michael Holquist, trans. Caryl Emerson and Michael Holquist (Austin, TX: University of Texas Press, 1981).

26 G. B. Shaw, *Back to Methuselah* (London: Constable, 1921), p. lxxxiv.

27 See Arthur C. Kirsch, *Jacobean Dramatic Perspectives* (Charlottesville: University Press of Virginia, 1972).

28 See Northrop Frye, 'The argument of comedy', in *Shakespeare's Comedies*, ed. Laurence Lerner (Harmondsworth: Penguin, 1967), pp. 315–25.

29 Jonson, *Timber, or Discoveries*, p. 79.
30 Charles Read Baskervill, *The Elizabethan Jig and Related Song Drama* (Chicago: University of Chicago Press, 1929); for a jig after a performance of Shakespeare's *Julius Caesar*, see Thomas Platter, *Thomas Platter's Travels in England, 1599*, trans. Clare Williams (London: Jonathan Cape, 1937).
31 A good selection is to be found in David Lindley (ed.), *Court Masques* (Oxford: Oxford University Press, 1995).
32 George Chapman, *The Comedies of George Chapman*, ed. T. M. Parrott (London: George Routledge and Sons, 1914), p. 439.
33 *Ben Johnson's Conversations with William Drummond of Hawthornden*, ed. R. F. Patterson (London: Blackie and Sons, 1923), p. 6.
34 Richard Tottel (ed.), *Songs and Sonnets* (London, 1557), sig. A1^v.
35 From Dowland's *Second Book of Songs* (London, 1600); see Diana Poulton, *John Dowland* (London: Faber and Faber, 1972), pp. 123–32.
36 'His Defiance to Envy', 76–7, *Virgidemiarum* (London, 1598).
37 Henry Crosse, *Virtue's Commonwealth* (London, 1603), sig. P3.
38 John Milton, *The Works of John Milton*, ed. Frank Allen Patterson et al., 18 vols (New York: Columbia University Press, 1931–8), vol. 3, p. 329.
39 See Malcolm Jones, '"Such pretty things would soon be gone": the neglected genres of popular verse', in *A Companion to English Renaissance Literature and Culture*, ed. Michael Hattaway (Oxford: Blackwell, 2000), pp. 442–63.
40 An excellent essay is Stanley Wells, 'Shakespeare and romance', in *Later Shakespeare*, ed. J. R. Brown and Bernard Harris (London: Edward Arnold, 1966), pp. 49–79.

Chapter 4   Defining the Past

1 Sir John Hayward, *The First Part of the Life and Reign of King Henry IV* (London, 1599), sigs A3^v–A4^r.
2 [Thomas Dekker], 'The horror of the plague', *News from Gravesend, Sent to Nobody* (London, 1604).
3 Henry Cornelius Agrippa, 'Of Histories', *Of the Vanity and Uncertainty of Arts and Sciences* [1530], trans. James Sandford (London, 1569), p. 13.
4 Sir Thomas More, *The History of King Richard III*, ed. J. R. Lumby (Cambridge: Cambridge University Press, 1893), p. 79.
5 Plutarch, *The Lives of the Noble Grecians and Romans*, trans. Sir Thomas North (London, 1579), sig. *vii^v.
6 See John Foxe, *Acts and Monuments of Matters Most Special in the Church* [1583] (Oxford: Oxford University Press, 1999), CD-ROM.

7 See William Haller, *Foxe's Book of Martyrs and the Elect Nation* (London: Jonathan Cape, 1963); David Loades (ed.), *John Foxe and the English Reformation* (Aldershot: Scolar Press, 1997); Sharon Achinstein, 'John Foxe and the Jews', *Renaissance Quarterly*, 54 (2001), pp. 86–120.

8 E. M. W. Tillyard, *Shakespeare's History Plays* (London: Chatto and Windus, 1944), p. 321.

9 Geoffrey Chaucer, *Works*, ed. F. N. Robinson (London: Oxford University Press, 1957), p. 189.

10 Walter Benjamin, 'The storyteller', trans. H. Zohn, *Illuminations* (London: Fontana, 1973), pp. 83–109, at p. 96.

11 Raphael Holinshed, *Chronicles of England, Scotland, and Ireland* [1587], 6 vols (London: J. Johnson et al., 1808), vol. 2, p. 737.

12 This sardonic populist tone is to be heard elsewhere in the margins, as, for example, when the death of the Duke of York is explained as 'a purchase of God's curse with the pope's blessing' (Holinshed, *Chronicles*, vol. 2, p. 269).

13 Benjamin, 'What is epic theater', *Illuminations*, p. 153.

14 Linda Hutcheon, *A Poetics of Postmodernism* (London: Routlege, 1988), p. ix.

15 [Thomas Nashe?], *The Return of the renowned Cavaliero Pasquil of England, from the other side the Seas, and his meeting with Marforius at London upon the Royal Exchange, where they encounter with a little household talk of Martin and Martinism* [the Marprelate controversy], *discovering the scab that is bred in England; and conferring together about the speedy dispersing of the Golden Legend of the Lives of the Saints* (n.p. 1589), p. 8.

16 Francis Bacon, *The Advancement of Learning* (1605), II. xxii. 9.

17 Gabriel Harvey, *Letter-Booke of Gabriel Harvey, AD 1573–1580*, ed. E. J. L. Scott, Camden Society New Series 33 (Westminster, 1884), p. 79; compare Leonard F. Dean, 'Sir Francis Bacon's theory of civil history-writing', *English Literary History*, 8 (1941), pp. 161–83.

18 Tacitus, *The End of Nero and Beginning of Galba. Four Books of the Histories of Cornelius Tacitus*, trans. Sir Henry Savile ([London], 1591). The *Annals* appeared in 1598. The translator Richard Greneway's Epistle Dedicatory, to the Earl of Essex, reads in part: 'For if history be the treasure of times past and, as well as a guide, a[n] image of man's present estate, a true and lively pattern of things to come, and, as some term it, the work-mistress of experience which is the mother of prudence, Tacitus may by good right challenge the first place among the best.' The influence of Tacitus on later drama is set out by Alan T. Bradford, 'Stuart absolutism and the "utility" of Tacitus,' *Huntington Library Quarterly*, 46 (1983), pp. 127–51; see also J. H. M. Salmon, 'Seneca and Tacitus in Jacobean England', in *The Mental World of the Jacobean Court*,

ed. Linda Levy Peck (Cambridge: Cambridge University Press, 1991), pp. 169–88.

19   Richard Tuck, *Philosophy and Government 1572–1651* (Cambridge: Cambridge University Press, 1993), p. 105; it may have been written by Anthony Bacon.

20   *Annals*, trans. Richard Greneway (1598), book 1, section 5, p. 8.

21   After narrating how Augustus had refashioned the state, Tacitus wrote 'How many were there which had seen the ancient form of government of the free commonwealth?' (*Annals*, book 1, section 2, p. 3).

22   *Annals*, book 1, section 4, p. 7.

23   *Histories*, sig ¶3^{r-v}.

24   *The first and second parts of John Hayward's 'The life and raigne of King Henrie IIII'*, ed. J. J. Manning (London: Royal Historical Society, 1991), p. 63.

25   Ibid., pp. 2, 38.

26   Sir Henry Wotton, *The State of Christendom* (London, 1667), p. 5; compare Erasmus, *The Complaint of Peace* (1517).

27   Bacon, *The Advancement of Learning*, II. ii. 5.

28   Ibid., II. iii. 3.

29   *The Works of Sir Walter Raleigh*, ed. William Oldys and Thomas Birch, 8 vols (Oxford: Oxford University Press, 1829), vol. 2, p. 5.

30   See, for example, ibid., vol. 2, p. 25.

31   Ibid., vol. 2, p. 47.

32   Ibid.

33   Ibid., vol. 4, pp. 616–17; compare vol. 5, pp. 10–11.

34   Jean Leclercq, *The Love of Learning and the Desire for God* (New York: New American Library, 1961), p. 88.

35   See British Library MSS Harl. 6788, ff.509^{r}, 549^{r}, etc.

36   *Works of Sir Walter Raleigh*, vol. 2, p. 202.

37   Ibid., vol. 4, p. 617; compare vol. 2, p. 144 etc.

38   Ibid., vol. 2, p. 300.

39   Ibid, p. 301.

40   Ibid., pp. 178–84 and vol. 3, pp. 192–7.

41   Ibid., vol. 2, p. 68.

42   Ibid., p. 73.

43   Ibid., p. 163; the root of this belief lies in Romans 1: 19.

44   Jean Seznec, *The Survival of the Pagan Gods: The Mythological Tradition and its Place in Renaissance Humanism and Art*, trans. Barbara F. Sessions (New York: Pantheon Books, 1953), pp. 11ff.

45   *Works of Sir Walter Raleigh*, vol. 2, p. 167.

46   Ibid., vol. 2, pp. 62, 75; vol. 3, p. 235.

47   V. Luciani, 'Ralegh's *Discourse of War* and Machiavelli's *Discorsi*', *Modern Philology*, 46 (1948), pp. 122–31; Mario Praz, 'Un machiavellico inglese:

Sir Walter Raleigh', in *Machiavelli in Inghilterra ed altri saggi* (Rome, 1943), pp. 149–64.
48 *Works of Sir Walter Raleigh*, vol. 5, pp. 50–1.

Chapter 5 Designing the Present

1 G. R. Elton (ed.), *The Tudor Constitution: Documents and Commentary* (Cambridge: Cambridge University Press, 1972), p. 344.
2 See Frances Yates, 'Elizabethan chivalry: the romance of the Accession Day tilts', in *Astraea: The Imperial Theme in the Sixteenth Century* (London: Routledge and Kegan Paul, 1985 edn), pp. 88–111.
3 See Sir Henry Wotton, *The State of Christendom* (London, 1667), p. 202 where Wotton conveniently summarizes arguments of this kind.
4 See, for example, [Philippe Duplessis Mornay?], *A Defence of Liberty against Tyrants*, ed. H. J. Laski (London: Bell, 1924).
5 See Debora Shuger, *Political Theologies in Shakespeare's England* (Basingstoke: Palgrave, 2001), pp. 11, 21–38.
6 Patrick Collinson, *The Religion of Protestants: The Church in English Society 1559–1625* (Oxford: Oxford University Press, 1982), pp. 141–88.
7 Thomas More, *Utopia*, ed. Richard Marius, trans. Ralph Robinson (London: Everyman, 1994), p. xxv.
8 See J. H. Hexter, *More's 'Utopia': The Biography of an Idea* (Princeton, NJ: Princeton University Press, 1952).
9 More, *Utopia*, p. 20.
10 Ibid., p. 26.
11 Ibid., pp. 100–101.
12 Ibid., p. 102.
13 Desiderius Erasmus, *The Praise of Folly*, trans. Sir Thomas Chaloner (London, 1549), sig. A1^v.
14 Ibid., sig. Div^{r-v}.
15 M. P. Tilley, *A Dictionary of the Proverbs in England in the Sixteenth and Seventeenth Centuries* (Ann Arbor: University of Michigan Press, 1950), E154.
16 Thomas Nashe, *The Unfortunate Traveller* (London, 1594), p. 55.
17 See Gamini Salgado (ed.), *Coney-catchers and Bawdy-baskets* (Harmondsworth: Penguin, 1972).
18 Erasmus, *The Praise of Folly*, sig. Civ^r.
19 Edmund Gayton, *Pleasant Notes upon Don Quixot* (London, 1654), pp. 24–5.
20 See Mikhail Bakhtin, *Rabelais and his World*, trans. Hélène Iswolsky (Bloomington, IN: Indiana University Press, 1984).

21　See Keith Thomas, 'The place of laughter in Tudor and Stuart England', *The Times Literary Supplement*, 21 January (1977), pp. 77–81.

22　Erasmus, *The Praise of Folly*, sig. Liv^v–M1^r.

23　*The Essayes of Michael Lord of Montaigne*, trans. John Florio, 3 vols (London: Everyman, 1910), vol. 2, p. 229.

24　Sir Walter Ralegh, *The Discovery of . . . Guiana* (London, 1596), pp. 10, 96.

25　Pietro Martire d'Anghiera, *The Decades of the New World or West India*, trans. Richard Eden (London, 1555), sig. aii^v.

26　Mark Girouard, *Life in the English Country House* (Harmondsworth: Penguin, 1980), p. 5.

27　See Anne Barton, 'Harking back to Elizabeth: Ben Jonson and Caroline nostalgia', *English Literary History*, 48 (1981), pp. 706–31.

28　See Raymond Williams, *The Country and the City* (London: The Hogarth Press, 1973).

29　John Stow, *The Survey of London*, ed. Henry B. Wheatley (London: Everyman, 1912), pp. 495–6.

30　W. B. Rye, *England as Seen by Foreigners in the Days of Elizabeth and James the First* (London: John Russell Smith, 1865), pp. 8–9.

31　For attitudes towards foreign workers, see David Scott Kastan, 'Workshop and/as playhouse: *The Shoemaker's Holiday*', *Studies in Philology*, 84 (1987), pp. 324–37.

32　D. M. Palliser, *The Age of Elizabeth: England under the Later Tudors* (London: Longman, 1983), p. 215.

33　Stow, *The Survey of London*, p. 496.

34　A. L. Beier, *Masterless Men: The Vagrancy Problem in England 1560–1640* (London: Methuen, 1985), p. 40.

35　*An Itinerary Written by F. Moryson, Gent.* (London, 1616), sig. Rrr2^r.

36　Thomas Dekker, *The Shoemaker's Holiday*, ed. R. L. Smallwood and Stanley Wells (Manchester: Manchester University Press, 1979), p. 47.

37　See Brian Gibbons, *Jacobean City Comedy* (London: Methuen, 1980 edn), p. 30.

38　Francis Bacon, 'Of Usury', in *Essays*, ed. W. Aldis Wright (London: Macmillan and Co., 1865), p. 169.

39　Thomas Middleton, *A Trick to Catch the Old One*, 1.3.

40　Margot Heinemann, *Puritanism and Theatre: Thomas Middleton and Opposition Drama under the Early Stuarts* (Cambridge: Cambridge University Press, 1980), pp. 88–9; for a more accurate account of 'Puritanism', see Patrick Collinson, *The Puritan Character: Polemics and Polarities in Early Seventeenth-century English Culture* (Los Angeles: William Andrews Clark Memorial Library, 1989).

41　Thomas Dekker, *The Wonderful Year*, Elizabethan and Jacobean Quartos 13 (Edinburgh: Edinburgh University Press, 1966), pp. 17–20, 44.

42 See Ian W. Archer, *The Pursuit of Stability: Social Relations in Elizabethan London* (Cambridge: Cambridge University Press, 1991).

Chapter 6 Fictive Persons and Places

1 Samuel Taylor Coleridge, *Coleridge's Essays and Lectures on Shakespeare* (London: Everyman, n.d.), p. 177.

2 Gordon Williams, *A Glossary of Shakespeare's Sexual Language* (London: Athlone, 1997), pp. 340–41.

3 See Malcolm Jones, 'The English print, c.1550–c.1650', in *A Companion to English Renaissance Literature and Culture*, ed. Michael Hattaway (Oxford: Blackwell, 2000), pp. 352–66.

4 See Stephen Orgel and Roy Strong (eds), *Inigo Jones: The Theatre of the Stuart Court*, 2 vols (London: Sotheby Parke Bernet, 1973).

5 Carol Chillington Rutter (ed.), *Documents of the Rose Playhouse* (Manchester: Manchester University Press, 1984), pp. 135–6.

6 William Shakespeare, *Titus Andronicus*, ed. Alan Hughes (Cambridge: Cambridge University Press, 1994), p. 16.

7 For a case for a later date, see M. P. Jackson, 'Shakespeare's *Richard III* and the Anonymous *Thomas of Woodstock*', *Medieval and Renaissance Drama in England*, 14 (2001), pp. 17–65.

8 E. K. Chambers, *The Elizabethan Stage*, 4 vols (Oxford: Clarendon Press, 1923), vol. 2, p. 365.

9 See N. B. Harte, 'State control of dress and social change in pre-industrial England', in *Trade, Government and Economy in Pre-industrial England*, ed. D. C. Coleman and A. H. John (London: Weidenfeld and Nicolson, 1976), pp. 132–65.

10 See Raymond Klibansky, Erwin Panofsky and Fritz Saxl, *Saturn and Melancholy: Studies in the History of Natural Philosophy, Religion and Art* (London: Nelson, 1964).

11 See Lisa Jardine, *Still Harping on Daughters: Women and Drama in the Age of Shakespeare* (London: Harvester Wheatsheaf, 1989).

12 Francis Bacon, *History of the Reign of King Henry VII*, ed. J. R. Lumby (Cambridge: Cambridge University Press, 1881), p. 111.

13 Michael Shapiro, *Gender in Play on the Shakespearean Stage: Boy Heroines and Female Pages* (Ann Arbor: University of Michigan Press, 1994).

14 Ludwig Wittgenstein, *Lectures and Conversations on Aesthetics, Psychology and Religious Belief*, ed. Cyril Barrett (Berkeley, CA: University of California Press, 1966), p. 33.

15 The text is available on: http://www.leeds.ac.uk/classics/resources/rhetoric/progaph.htm (accessed December 2004).

16 See also Nancy Vickers, '"The blazon of sweet beauty's best": Shake-speare's Lucrece', in *Shakespeare and the Question of Theory*, ed. Patricia Parker and Geoffrey Hartman (London: Methuen, 1985), pp. 95–115.

17 Charles Sorel, *The Extravagant Shepherd, or the History of Lysis: An Anti-Romance* [1654], trans. John Davies (London, 1660), p. 25.

18 Sir Philip Sidney, *The Countess of Pembroke's Arcadia*, ed. Maurice Evans (Harmondsworth: Penguin, 1977), p. 66.

19 Thomas Nashe, *The Unfortunate Traveller and Other Works*, ed. J. B. Steane (Harmondsworth: Penguin, 1985), p. 369.

20 See Michael Hattaway, *Elizabethan Popular Theatre* (London: Routledge, 1982), p. 38.

21 Rutter, *Documents of the Rose Playhouse*, p. 38.

22 Roland Barthes, 'The reality effect', trans. R. Carter, in *French Literary Theory Today*, ed. Tzvetan Todorov (Cambridge: Cambridge University Press, 1982), p. 16.

23 Sidney, *Arcadia*, pp. 69–70.

24 See Ruth Webb, 'Ekphrasis ancient and modern: the invention of a genre', *Word and Image*, 15 (1999), pp. 7–18.

25 Ernst Robert Curtius, *European Literature and the Latin Middle Ages*, trans. Willard R. Trask (London: Routledge and Kegan Paul, 1953), pp. 194–200.

26 See Eric Cheyfitz, *The Poetics of Imperialism* (New York: Oxford University Press, 1991), pp. xii–xiii.

27 Michael Drayton, *Poly-Olbion* (London, 1613), 24, p. 46.

28 Curtius, *European Literature and the Latin Middle Ages*, p. 195.

Chapter 7   Godliness

1 George Wither, *Britain's Remembrancer* (London, 1628), p. 275.

2 [Robert Southwell], *An Humble Supplication to Her Majesty* (n.p., 1595), pp. 55–6.

3 Ibid., pp. 82–3.

4 Richard Corbett, *Certain Elegant Poems* (London, 1647), pp. 47–8; for the tunes, see Claude M. Simpson, *The British Broadside Ballad and its Music* (New Brunswick: Rutgers University Press, 1966), p. 740.

5 See John Florio, *A World of Words* (London, 1598), and *Queen Anna's New World of Words* (London, 1611).

6 William Habington, 'On the death of the Right Honourable, George Earle of S.', *Castara* (London, 1640 edn), p. 108.

7 *Book of Homilies* (London, 1587), sig. C3^r.

8   Sir Philip Sidney, *The Countess of Pembroke's Arcadia*, ed. Maurice Evans (Harmondsworth: Penguin, 1977), p. 815.

9   'Upon reformers' doctrine of predestination', *The Mirror of New Reformation* ([Rouen], 1634), p. 62.

10 T. S. Eliot, '*In Memoriam*', *Selected Prose*, ed. Frank Kermode (London: Faber and Faber, 1975), p. 245.

11 Lynn Sauls, 'Traherne's debt to Puente's *Meditations*', *Philological Quarterly*, 50 (1971), pp. 161–74.

12 T. S. Eliot, *George Herbert* (London: Longmans, Green, and Co., 1962), p. 24.

13 Friedrich Nietzsche, 'On Truth and Lies in an Extra-moral Sense' (1873) at http://www.geocities.com/thenietzschechannel/tls.htm (accessed May 2005).

14 Carlos M. N. Eire, *War against the Idols: The Reformation of Worship from Erasmus to Calvin* (Cambridge: Cambridge University Press, 1986), p. 315.

15 Lancelot Andrewes, *Ninety-six Sermons* (London, 1629), p. 188 (emphasis added); I owe my knowledge of this sermon to James Shapiro.

16 John Donne, *Eighty Sermons* (London, 1640), p. 544.

17 See Thomas Laqueur, *Making Sex: Body and Gender from the Greeks to Freud* (Cambridge, MA: Harvard University Press, 1990).

18 Donne, *Eighty Sermons*, p. 820.

19 Thomas Cranley, 'To the fair Amanda', *Amanda, or The Reformed Whore* (London, 1636), p. 38.

20 *The Works of William Drummond of Hawthornden*, ed. John Sage and Thomas Ruddiman (Edinburgh: James Watson, 1711), p. 143.

21 Baldassare Castiglione, *The Book of the Courtier*, trans. Sir Thomas Hoby [1561] (London: Everyman, 1928), pp. 318, 319, 321.

22 Edmund Spenser, *The Shorter Poems*, ed. William A. Oram et al. (New Haven, CT: Yale University Press, 1989), p. 690.

23 For Cupid in the neo-platonic tradition, see 'Blind Cupid' in Erwin Panofsky, *Studies in Iconology* (New York: Harper and Row, 1939), pp. 95–128.

24 Spenser, *The Shorter Poems*, p. 722.

25 Ibid.

26 Panofsky, *Studies in Iconology*, pp. 142–3.

27 Frank Kermode, 'The banquet of sense', in *Renaissance Essays* (London: Routledge and Kegan Paul, 1971), pp. 84–115.

28 Cherry A. Hankin (ed.), *Letters between Katherine Mansfield and John Middleton Murry* (New York: New Amsterdam, 1991), p. 344.

29 D. J. Gordon, 'Chapman's *Hero and Leander*', *English Miscellany*, 5 (1954), pp. 41–92.

Bibliography

This bibliography is designed to suggest further reading to accompany each chapter in the text. It can be supplemented by consulting the essays and reading lists in Michael Hattaway (ed.), *A Companion to English Renaissance Literature and Culture* (Oxford: Blackwell, 2000), David Scott Kastan (ed.), *A Companion to Shakespeare* (Oxford: Blackwell, 1999) and Arthur F. Kinney (ed.), *A Companion to Renaissance Drama* (Oxford: Blackwell, 2002). I have not included studies of particular authors or texts: many of these can be found in the notes.

Chapter 1   Speaking and Writing

Altman, Joel B., *The Tudor Play of Mind: Rhetorical Inquiry and the Development of Elizabethan Drama* (Berkeley, CA: University of California Press, 1978).

Bentley, Gerald Eades, *The Professions of Dramatist and Player in Shakespeare's Time, 1590–1642* (Princeton, NJ: Princeton University Press, 1986).

Bolgar, R. R., *The Classical Heritage and its Beneficiaries* (Cambridge: Cambridge University Press, 1954).

Carper, Thomas and Attridge, Derek, *Meter and Meaning* (London: Routledge, 2003).

Castiglione, Baldassare, *The Book of the Courtier*, trans. Sir Thomas Hoby [1561] (London: Everyman, 1928).

Dixon, Peter, *Rhetoric* (London: Methuen, 1971).

Doran, Madeleine, *Endeavors of Art: A Study of Form in Elizabethan Drama* (Madison: University of Wisconsin Press, 1954).

Howell, Wilbur Samuel, *Logic and Rhetoric in England, 1500–1700* (Princeton, NJ: Princeton University Press, 1956).

Lanham, Richard A., *A Handlist of Rhetorical Terms: A Guide for Students of English Literature* (Berkeley, CA: University of California Press, 1968).

Lewalski, Barbara Kiefer, *Writing Women in Jacobean England* (Cambridge, MA: Harvard University Press, 1994).

Mack, Peter, *Renaissance Rhetoric* (Basingstoke: Macmillan, 1994).

Mueller, Janel M., *The Native Tongue and the Word: Developments in English Prose Style, 1380–1580* (Chicago: University of Chicago Press, 1984).

Parker, Patricia A., *Literary Fat Ladies: Rhetoric, Gender, Property* (London: Methuen, 1987).

Shuger, Debora K., *Sacred Rhetoric: The Christian Grand Style in the English Renaissance* (Princeton, NJ: Princeton University Press, 1988).

Tilley, M. P., *A Dictionary of the Proverbs in England in the Sixteenth and Seventeenth Centuries* (Ann Arbor: University of Michigan Press, 1950).

Trousdale, Marion, *Shakespeare and the Rhetoricians* (Chapel Hill, NC: University of North Carolina Press, 1982).

Tuve, Rosemond, *Elizabethan and Metaphysical Imagery* (Chicago: University of Chicago Press, 1947).

Vickers, Brian, *In Defence of Rhetoric* (Oxford: Clarendon Press, 1989).

Zunder, William and Trill, Suzanne (eds), *Writing and the English Renaissance* (London: Longman, 1996).

Chapter 2   Reading, Publication, Performance

Allison, A. F. and Rogers, D. M. (eds), *The Contemporary Printed Literature of the English Counter-Reformation between 1558 and 1640: An Annotated Catalogue*, 2 vols (Aldershot: Scolar Press, 1994).

Barish, Jonas A., *The Antitheatrical Prejudice* (Berkeley, CA: University of California Press, 1981).

Barnard, John and McKenzie, D. F. (eds), *The Cambridge History of the Book in Britain, 1557–1695* (Cambridge: Cambridge University Press, 2002).

Bennett, Henry Stanley, *English Books and Readers, 1475 to 1557*, 2nd edn (Cambridge: Cambridge University Press, 1969).

——, *English Books and Readers 1558 to 1603* (Cambridge: Cambridge University Press, 1965).

——, *English Books and Readers, 1603 to 1640* (Cambridge: Cambridge University Press, 1970).

Cerasano, S. P. and Wynne-Davies, Marion, *Renaissance Drama by Women: Texts and Documents* (London: Routledge, 1996).

Chartier, Roger, *The Order of Books: Readers, Authors, and Libraries in Europe between the Fourteenth and Eighteenth Centuries*, trans. Lydia Cochrane (Cambridge: Cambridge University Press, 1994).

Cressy, David, *Literacy and the Social Order: Reading and Writing in Early Modern England* (Cambridge: Cambridge University Press, 1980).

Dutton, Richard, *Licensing, Censorship, and Authorship in Early Modern England* (Basingstoke: Palgrave, 2000).

Eisenstein, Elizabeth, *The Printing Press as an Agent of Change*, 2 vols (Cambridge: Cambridge University Press, 1979).

Evans, G. Blakemore, *Elizabethan–Jacobean Drama* (London: A and C Black, 1988).

Fox, Adam, *Oral and Literate Culture in England 1500–1700*. Oxford Studies in Social History (Oxford: Clarendon Press, 2000).

Gair, W. Reavley, *The Children of Paul's: The Story of a Theatre Company, 1553–1608* (Cambridge: Cambridge University Press, 1982).

Gurr, Andrew, *Playgoing in Shakespeare's London*, 2nd edn (Cambridge: Cambridge University Press, 1996).

Hattaway, Michael, *Elizabethan Popular Theatre: Plays in Performance* (London: Routledge and Kegan Paul, 1982).

Marotti, Arthur F., *Manuscript, Print, and the English Renaissance Lyric* (Ithaca, NY: Cornell University Press, 1995).

Milward, Peter, *Religious Controversies of the Jacobean Age: A Survey of Printed Sources* (London: Scolar Press, 1978).

Montrose, Louis, *The Purpose of Playing: Shakespeare and the Cultural Politics of the Elizabethan Theatre* (Chicago: University of Chicago Press, 1996).

Pollard, Tanya (ed.), *Shakespeare's Theater: A Sourcebook* (Oxford: Blackwell, 2004).

Shuger, Debora, *The Renaissance Bible: Scholarship, Sacrifice, and Subjectivity* (Berkeley, CA: University of California Press, 1994).

Spufford, Margaret, *Small Books and Pleasant Histories: Popular Fiction and its Readership in Seventeenth-century England* (Cambridge: Cambridge University Press, 1981).

Watt, Tessa, *Cheap Print and Popular Piety, 1550–1640* (Cambridge: Cambridge University Press, 1991).

Wheale, Nigel, *Writing and Society: Literacy, Print and Politics in Britain, 1590–1660* (London: Routledge, 1999).

White, Paul Whitfield and Westfall, Suzanne R., *Shakespeare and Theatrical Patronage in Early Modern England* (Cambridge: Cambridge University Press, 2002).

Wickham, Glynne, Berry, Herbert and Ingram, William (eds), *English Professional Theatre, 1530–1660: Theatre in Europe, A Documentary History* (Cambridge: Cambridge University Press, 2000).

Chapter 3   Forms Ancient and Modern

Aughterson, Kate (ed.), *The English Renaissance: An Anthology of Sources and Documents* (London: Routledge, 1998).

Eagleton, Terry, *Sweet Violence: The Idea of the Tragic* (Oxford: Blackwell, 2002).

Gibbons, Brian, *Jacobean City Comedy* (London: Methuen, 1980).

Greenblatt, Stephen (ed.), *Power of Forms in the English Renaissance* (Norman, OK: Pilgrim Books, 1982).

Henderson, Diana E., *Passion Made Public: Elizabethan Lyric, Gender, and Performance* (Urbana: University of Illinois Press, 1995).

Hunter, G. K., *English Drama 1586–1642: The Age of Shakespeare* (Oxford: Oxford University Press, 1997).

Keach, William, *Elizabethan Erotic Narratives: Irony and Pathos in the Ovidian Poetry of Shakespeare, Marlowe, and their Contemporaries* (New Brunswick: Rutgers University Press, 1977).

Kernan, Alvin Bernard, *The Cankered Muse: Satire of the English Renaissance* (New Haven, CT: Yale University Press, 1959).

Kerrigan, John, *Revenge Tragedy: Aeschylus to Armageddon* (Oxford: Oxford University Press, 1996).

Klein, David, *The Elizabethan Dramatists as Critics* (London: Peter Owen, 1963).

Lever, J. W., *The Elizabethan Love Sonnet* (London: Methuen, 1956).

Lewalski, Barbara Kiefer (ed.), *Renaissance Genres: Essays on Theory, History, and Interpretation* (Cambridge, MA: Harvard University Press, 1986).

Mazzeo, Joseph Anthony, *Renaissance and Revolution* (New York: Pantheon Books, 1965).

Praz, Mario, *The Flaming Heart* (New York: Doubleday, 1958).

Neill, Michael, *Issues of Death: Mortality and Identity in the Drama of Shakespeare and his Contemporaries* (Oxford: Oxford University Press, 1997).

Salingar, Leo, *Shakespeare and the Traditions of Comedy* (Cambridge: Cambridge University Press, 1974).

Simpson, James, *The Oxford English Literary History, 1350–1547: Reform and Cultural Revolution*, ed. Jonathan Bate, vol. 2 (Oxford: Oxford University Press, 2002).

Vickers, Brian (ed.), *English Renaissance Literary Criticism* (Oxford: Oxford University Press, 1999).

Wells, Robin Headlam, *Elizabethan Mythologies: Studies in Poetry, Drama and Music* (Cambridge: Cambridge University Press, 1994).

Chapter 4   Defining the Past

Anderson, Judith H., *Biographical Truth: The Representation of Historical Persons in Tudor–Stuart Writing* (New Haven, CT: Yale University Press, 1984).

Burke, Peter, *The Renaissance Sense of the Past: Documents of Modern History* (London: Edward Arnold, 1969).

Cressy, David, *Bonfires and Bells: National Memory and the Protestant Calendar in Elizabethan and Stuart England* (London: Weidenfeld and Nicolson, 1989).

Dorey, Thomas Alan (ed.), *Tacitus* (London: Routledge and Kegan Paul, 1969).

Ferguson, Arthur B., *Clio Unbound: Perception of the Social and Cultural Past in Renaissance England* (Durham, NC.: Duke University Press, 1979).

Fussner, Frank Smith, *The Historical Revolution: English Historical Writing and Thought, 1580–1640* (London: Routledge and Kegan Paul, 1962).

Hirst, Derek, *Authority and Conflict: England 1603–1658* (London: Edward Arnold, 1986).

Hutton, Ronald, *The Rise and Fall of Merry England: The Ritual Year 1400–1700* (Oxford: Oxford University Press, 1994).

Kamps, Ivo, *Historiography and Ideology in Stuart Drama* (Cambridge: Cambridge University Press, 1996).

Kelley, Donald R. and Sacks, David Harris (eds), *The Historical Imagination in Early Modern Britain: History, Rhetoric, and Fiction, 1500–1800* (Cambridge: Cambridge University Press, 1997).

Parry, Graham, *The Trophies of Time: English Antiquarians of the Seventeenth Century* (Oxford: Oxford University Press, 1995).

Patterson, Annabel M., *Reading Holinshed's Chronicles* (Chicago, IL: University of Chicago Press, 1994).

Pocock, J. G. A., *The Ancient Constitution and the Feudal Law: A Study of English Historical Thought in the Seventeenth Century*, 2nd edn (Cambridge: Cambridge University Press, 1997).

Rackin, Phyllis, *Stages of History: Shakespeare's English Chronicles* (London: Routledge, 1990).

Seznec, Jean, *The Survival of the Pagan Gods: The Mythological Tradition and its Place in Renaissance Humanism and Art*, trans. Barbara F. Sessions (New York: Pantheon Books, 1953).

Thomas, Keith, *The Perception of the Past in Early Modern England: The Creighton Trust Lecture, 1983* (London: University of London, 1983).

Woolf, D. R., *The Idea of History in Early Stuart England: Erudition, Ideology and 'The Light of Truth' from the Accession of James I to the Civil War* (Toronto: University of Toronto Press, 1990).

Chapter 5   Designing the Present

Agnew, Jean-Christophe, *Worlds Apart: The Market and the Theater in Anglo-American Thought, 1550–1750* (Cambridge: Cambridge University Press, 1986).

Braddick, Michael J., *State Formation in Early Modern England, c.1550–1700* (Cambridge: Cambridge University Press, 2000).

Butler, Martin, *Theatre and Crisis, 1632–1642* (Cambridge: Cambridge University Press, 1984).

Caspari, Fritz, *Humanism and the Social Order in Tudor England* (Chicago: University of Chicago Press, 1954).

Dollimore, Jonathan, *Radical Tragedy: Religion, Ideology and Power in the Drama of Shakespeare and his Contemporaries* (Brighton: Harvester Press, 1984).

Gillies, John, *Shakespeare and the Geography of Difference* (Cambridge: Cambridge University Press, 1994).

Greenblatt, Stephen Jay, *Marvelous Possessions: The Wonder of the New World* (Chicago: University of Chicago Press, 1991).

Hadfield, Andrew, *Literature, Travel, and Colonial Writing in the English Renaissance, 1545–1625* (Oxford: Oxford University Press, 1998).

Heinemann, Margot, *Puritanism and Theatre: Thomas Middleton and Opposition Drama under the Early Stuarts* (Cambridge: Cambridge University Press, 1980).

Helgerson, Richard, *Forms of Nationhood: The Elizabethan Writing of England* (Chicago: University of Chicago Press, 1992).

Kaiser, Walter Jacob, *Praisers of Folly: Erasmus, Rabelais, Shakespeare* (London: Victor Gollancz, 1964).

King, John. N., *Tudor Royal Iconography: Literature and Art in an Age of Religious Crisis* (Princeton, NJ: Princeton University Press, 1989).

Lamont, William and Oldfield, Sybil (ed.), *Politics, Religion and Literature in the Seventeenth Century* (London: Everyman, 1975).

McEachern, Claire, *The Poetics of English Nationhood 1590–1612* (Cambridge: Cambridge University Press, 1996).

Manley, Lawrence, *Literature and Culture in Early Modern London* (Cambridge: Cambridge University Press, 1995).

Maquerlot, Jean-Pierre and Willems, Michèle (eds), *Travel and Drama in Shakespeare's Time* (Cambridge: Cambridge University Press, 1996).

Neill, Michael, *Putting History to the Question: Power, Politics, and Society in English Renaissance Drama* (New York: Columbia University Press, 2000).

Parry, Graham, *The Seventeenth Century: The Intellectual and Cultural Context of English Literature, 1603–1700* (London: Longman, 1989).

Peck, Linda Levy (ed.), *The Mental World of the Jacobean Court* (Cambridge: Cambridge University Press, 1991).

Sharpe, J. A., *Crime in Early Modern England 1550–1750* (London: Longman, 1984).

——, *Early Modern England: A Social History, 1550–1760* (London: Longman, 1987).

Thomas, Keith, *Man and the Natural World: Changing Attitudes in England, 1500–1800* (London: Allen Lane, 1983).

Tuck, Richard, *Philosophy and Government 1572–1651* (Cambridge: Cambridge University Press, 1993).

Turner, James, *The Politics of Landscape* (Cambridge, MA: Harvard University Press, 1979).

Walker, Greg, *The Politics of Performance in Early Renaissance Drama* (Cambridge: Cambridge University Press, 1998).

Welsford, Enid, *The Fool: His Social and Literary History* (London: Faber and Faber, 1935).

Wiles, David, *Shakespeare's Clown: Actor and Text in the Elizabethan Playhouse* (Cambridge: Cambridge University Press, 1987).

Wrightson, Keith, *English Society 1580–1680* (London: Routledge, 2003).

Yates, Frances, *Astraea: The Imperial Theme in the Sixteenth Century* (London: Routledge and Kegan Paul, 1985 edn).

Chapter 6 Fictive Persons and Places

Auerbach, Erich, *Mimesis: The Representation of Reality in Western Literature* (Garden City, NY: Doubleday, 1957).

Clifford, Gay, *The Transformations of Allegory* (London: Routledge and Kegan Paul, 1974).

Curtius, Ernst Robert, *European Literature and the Latin Middle Ages*, trans. Willard R. Trask (London: Routledge and Kegan Paul, 1953).

Dessen, Alan C., *Elizabethan Stage Conventions and Modern Interpreters* (Cambridge: Cambridge University Press, 1984).

Fish, Stanley, *Self-consuming Artifacts: The Experience of Seventeenth-century Literature* (Berkeley, CA: University of California Press, 1972).

Fletcher, Angus, *Allegory: The Theory of a Symbolic Mode* (Ithaca, NY: Cornell University Press, 1964).

Greenblatt, Stephen J., *Renaissance Self-fashioning: From More to Shakespeare* (Chicago: University of Chicago Press, 1980).

Hendricks, Margo (ed.), *Women, 'Race' and Writing in the Early Modern Period* (London: Routledge, 1993).

Lee, John, *Shakespeare's 'Hamlet' and the Controversies of Self* (Oxford: Oxford University Press, 2000).

MacDonald, Michael, *Mystical Bedlam: Madness, Anxiety and Healing in Seventeenth Century England* (Cambridge: Cambridge University Press, 1981).

Maus, Katharine Eisaman, *Inwardness and Theater in the English Renaissance* (Chicago: University of Chicago Press, 1995).

Norbrook, David, *Writing the English Republic: Poetry, Rhetoric and Politics, 1627–1660* (Cambridge: Cambridge University Press, 1999).

Orgel, Stephen, *Impersonations: The Performance of Gender in Shakespeare's England* (Cambridge: Cambridge University Press, 1988).

Shapiro, Michael, *Gender in Play on the Shakespearean Stage: Boy Heroines and Female Pages* (Ann Arbor: University of Michigan Press, 1994).

Traub, Valerie, Kaplan, M. Lindsay and Callaghan, Dympna (eds), *Feminist Readings of Early Modern Culture: Emerging Subjects* (Cambridge: Cambridge University Press, 1996).

Wells, Robin Headlam, *Shakespeare on Masculinity* (Cambridge: Cambridge University Press, 2000).

Chapter 7   Godliness

Collinson, Patrick, *The Reformation* (London: Weidenfeld and Nicolson, 2003).

——, *The Religion of Protestants: The Church in English Society 1559–1625* (Oxford: Oxford University Press, 1982).

Haigh, Christopher, *English Reformations: Religion, Politics and Society under the Tudors* (Oxford: Oxford University Press, 1993).

King, John N., *English Reformation Literature: The Tudor Origins of the Protestant Tradition* (Princeton, NJ: Princeton University Press, 1982).

Lewalski, Barbara Kiefer, *Protestant Poetics and the Seventeenth-century Religious Lyric* (Princeton, NJ: Princeton University Press, 1984).

Martz, Louis, *The Poetry of Meditation: A Study of English Religious Literature of the Seventeenth Century* (New Haven, CT: Yale University Press, 1962).

Norbrook, David, *Poetry and Politics in the English Renaissance*, rev. edn (Oxford: Oxford University Press, 2002).

Nuttall, A. D., *Overheard by God: Fiction and Prayer in Herbert, Milton, Dante, and St John* (London: Methuen, 1980).

Panofsky, Erwin, *Studies in Iconology* (New York: Harper and Row, 1939).

Shell, Alison, *Catholicism, Controversy, and the English Literary Imagination, 1558–1660* (Cambridge: Cambridge University Press, 1999).

Southern, A. C., *Elizabethan Recusant Prose, 1559–1582* ([Norwood, PA]: Norwood editions, 1978).

Thomas, Keith, *Religion and the Decline of Magic* (Harmondsworth: Penguin, 1973).

Index

Printed in the United States
137589LV00007B/18/P